FOR A LIVING

FOR A LIVING

The Poetry of Work

Edited by
Nicholas Coles & Peter Oresick

UNIVERSITY OF ILLINOIS PRESS
Urbana and Chicago

Library of Congress Cataloging-in-Publication Data

For a living : the poetry of work / edited by Nicholas Coles and Peter
    Oresick.
        p.   cm.
    Includes index.
    ISBN 0-252-02122-3.—ISBN 0-252-06410-0 (paper)
    1. Working class writings, American. 2. American poetry—20th
century. 3. Work—Poetry. I. Coles, Nicholas. II. Oresick,
Peter.
PS591.W65F67 1995
811'.54080355–dc20   94-4377
                                                                            CIP

CONTENTS

INTRODUCTION

Most of us work at jobs for a living—even writers. Wallace Stevens, the great modernist poet, spent his working life as a lawyer and insurance executive. He carried a briefcase with his business papers in one compartment and his poems in another, in order, he said, to "keep them completely separated."[1] By tradition, it seems, most poetry avoids the subject of work. The poet and critic Dana Gioia, for many years an executive with General Foods, complains of the dominant confessional mode in American poetry that, "while it has unlocked the doors to a poet's study, living room, and bedroom, it has stayed away from his office."[2] And, we might add, from the other spaces—factories, kitchens, hospitals, courthouses, banks, schools, stores, and restaurants—in which women and men do what they do "for a living."

Why has poetry traditionally ignored the working life? For the English Romantics, poetry was a preserve of culture against the barbarism of industrial society. For the moderns, poetry was what Eliot's hollow men needed but could not hear. In John Ashbery's "The Instruction Manual," the poem is an occasion for an imaginative vacation from work: the technical writer/poet gazes out of the window of the office in which he sits trying to write "the instruction manual on the uses of new metals" and conjures in its place a "dream of Guadalajara," an exotic world of possibility beyond the world of work. Spinning out this dream, the poem becomes ironically an instruction manual for poets on the art of transcending the mundane and the technical.

It may be, however, that the traditional reticence about work is not so much that of poets themselves as of those who collect and edit their work, since to write about work is usually to write about issues of politics and class, which remain unpopular topics for literature textbooks. In our reading of American poets of the past decade or so, we see evidence that the customary separation between poetry and the working life is breaking down. Our first anthology, *Working Classics: Poems on Industrial Life* (University of Illinois Press, 1990), demonstrated the prevalence, among some of the best-known contemporary writers, of poems about U.S. mills and mines and blue-collar neighborhoods. In this companion volume we feature poems that address the nature and culture of nonindustrial work: that is, work that has in common the production of "services" or "information" rather than more tangible or durable "goods"; work that could be categorized as white collar, pink collar, domestic, clerical, technical, managerial, or professional.[3] The range of jobs represented in *For A Living* crosses lines of status and class, from flipping burgers (Daniels) or mopping floors (Espada) to television news reporting (Ai) or Wall Street brokerage (Holden). Along with poems about the newer forms of clerical drudgery—data processing and telemarketing, for instance— the collection includes the traditional professions of law, medicine, and teaching. Also represented are the ancient unremunerated professions of homemaking and child raising, from the points of view of both full-time homemakers and mothers with employment outside the home who explore in poetry "the lack of fit of this sort of making—mothering—into / what we call our business / or life" (Casey).[4]

Most of the poems here were written in the 1980s and 1990s and represent predominant forms of work in the "postindustrial" era. According to *The American Almanac of Jobs and Salaries,* the number of Americans now engaged in traditional blue-collar jobs, primarily industrial manufacturing, has declined dramatically: "Today more than three-quarters of all Americans work in such areas as accounting, banking, engineering, consumer services, education, health care, legal work, transportation, and wholesale and retail trade."[5] Another six million are employed in federal, state, and local governments. One notable development is that the largest influx into jobs in the service economy has been among women and among Asian, Hispanic, and African Americans—a trend that is reflected in our selections for this anthology.

Some of the poems here comment directly on the effects of this recent shift to a service economy. In a poem from *Working Classics: Poems on Industrial Life,* a laid-off steelworker addressed his situation in response to a pep talk by then-president Ronald Reagan.

> "I'm fifty-nine years old, for God's sake Mr. Reagan
> fifty-nine years old. You want me to study computers
> and biology now? You want me to work at McDonald's;
> sixteen-year-old kids and three thirty-five an hour?"
> (Michael O'Connor, "Reaganomics Comes to
> Pittsburgh," 173)

In this companion volume, Mark Defoe's poem "The Former Miner Returns from His First Day as a Service Worker" gives us a glimpse of what that shift was like for those obliged to make it. In a "McDonald's—somewhere in Appalachia,"

> All day he rubbed his eyes in the crisp light.
> All day the blue tile, the polished chrome, said
> Be nimble, be jolly, be quick.
>
> All day he grinned while the public, with bland
> Or befuddled faces, scowled over his head

at the illuminated menu. By the day's end, "He has never been so tired. / His hands have never been so clean."

For displaced industrial workers such as Defoe's, forced entry into the lowest levels of the service economy can be dramatic and damaging: in exchange for being able to keep relatively clean in their new jobs, they have lost pay, pride, and, not coincidentally, the protection of unions. For those who go to work in shiny buildings downtown, trained and dressed for success, the reflected status of working where "the real money's made these days" may mask some of the costs (Skinner, "The Moment when the Workers of the Night Pass By the Workers of the Day").[6] The secretary in Judith Berke's "Ms" admires her female boss's manipulation of the old boys' pecking order, but she also sees how tenuous and circumscribed her boss's power really is:

> she's part of the tribe now.
> That's why she wears the jacket
> with the shoulders. Sometimes we eat lunch
> here in her office, and there she is,
> her head back in the chair, swiveling,
> and the jacket, like another person,
> in back of her.

Occasionally these other persons are directly encountered in these poems (see Subject Index under "Bosses"); more often they are recessed on the upper floors, where in

> the sudden hush of mahogany row, puce carpet
> of deepest pile, the carved wooden doors
> that once opened a sacred Hindu temple, each
> as large as four large men, now block the CEO from non-
> essential eyes.
> (Skinner, "The Moment when the Workers of
> the Night Pass By the Workers of the Day")

Many of these poems suggest that less has changed in the ways people work, and feel about their work, than the epochal terms "postindustrial" and "information age" imply. While forms of work such as high technology are notably new, the largest element of change in the work force is in fact an expansion of the lowest-paid, least secure traditional working-class jobs: domestic, clerical, product distribution, food service. Many of these jobs are as boring and repetitive as assembly-line work, as the form of Wanda Coleman's "Drone" makes clear:

> i am a clerk
> i am a medical billing clerk

> i sit here all day and type
> the same type of things all day long
> insurance claim forms
> for people who suffer chronic renal failure
> fortunately these people I rarely see
> . . . .
> there are few problems here. i am a very good clerk
> i sit here all day and type
> i am a medical billing clerk
> i am a clerk
> i clerk.

The nature of the work performed reduces the worker's identity (a lowercase "i") to the status of the function she performs (clerk), so that it is preferable not to see the persons whose cases pass through her hands.

Other service jobs—receptionist, nurse, waitress—are performed in direct contact or confrontation with others designated as "people," "the public," "the customer," "client," "patient," the consumer of the services delivered by the worker. Since the success of this transaction depends on its face-to-face quality, it requires an investment of "personal" characteristics—looks, deportment, dress, smile, tone of voice, bedside manner, "personality"—each of which becomes an element of job qualification, and also a salable "feature" of the service the worker represents. In this kind of employment, the person of the worker could be said to become literally commodified, even more than that of the industrial worker whose labor is abstracted and mingled with the commodities he or she produces. We can see this most directly in work that relies on physical attractiveness for its value, as with the usherette at the Los Angeles Forum in Maxine Scates's "The Body," who in "her toga and her white boots" must endure without noticeable revulsion the "lewd whispers" of her customers:

> I took pride in knowing how to do my job.
> I exhibited restraint in the public arena,
> where no one had to know what he was saying
> where he got to say what he wanted to say.
> After all, I was a Forum girl.

This is her first job, yet she already has the sophisticated professional sense that sexual harassment, as we call it today, is itself the commodity offered to the public through her work.

Even when the work described is predominantly "mental"—administrative, managerial, technical, professional—these poems show it to be still pervaded by what, in political terms, we would call exploitation, the sense of energies spent and used up for other people's purposes. A worker's thinking process, and the words in which it materializes, are commodities in the marketplace, available for hire, as in the case of the New York lawyer in Lawrence Joseph's "Any and All":

> Another day
>
> you contemplate your strategy:
> think about how they think about you
>
> thinking about them and the look on your face
> to prove you have the proper attitude.
>
> Let no laughter reveal moods. Let
> Charlotte Stone reveal that her father
>
> over the weekend purchased a peninsula in Rhode Island
> for Harry and her, let her teeth
>
> be too large and too gray: there is blood
> and there is blood-letting; this is not your blood.
>
> Shut the door and wait. Someone else's father
> forgives you when you know not what you do,
>
> reminds you, "He's a weasel but he's my friend."
> You're a monkey and you work for him,
>
> decide for him whether his clauses should be restrictive,
> whether to replace every "any" with "all."

This formal alienation—the withholding of one's own blood behind the proper face, attitude, or dress—produces in other poems a surreal sense that the worker has disappeared inside whatever motions she or he may be going through:

> We work in this building and we are hideous
> in the fluorescent light, you know our clothes
> woke up this morning and swallowed us like jewels
> and ride up and down the elevators, filled with us.
>   (Denis Johnson, "White, White Collars")

Or, in the place of the recurrent motions of the building, signifying that business is getting done, the poem conjures a submerged stillness between the walls of the office:

> You cannot find yourself in this calm
> . . . .

> . . . you are suspended between
> the two points of departure and arrival,
> and you can insist on neither.
> (Stanley Marcus, "At the Office")

In this calm, nevertheless, decisions are made and actions taken whose effects, in a ghostly analogy to the manufacturing assembly line, happen in another region or department. At all levels of work in tall buildings, workers feel subject to uncontrollable "forces"—the economy, sales, bosses—larger and more powerful than themselves, and the winning and losing of that contest wears them down:

> He did not look well,
> the paunch of too many receptions and dinners
> at too many conferences
> in too many hotels.
>
> . . . .
> "That last profit forecast was rotten,
> really a killer."
> (James A. Autry, "Business Is Bad, II")

In fact, the notion that hard work never killed anyone is as inaccurate in reference to corporate work as it is to physically more dangerous jobs. Ted Kooser puts it this way:

> So it is that men die at the whims of great companies,
> their neckties pulling them speechless into machines,
> their wives finding them slumped in the shower,
> their hearts blown open like boiler doors.
> ("The Goldfish Floats to the Top of His Life")

Just as the industrial accident symbolizes the extent to which the worker too is raw material for manufacturing, so the heart attack and other stress-related diseases register the damage done by the political structure of work in the corporate economy.

These poems make clear that subordination is still the dominant relation in our "transformed" economy. Class division and class antagonism persist as vigorously as ever, and it is above all in our experience of work that we bump into class boundaries. Most workers in white-collar jobs perhaps think of themselves as middle class, upwardly mobile, socially superior to their blue-collar relatives or childhood friends. They may identify with management and the corporate enterprise and see no need for unions. Yet as the public arguments about the state of the economy during the 1992 election campaign demonstrated, the Reagan-era economics of government deregulation, unfettered business, corporate takeovers, and a booming service economy produced ironic effects: lower real pay for most Americans, a decline in health and pension benefits, longer workdays, higher rates of unemployment and underemployment, greater job insecurity, and an increase in the number of families in which two people must work in order to make ends meet. As Barbara Ehrenreich argues in *Fear of Falling,* while the rich get richer and the poor get poorer and the middle shrinks, most people remain, by any definition except the color of their collars, working class.[7]

Though they don't necessarily have occasion to worry about it much:

> I was at the 7-11.
> I ate a burrito.
> I drank a Slurpee.
> I was tired.
> It was late, after work—washing dishes.
> The burrito was good.
> I had another.
>
> . . . .
> On the way out I bought a quart of beer for $1.39.
> I was aware of social injustice
> In only the vaguest possible way.
> (Campbell McGrath, "Capitalist Poem #5")

• • •

One of the pleasures of editing an anthology like this is that, even while its subject is restricted—in this case, to the working life—the collection comes to represent, in the poems' forms and styles and strategies, the diverse range of contemporary American poetry. Alongside free verse poems by current masters of the form such as Sharon Olds and Philip Levine, there are longer New Narrative poems here, including one (Robert McDowell's "My Corporate Life") in iambic pentameter. There are several examples of the New Formalism, including poems by two of the movement's protagonists, Dana Gioia and Brad Leithauser, as well as a sonnet by Maggie Anderson, a sestina by Jan Clausen, a villanelle by Laurie Henry, and a pantoum by Michael McFee. There are prose poems, found poems, list poems, and joke poems. There is also a "language poem" here, Miriam Solan's "Check-up," which works through perpetually interrupted prose to render the bewildering simultaneity of actions, commands, and responses in a overworked doctor's office. Deb Casey's "ZOOOOOOOM: A Familiar Story: Drop-off/Pick-up Panic" similarly uses every typographical trick on the word processor to render the breathless collision of needs and responsibilities of a working mother dealing with the intricate timing of day care, parking, meetings, breast feeding, and so on. It

seems that new or unfamiliar material interacting with available poetic con-
ventions produces a good deal of formal experimentation.

We saw little evidence, in the selection process for this anthology, of the
sameness and staleness complained of by a number of observers of the
contemporary poetry scene, usually attributed to the rise of university writing
programs and the employment of so many practicing American poets as
university faculty.[8] Perhaps this is due to the nature of our subject. It may be
because work is for many the most public aspect of life that these poems
escape the individual and private obsession of the so-called "workshop poem."
While many of the poems in *For a Living* have autobiographical bases, it is
not easy to tell whether the poet has done the kind of work represented by
the poem or is entering another's workspace via the empathic observation
and imagination that Tillie Olsen calls "trespass vision." The cluster of poems
on medical care, for example, demonstrate an array of positions—doctor,
nurse, receptionist, orderly, lab technician, patient—and of attitudes on these
actors' common work: awestruck, disgusted, caring, exploited, businesslike.

The strength and variety of these poems lead us to agree with Jonathan
Holden that "the fate of American poetry" (to borrow the title of his book) is
currently relatively promising.[9] Poets in the United States are in general
better supported economically than in any other nation or time. Their
audience, while not by any means "popular," is vastly expanded by virtue of
the democratic opening of universities and colleges to working-class and
minority students since the sixties. Poetry seems to be recovering from the
Romantic legacy of the feeling-obsessed lyric, as well as from the reaction to
Romanticism in high modernist density and abstraction. According to Holden,
contemporary poetry is reclaiming not only the cultural work of story telling
that had been ceded to prose fiction but also the didactic work of sermon and
proverb and the discursive or political work of the essay.

We can see this in James A. Autry's poems, reprinted from his bestseller
Love and Profit: The Art of Caring Leadership, which offer a kind of moral
education in humane business management; in the poems from Marilyn
Krysl's book published by the National League for Nursing to promote a new
consciousness of care giving as an alternative to high-tech medicine; and in
Tom Wayman's "Paper, Scissors, Stone," a witty critique of the wage system
arguing that all workers should be paid equitably for the different kinds of
work we do. Holden also credits the emergence of a strongly identified
women's poetry for having brought forth not only the "naked and fiery
forms" named by the poet-critic Suzanne Juhasz but also a commitment to
ideas, a tendency to "deal realistically with questions of history, ideology,
social and personal responsibility."[10] This, he argues, is poetry's mainstream
work of "realism," which "has always gained its force from the act of exposure
of uncomfortable and inadequately acknowledged truths." These work poems,

we believe, serve realism by puncturing the everywhere-dominant rhetoric of the "new" and of "progress" that drives and legitimizes the expansion of the service and information economies. They allow us to ask: What kinds of jobs are these, What are their effects on those who do them, What cultural value do they produce and circulate to their consumers?

The diversity of forms and purposes in the poems collected here is, in part, a result of the relatively open and public way in which we assembled *For a Living.* Instead of just combing through contemporary poetry books, chapbooks, and journals, as we did for our previous volume, this time we also mailed a call for manuscripts to each of the five thousand practicing poets listed in *A Directory of American Poets and Fiction Writers.* [11] We announced that we were compiling an anthology of poems about work in the service and information economies and we listed several specific job categories. "Also of interest," we wrote, "are varied points of view, including those of managers and the managed, paid and unpaid domestic workers, entrepreneurs and entry-level employees." It took us two years to work through the thousands of entries and suggestions we received and to shape them into the present collection. We feel we got what we asked for, and more. We hope you find the results as enjoyable and provocative as we have.

NOTES

1. Quoted by Dana Gioia, "Business and Poetry," in *Can Poetry Matter?: Essays on Poetry and American Culture* (Saint Paul: Graywolf Press, 1992), 133.

2. Gioia, "Business and Poetry," 126.

3. Agricultural and other forms of outdoor work, such as logging and longshoring, are not included. For a selection of such poems, see Tom Wayman, *Going for Coffee: An Anthology of Contemporary North American Working Poems* (Madeira Park, B.C.: Harbour, 1981).

4. For a full listing of topics, jobs, and workplaces, see the Subject Index.

5. John W. Wright and Edward J. Dwyer, *The American Almanac of Jobs and Salaries* (New York: Avon, 1991), xx.

6. "Reflected status" is a key term in Rosabeth Moss Kanter's *Men and Women of the Corporation* (New York: Basic, 1977).

7. Barbara Ehrenreich, *Fear of Falling: The Inner Life of the Middle Class* (New York: HarperCollins, 1989), 8.

8. See, for instance, Wendell Berry, "The Specialization of Poetry," *Hudson Review* 38 (Spring 1985); Joseph Epstein, "Who Killed Poetry?" *Commentary* 86 (August 1988); and Gioia, *Can Poetry Matter?*

9. Jonathan Holden, *The Fate of American Poetry* (Athens: University of Georgia Press, 1991).

10. Ibid., 30.

11. *A Directory of American Poets and Fiction Writers* (New York: Poets and Writers, Inc.), published annually.

FOR A LIVING

EXCERPTS FROM
Evidence: From a Reporter's Notebook

2

"You some reporter, right?" she says.
"It was a white man did this.
Said it is to show you niggers
who climbed from back of bus
to sit with us.
You nigger bitch, you get what you deserve,
and then he twist my arm behind me.
See the scratches, the splotches.
He drags me through some bushes and I got cuts.
You see 'em. You do.
He bit me too."
She tears at her skirt
and raises her knee, so I can see
high up her inner thigh,
too high, almost to knotted hair where underwear
of shiny fabric, nylon, I guess, begins.
"And when he finished with me," she says,
"he spit between my legs and rub it in."
I have learned not to wince
when such details are given;
still, I feel a slight
tightening of stomach muscles
before I make myself unclench
and do the true reporter thing,
which is to be the victim,
to relive with her again, again,
until it is my own night of degradation,
my own graduation from the shit to shit.
"Go on," she says, "write it down or somethin',
tape it, film it.
We got to hit him hard, hurt him. OK?"
"We will," I say, my smile in place now
like my hair, my friendship a brand-new dress

I wear until I wear it out or down,
but even as I take her hand extended to me,
so that we are banded together
in her stormy weather,
both without raincoats, umbrellas,
I flash on the report just read—
questionable rape, no tears, no bleeding there
or in the other place,
and bites that could be self-inflicted.
"Dirty sonofabitch," I say,
"is this United States of Revenge, or what?
We've got everything we need, got television,
and I have got your story
before the competition."

Six straight days, she's front-page news.
She makes guest appearances by dozens.
Everybody's cousin wants their piece
of tender meat,
but I've already eaten there
and I'm still hungry.
I'm suffocating too and I need air,
I need a long vacation from myself
and from my protégée
in all the ways manipulation pays,
when you play off the outrage
and the sympathy of others.
And she's a natural, she was born to do it,
should have her own byline in *New York Times,*
and I should have a Watergate,
should get my chance for Pulitzer glory,
but even Woodward faded like a paper rose
once he got his story.
I mean, you've got to know when to let it ride
and let it go, or else you wind up
some side show in Hackensack, or Tupelo.
You see, I couldn't prove that she was lying
and I couldn't prove she wasn't,
but that doesn't mean I abandoned her.
I swear the story led me somewhere else,
to the truth,
whatever that is, an excuse, I know, but valid.
Reality is a fruit salad anyway.
You take one bite, another, all those flavors,
which one is right?
She chose the role of victim
and for a while, I went along,
until tonight, when I look out
my window over Central Park

and think of other women whimpering
and bleeding in the darkness,
an infinity of suffering and abuse
to choose my next big winner from.
What I do, I take my own advice.
I whip my horse across the finish line
before I shoot it.
I step over her body
while the black sun rises behind me,
smoking like an old pistol.
The unofficial rules of this game
are that once found out,
you aim your tear-stained face into the camera.
You make your disgrace, your shame, work for you.
They don't burn bitches anymore,
they greet them at the back door with corsages
and slide them out the front into a reed basket
to float down the Nile, repentance,
into the arms of all us Little Egypts.
Welcome back.

4

My latest eyewitness news report,
focused on false accusations,
took as a prime example
my own delectable sample of the sport.
Even Warhol would have been proud,
would have remained in awe
long enough to list her name in his diaries,
might have understood her appetite,
have gained insight into her need,
though even her staunchest supporters
cannot explain away all contradictions,
all claims of violation that don't add up.
But really, if they only knew, in spite of that,
the lens through which we view the truth
is often cracked and filthy with the facts.
It could have happened. That is the bridge
that links the world of Kafka to us still,
the black pearl in pig's mouth
that won't be blasted out no matter what we do,
that finds us both on Oprah
or on Donahue, facing the packed pews
of the damned and the saved,
to send our innocence,
our guilt, across the crowded airwaves
to be filtered through
the ultimate democracy of TV,
which equalizes everything it sees
and freezes us to the screen between commercials
for movies of the week and shaving cream,
each show a rehearsal for the afternoon
when with a cry
she spreads her chocolate thighs
while I kneel down to look,
but still I find no evidence

of racist's or even boyfriend's semen.
I press my fingers hard against her,
then hold them up before the audience,
wet only with the thick spit of my betrayal.

Sonnet for Her Labor

My Aunt Nita's kitchen was immaculate and dark,
and she was always bending to the sink
below the window where the shadows off the bulk
of Laurel Mountain rose up to the brink
of all the sky she saw from there. She clattered
pots on countertops wiped clean of coal dust,
fixed three meals a day, fried meat, mixed batter
for buckwheat cakes, hauled water, in what seemed lust
for labor. One March evening, after cleaning,
she lay down to rest and died. I can see Uncle Ed,
his fingers twined at his plate for the blessing;
my Uncle Craig leaning back, silent in red
galluses. No one said a word to her. All that food
and cleanliness. No one ever told her it was good.

Juan Angel

—A Man in Rock & Roll Purgatory

Lately I've been trying to visualize
          things. Like attracts like. Like if I
think I might get famous why I'll
          get famous. Juan might become JUAN,
in neon. I'm sure of it. I'm Fame's
          angel. ANGEL. *West Side Story* taught
Puerto Ricans to walk, like they're
          suddenly going to explode into . . . a
dance. All latins are lovers and
          are required by law to be able to mambo
and samba and tango and salsa
          and do any forbidden dance . . .
It's as if you have to want to become
          Charro or the Spiderwoman who kisses the
American William Hurt to death. Like,
          like they couldn't find one unemployed
Latino actor to take over the role!
          Or were they afraid of giving a Hispanic
the Academy Award? Anyway, it's safe.
          And it was Puerto Rican drag queens and
Black drag queens that started
          the Stonewall riots. Judy dared to die.
The hard part of living alone is
          trying to take pictures of yourself.
Not always in drag. It's always a
          closeup—unless, of course, your arms
grow unusually long. I love
          pictures! I keep trying to choose
the ones that are going to make the
          best album covers. I told you I'm
trying out this visualizing thing.
          Like thinking myself into record stores,
Like I can see it already.
          Oasis Records and a fan looks up, spots
me. Screams. Fans start chasing

me. ME! Like what happened to the

Beatles in *A Hard Day's Night.* I'm

running and running so my fans don't

catch up or lose me either. It's

a delicate balance. I mean—look at

Elvis's ghost. It can't haunt

Graceland in privacy. God gave me my

privates for a reason. I've been

practicing! For the video shows. I

not only know how to lip sync,

I hip sync! I'm so good in my empty bed:

Hello
I'm blonde
Goodbye
I'm brunette
After two vodkas
you're easy to forget
Hey you
I'm easy
But man you're sleazy
Sure
I want everything
Everything
that has a sting
I have to feel it
to make it real
I have to feel it

Oh, once I started a band but

all of us wanted to be the star power.

When the neighbors called the cops

we told them we were on *Star Search.*

Fame! I'm going to live forever.

I'm Juan Angel. I'm keeping my name.

I mean people know Gloria Estefan.

Trini Lopez. Rita Moreno. Julio Iglesias

showed up once on the *Golden Girls.*

My mother was born in the village in
Puerto Rico that Jose Feliciano was.
A sign! That I'm Juan in a million.
Juan-derful. Juan is the one. Juan toss
of the dice. Juan chance of a lifetime.
Juan-na dance! Gotta dance!
Out of my way Madonna. I mean, why did
she get the #1 hit, *La Isla Bonita?*
Barry Manilow and that *Copacabana.*
Father used to sing me to sleep with
La Bamba. Why didn't I record it first?
I dream big, but no matter how big I
dream I'm smaller than life, smaller.
I'm tired of waiting for the big break,
the big man, the big boys, the big game.
I'm tired of waiting. Reminds me of
that old Spanish joke about us that
while waiting for a new life in
America we're waiting on tables.
I want to be in America. *Born in*
the USA. See you on an album cover
near you. Hello, I'm Juan Angel.

The Instruction Manual

As I sit looking out of a window of the building
I wish I did not have to write the instruction manual on
    the uses of a new metal.
I look down into the street and see people, each walking
    with an inner peace,
And envy them—they are so far away from me!
Not one of them has to worry about getting out this
    manual on schedule.
And, as my way is, I begin to dream, resting my elbows
    on the desk and leaning out of the window a little,
Of dim Guadalajara! City of rose-colored flowers!
City I wanted most to see, and most did not see, in
    Mexico!
But I fancy I see, under the press of having to write the
    instruction manual,
Your public square, city, with its elaborate little band-
    stand!
The band is playing *Scheherazade* by Rimsky-Korsakov.
Around stand the flower girls, handing out rose- and
    lemon-colored flowers,
Each attractive in her rose-and-blue striped dress (Oh!
    such shades of rose and blue).
And nearby is the little white booth where women in
    green serve you green and yellow fruit.
The couples are parading; everyone is in a holiday mood.
First, leading the parade, is a dapper fellow
Clothed in deep blue. On his head sits a white hat
And he wears a mustache, which has been trimmed for
    the occasion.
His dear one, his wife, is young and pretty; her shawl is
    rose, pink, and white.
Her slippers are patent leather, in the American fashion,
And she carries a fan, for she is modest, and does not
    want the crowd to see her face too often.
But everybody is so busy with his wife or loved one
I doubt they would notice the mustachioed man's wife.

13

Here come the boys! They are skipping and throwing
    little things on the sidewalk
Which is made of gray tile. One of them, a little older,
    has a toothpick in his teeth.
He is silenter than the rest, and affects not to notice the
    pretty young girls in white.
But his friends notice them, and shout their jeers at the
    laughing girls.
Yet soon all this will cease, with the deepening of their
    years,
And love bring each to the parade grounds for another
    reason.
But I have lost sight of the young fellow with the tooth-
    pick.
Wait—there he is—on the other side of the bandstand,
Secluded from his friends, in earnest talk with a young
    girl
Of fourteen or fifteen. I try to hear what they are saying
But it seems they are just mumbling something—shy
    words of love, probably.
She is slightly taller than he, and looks quietly down into
    his sincere eyes.
She is wearing white. The breeze ruffles her long fine
    black hair against her olive cheek.
Obviously she is in love. The boy, the young boy with the
    toothpick, he is in love too;
His eyes show it. Turning from this couple,
I see there is an intermission in the concert.
The paraders are resting and sipping drinks through
    straws
(The drinks are dispensed from a large glass crock by a
    lady in dark blue),
And the musicians mingle among them, in their creamy
    white uniforms, and talk
About the weather, perhaps, or how their kids are doing
    at school.

14

Let us take this opportunity to tiptoe into one of the side
   streets.
Here you may see one of those white houses with green
   trim
That are so popular here. Look—I told you!
It is cool and dim inside, but the patio is sunny.
An old woman in gray sits there, fanning herself with a
   palm leaf fan.
She welcomes us to her patio, and offers us a cooling
   drink.
"My son is in Mexico City," she says. "He would wel-
   come you too
If he were here. But his job is with a bank there.
Look, here is a photograph of him."
And a dark-skinned lad with pearly teeth grins out at us
   from the worn leather frame.
We thank her for her hospitality, for it is getting late
And we must catch a view of the city, before we leave,
   from a good high place.
That church tower will do—the faded pink one, there
   against the fierce blue of the sky. Slowly we enter.
The caretaker, an old man dressed in brown and gray,
   asks us how long we have been in the city, and how
   we like it here.
His daughter is scrubbing the steps—she nods to us as
   we pass into the tower.
Soon we have reached the top, and the whole network of
   the city extends before us.
There is the rich quarter, with its houses of pink and
   white, and its crumbling, leafy terraces.
There is the poorer quarter, its homes a deep blue.
There is the market, where men are selling hats and
   swatting flies.
And there is the public library, painted several shades of
   pale green and beige.
Look! There is the square we just came from, with the

promenaders.
There are fewer of them, now that the heat of the day has
    increased,
But the young boy and girl still lurk in the shadows of the
    bandstand.
And there is the home of the little old lady—
She is still sitting in the patio, fanning herself.
How limited, but how complete withal, has been our
    experience of Guadalajara!
We have seen young love, married love, and the love of
    an aged mother for her son.
We have heard the music, tasted the drinks, and looked
    at colored houses.
What more is there to do, except stay? And that we
    cannot do.
And as a last breeze freshens the top of the weathered
    old tower, I turn my gaze
Back to the instruction manual which has made me
    dream of Guadalajara.

Leaving It All Behind

There were days when we still didn't get it,
that this wasn't like school or the military,
that we wouldn't graduate or get out
and leave it all behind.
We brought lunches in brown paper bags
and folded airplanes
to fly in the park,
and lusted after secretaries
just in from the small towns
and still learning how to dress.

We pitied the older guys
playing out their big-time businessman roles
as if most of them were not just some kind
of free-market bureaucrats.
Somehow we knew we'd do better
and we knew we'd be different,
without that need to cover our asses,
without that fear of failure.
We would give young guys like us
plenty of room to make us look good,
and we would ignore stupid policies and politics
and get rid of deadwood vice presidents
who wasted time and money and office space.
We would have the guts to take our money and run
before the job pushed us too hard
and the next title became too important,
before we found ourselves on airplanes every week
and in the office every weekend,
before our kids stopped caring if we were around,
and our wives drank too much
at too many ladies' luncheons
where they were going to have just a sherry
or one glass of wine,
before we got tired of smiling at every jerk
who might spend a dime with us,

before we ate every oversauced meal
and sniffed every cork and drank every bottle of wine,
before we went to every sunny resort
and heard every self-improvement speaker
and danced at every black-tie dinner
and applauded every chairman and program committee
and carried home every printed tote bag
and monogrammed vinyl notebook
and T-shirt,
and put every smiling group picture in a scrapbook.

Before all that,
we would get out.

Business Is Bad, I

How do you know when you've gone too far?
Maybe it's when someone asks,
"How are you?"
And you tell them how business is.
Maybe it's when business is bad
and it feels like a death in the family,
and you wonder how anybody can be happy,
the way you feel when you're on the way to a funeral
and find yourself wondering
why all those other people in the airport
are laughing and smiling as if no one had died.
Don't they know, don't they know?
Business is bad.

Maybe it's when you find yourself angry
in the midst of another, yet another,
birthday coffee or promotion party,
or when someone asks you to join a baseball pool
or attend a fund-raising lunch,
or stop for an after-work drink
with the such-and-such department,
which is celebrating
another of those productivity milestones
we invent so we'll have something to celebrate.
"How do they have time for this crap?"
you ask yourself.
Don't they know, don't they know?
Business is bad.

Business Is Bad, II

He did not look well,
the paunch of too many receptions and dinners
at too many conferences
in too many hotels.
(Sometimes it's smiling too much
I think
and saying the same thing
over and over again,
a kind of social fatigue.)
And here he was,
eating and drinking,
this time with friends,
—never mind that we all work together,
that we talk about those same things—
in the home of another friend,
so I asked, "How are you doing?"
with an emphasis on the you.
And he shook his head
and frowned and tucked his chin
and swallowed like someone
whose mouth is dry
and said,
"That last profit forecast was rotten,
really a killer."

On Firing a Salesman

It's like a little murder,
taking his life,
his reason for getting on the train,
his lunches at Christ Cella,
and his meetings in warm and sunny places
where they all gather,
these smiling men,
in sherbet slacks and blue blazers,
and talk about business
but never about prices,
never breaking that law
about the prices they charge.

But what about the prices they pay?
What about gray evenings in the bar car
and smoke-filled clothes and hair
and children already asleep
and wives who say
"You stink"
when they come to bed?
What about the promotions they don't get,
the good accounts they lose
to some kid MBA
because somebody thinks their energy is gone?

What about those times they see in a mirror
or the corner of their eye
some guy at the club shake his head
when they walk through the locker room
the way they shook their heads years ago
at an old duffer
whose handicap had grown along with his age?

And what about this morning,
the summons,
the closed door,

and somebody shaved and barbered and shined
fifteen years their junior
trying to put on a sad face
and saying he understands?

A murder with no funeral,
nothing but those quick steps outside the door,
those set jaws,
those confident smiles,
that young disregard for even the thought
of a salesman's mortality.

Executive Health

Something happens,
a dizziness when you stand up,
a pain you never noticed before,
a heavy breath at the top of the stairs.
And you think about a friend in the hospital,
and wonder what's going to get you someday.
So you make another vow,
you buy a diet book
and new workout clothes
and a computerized treadmill
and meditation tapes,
and you renew the health-club membership
and get your racquet out of the closet
and inflate the tires on the bike
and walk three miles the very first day.

Then it's Monday,
and the broiled fish you were going to have
turns into pasta
and the dessert you'll always skip
becomes just sherbet,
and out of the office by five
means still there at seven.
On Tuesday you can't work out on an airliner,
and who in his right mind jogs
after dark in a strange city?
And the tapes you play for stress
put you to sleep at the wrong time,
so you lie awake later,
listening to the horns and the garbage trucks
and the sound of your own breathing,
and vow to make another start this weekend.

Retirement Party

They all come,
even the ones who think
he was a pain in the neck.
They come and talk
about how he will be missed,
most of them never noticing he was there.
They come for themselves,
like going to a funeral
out of the fear of being buried alone someday.

They line up for coffee
and punch and cookies,
there being no official alcohol on the premises.
They read telegrams from old customers and old vendors
and old office buddies long retired.
They give him the right gift,
the rod and reel
or the camp stove
or the camera
or the round-trip ticket to somewhere,
bought with the fives and ones and quarters
from the manila envelope that has
in his last month
made its way all around the company.

He is moved by the attention,
by the feeling he is loved
and will be missed
and things won't be the same without him,
and he says some words
about how he will never forget any of them.
He introduces his family, who came halfway across the country
just for the occasion,
then everybody drifts toward their offices
saying good-bye with things like
"You lucky bastard,"

and "You don't even have to get up tomorrow,"
and "Stay in touch,"
and "Come visit,"
and other words of comfort for times like these.

EXCERPT FROM
A Song of Survival

I worked as a licensed plumber, had my own tools
and truck, every morning met the sun, felt my muscles
pull against each other, working the pipe-wrenches
and shovels. I worked as a business executive for a
merchandise firm, meeting customers, having coffee
in cafes with prospective clients, feeling the sturdy
handshakes, wearing my new white shirts and suits of
different colors, driving automatic, power-steering
chevvies, travelling to small communities,
and I worked in Mexico as a rock-breaker, high on
the mountain, stood in the midday sunlight,
shirtless, my chest shimmering in perspiration, as I
brought the big hammer down on huge rocks,
cracking them,
and my chest heaving, my legs apart, both hands
gripped tight, and down again on the rock!
And I worked for myself as a dope dealer of
marijuana, sitting with friends on lawns,
in living rooms,
or by the sea, we'd sit and watch the sun going down,
glistening over a thousand tiny swelling curls of water,
exploding orange and yellow on the horizon,
and I wondered about my life, where I
wanted it to go, deciding what I wanted from life.
And I worked as a woodchopper in the mountains,
the snow was marvelous,
glittering in the morning with the smell of wood
everywhere, fresh wet bark, speckled with dew,
and broken sticks oozing sap, tree boughs
shaking with squirrels, deer on their pointing toes
watched me from a distance eyes brimming with sparks.
And I worked as a dishwasher,
two big stainless steel sinks filled with tumultuous
heaps of pans and skillets and chef-spoons,
big-bellied pots with burned black bottoms, with

sleeves rolled up and rubber apron on, I'd bend over,
scrubbing as fast as I could, while waitresses
zing'd back and forth, dumping pans and dishes,
giving me a word of consolation—I'd grump,
and they'd scurry away tired as myself.
I worked as a streetsweeper in the early morning
in my heavy old jacket and cap, pushing the broom,
picking up papers, musing over the display windows
of department stores, admiring women embarking
on the bus, their thighs pressed smoothly against
skirts, hair flowing, eyes jet dark and soft lips,
while their hair shook, and winds sped rowdily
down streets, against curtains of windows, against
shiny hair of businessmen, their shoes spit polished
to a gleam, briefcase in hand, and, soon, all the
people jumbling across stoplights, cars and trucks
sputtering in the early morning.
And I worked as a cook and bouncer in a niteclub,
cooking hamburgers and fish,
carrying out drunks and breaking up fights,
shooting pool with my friends as they choked
on the food, and the drunks staggered back in,
pushing cars late at night to get them started.
And I worked as a milker in a big dairy farm,
loving the cows,
I'd walk down the old path to the fields with a stick
in my hand, they'd all turn with groggy brown eyes,
slowly swishing tails and chewing cuds,
I'd give a whistle, they'd come to me, I'd follow
them down the path, talking to them as they
mosey'd on, and I'd tell them I loved them, their
big wet noses.
And I worked as a truckdriver in town at night,
in the small cab, with just me, the radio, the stars,
and the empty streets,
and I'd stop by a residential house with a big garden

27

and snip a few roses in the dark,
then jump back in my truck and drive down to my
woman's house, tap on the glass pane, I'd hear
her mother's worried voice ask who would come to
the window, and my woman would open the curtain,
smile sleepily, and run to the door to let me in.
And I worked as a metalworker on top of bridges,
tying strips of metal bars together before they
poured the cement, and at noon I'd have armwrestles
with the carpenters,
and eat chili, sitting on dirt mounds, my whole body
aching from work, yet I was proud, and I'd drive
the big scrapers, and direct the man in the crane,
and help carpenters, they'd invite me over
to their trailers in the evening,
and, finally, when the bridge was done, we all
stood there, looking proud in our dirty and
dust-smudged faces, and knew the bridge
meant something to us all.
I owned a chuckwagon filled with icy cokes and
candy bars and hot sandwiches, I would go around
to all the construction sites, and beep beep the gas
horn, and out of the massive and rambling
construction site, grubby workmen began appearing,
out of windows, out of brick heaps and holes in the
ground, plumbers, electricians, carpenters,
laborers, all lining up,
their tools and instruments jangling and knocking
from heavy leather belts at their waists, the sun
beating down fiercely. I'd give them cokes and
candy, and we'd joke, while they squatted down
and ate, smoked a cigarette, brushed dust from
their faces and hair, talked about the buildings,
blueprints, materials.
And I worked as a school custodian, pushing the
long dust-mop down the shiny scuffed halls,

passing the numbered doors, cleaning desks,
windows, scrubbing toilets and walls, watering
the grass and watching the kids play basketball,
I, the only person among all these books,
blackboards and little figures of cut paper
thumbtacked to boards, little gold and blue stars,
and colored drawings on paper, as I
swept up the dirt and carried my dustpan out,
emptying trashcans—
not only school, but the whole world, would be
empty, empty without children, the most
precious creatures of God, our hopes and loves.
And I went on working at different jobs,
as a chain-puller, a soda-jerk, a shoe salesman,
refrigeration mechanic, gardener, horse trainer,
appliance man, painter—I searched
for an occupation where I could expend my full
worth, I needed a job
where I could be free and creative, and I kept
searching, learning about people, about the
country, while I looked for something to define my
heart with the world into one, using my body and
mind and soul, into one,
and the search led me to my first cell in prison.

There's Me

There's me & Thelma & Louie & Lisa.
We're the kinda people, don't know too much about that place.
We know about factories all right, but not about how everybody
up there makes so much money.

Like Louie says, how you gonna make so much money
if you don't work? And Thelma says, sure people use their brains,
but a body works too. But a body costs a nickel, a mind costs
a million. And all them minds, what if there weren't no bodies
to work for them? Huh?

Up in that place, that's really something
uh Lisa, really something.

Here we are in clothes and talk and faces.
We know what's going on down here, but up there? Man . . .

So don't ask me why I carry a knife. Like
this, and don't ask me no questions, because I don't understand;
but take a cop wants to arrest somebody, and I'm walking
down the street, why me? He just wants to arrest somebody.
Not him, but someone told him to arrest somebody. And that
someone was told by someone else, who had little numbers in
a paper that say things ain't going too well. Now where'd
he get them numbers? Maybe from somebody with a computer
up there in one of them offices up there. Just a regular old man
or lady standing in front of a machine writing out numbers
and figuring stuff up.

Now why's he figuring something up? Ok Lisa
look: he's figuring up something, because someone else
somewhere wants him to. And you know someone who can make
him figure something up, is somebody big. Way up there . . .
probably got a whole bunch of things in this world like
boat companies and oil companies and things like that.

Just think, why does he want anyone to figure
up something? Cause one of the dudes that work for him told
him something was going wrong somewhere, and the figuring
needed to be done cuz it was messing things up.

And how does he know? I think he looks at
all these charts, you know, and if the line goes down, that

30

means the chump is losing. He's paid to win. So he's got
all these college dudes with degrees, thousands of them,
in a big ole building, working all day, so he can win.
They figure up everything.
    And from way up there, whatever comes out,
on a little piece of paper figured up by a thousand minds,
happens down here on the street. See what I mean?
    We're different man. You go to work Thelma
and spill coffee on tables, collect tips, smoke cigarettes,
you know, you know what's going on with yourself. And Louie
and Lisa and me, we all live, like getting good clothes,
dressing up for Friday night, riding down Central, getting
up in the morning and cursing at cockroaches, it's a good
life, better, because we know we're human beings. Know
what I mean?
    So there ain't nothing wrong with us man,
we're ok, we're good people, and our life ain't so bad man.
We'll make it, look out for each other.

LENORE BALLIRO

French Restaurant, 1982

We do it for six hours.
Everyone knows:

We write down on a pad
what it is they want,
but we don't let them see it.

They think we remember,
so we let them.

They watch what moves
under the black swing of skirt,

how the candles underlight
the faces that lean to clear
their plates.

We put our tips
in jars with our names, dipping in
with slippery fingers. After,

you invite me: to shoot pool,
far from Beaujolais Nouveau,
anything East Side or Ivy League. You invite me:
to drink shots and beer at Mike's 17 bar, downtown.
You invite me: respectfully,
to Mayo, Georgia, where your father
fishes in a pond in the backyard,
wearing a hat from the French Foreign Legion.
Permettez-moi.

The buses stop running,
and we walk through the tunnel.
The game is good, the sharp clack
of those balls that we whack
across Mike's table.

It's a good thing. We work the same shift.
And when we pass
in the aisles of our stations,
the small hairs on the back of our wrists
stiffen.

WALTER BARGEN

Heavenly Host

When lightning struck the transformer
during the night, leaving the exact
time on every wall clock in the office,
though not necessarily the same minute
and second, no one was troubled except

to stand on chairs, perhaps catching
the glance of an office mate, especially,
if the dress was short and the legs young,
but only for an instant, afraid such
attention might be noticed, that

allegiances might be called into question,
and rumors suggest all the impossibilities,
sure that an episodic life is less than
they have. No one noticed, how at eight
o'clock on a morning turned cold with patches

of ice on roads and clinging to corners of
windshields, suggesting with only a side
glance the uncataloged motions of passing
fields and buildings, a country just
happening—only to be left waiting

for the custodian to thaw the door's frozen
lock. No one really noticed, how at eight
o'clock the secretaries rose to the ceiling,
and in that rush of time resetting the clocks,
there was an unbearable ravelling, those

small black hands racing in circles, as if
someone were shouting from too far away to
be understood, and all anyone could do was
breathe and watch the secretaries step down
at one minute after, having lost their wings.

34

What We Want to Hear

On the ramp of the freeway
the engine dies, though
the car continues to roll,
and shifting back into gear,
the ignition turned on,
and letting the clutch out,
the car lurches, the engine
kicks-in, and I'm off, and it's
running, but at the first stop
sign off the highway it dies
again, and I push it onto
the gravel shoulder letting
the morning traffic rush
past, and after opening
the hood and removing
the air filter it starts
again, only to fail
at the next stoplight,
the inside lane engulfed
in a ghost of blue smoke
that blows over the windshields
of blocked cars and frantic
drivers until it sputters
and is coaxed along only
to utterly stop in the turn
lane in front of my destination,
and three suited men push
through the intersection
rolling the car into the parking
lot where after work it starts
right up.

Thomas Hill Power Plant Car Pool

Cold rain explodes into slush
on the windshield.

It's deer season
and the stories are bragged freely
about a cousin or uncle
who shot the biggest buck
in Randolph County—
three-hundred pounds.

That moment we see
three does race
across the road.
The last one to leap
the fence falls
to its knees,
does a full somersault,
keeps running,
never breaking its stride.
The driver shouts,
"They must be late for work!"

The beer cooler open
the pop-tops fire
indiscriminately.

Another Hour

Behind steel and imitation
walnut desks, we sit across
from each other. The sun sets on
the other side of the building.
The pictures taped on the walls
give off little light. Without
speaking we think the same
thought. We drift into the music
on the radio, into the hotel lounge
where it is being played. The chandelier
is lost in its own glow, and
the wide chairs float like rafts
that never touch the shore
of this day. Soon the snare
drum and bass drop away
leaving a solitary piano
to slowly shape the soft air
of evening, leaving us alone
to stare out the window-walls
into a growing curtain of fog.
The glass is so invisible
we are tempted to walk through,
leaving the one or two others
alone over their drinks,
not even shocked, as if
this has happened before,
that men have entered rooms
they could not leave
and dreamed of other desks.

JANE BARNES

Right Now

you're out in a village in the Berkshires
and your waiter is serving your steak.
You're on your third Sombrero and
one of the engineers is telling a joke.

I'm home with the TV news on so everything
will seem normal. I've invited Marcie over for a beer.
It already seems odd to have done it.

Now you're cutting the steak. It is thick and rare
and the boss is paying for it. You laugh.
This is the life! You're glad you smoked that joint.
You see two lovers in the corner
and try not to miss me and spoil it.

I drink Lites with Marcie; we talk about teaching.
She says how nice I'm still with my lover.
She goes home and I spread the newspaper out
on your side of the bed and drink cold tea.

You're going into the lounge for a brandy
with the detail man. The guys make jokes
about the location of your room.
I lay two pillows alongside me in bed.

The Back-up Singer

The Father of the Stethoscope:
René Theophile Hyacinthe Laënnec,
mellifluous name.
In 1816 he rolled a *cornet de papier,* then held it
against the first chest
of the first heart to open its argument
to another man that way, through flesh
and conducting bone. Later
the instrument was crafted of wood, and a small hole bored
for the passage of human sound.

Is it wrong to want to be the only one?
To wish the wedding ring of the spotlight
slipped over me in a moment
that finally holds?
Houselights rise then lower like the rush of blood
through narrowed vessels.
The cymbal solo and high hat
shimmer me forward, but in the blur
and slip of horns I'm singing *do wop*
and *shing, shing-a-ling*
behind a lame pimp and his big-haired girls.

I like to read the old school books.
The page of René Laënnec
turned down in particular, and nearly worn through,
which is also the nature of hope.
A young girl's hands turned
whole lifetimes down.
I'd listen to the telegraphing night bugs'
double ardor, and eventually to darkness
siphoned off by dawn
like the sounds I'd make with my perfect pitch
and years of training under that same blue
no-protection sky.

But there are planetary systems in the blood.
A grand opera of fate brings chances
we can't see but choose somehow.
Later, we see how we went wrong.
Now August says he never, ever
wanted anyone so badly. But there's rehab first,
and the business with his wife.
And the last abortion having left
a disability of my womb
I've come to think of as a million tiny birdsfeet tracking
over muddied ground. Some nights

it's too much like this
on the girls' bus. Regret or Spend It Now,
towels around our throats.
More often it's regret
rolling its bullet casings at our feet—
Lissanne, Yvette, me—
its spent and blackened flashbulbs.
Then I recall the lessons I never quite learned
for their sweetness alone.
On a single mating flight
the queen bee will store enough spermatozoa
to hold her the rest of her working days.
In the blue runways of iris and morning glory,
from ultraviolet
nectar guides, she'll fertilize as she goes.

Call it love that keeps me here.
Call it the final, female talent for demurring
when life takes over.
I call it a living, discovering at sixteen
that come in my mouth doesn't taste
remotely like white flowers.
Ten years later I'm waiting for the bus to stop
or lurch me to my next home.

I'm housewife to an act that pays and pays and pays.
Under lights hotter than God
I activate the angels in my voice and take
three steps backward, *cha cha cha*.
But I call it a science more mine
than either sex or shame
to be this alone, in time, among others.
Some days I get up before noon just to hear
the first notes of the treble world
break from my throat
over the heads of everyone listening but me.

JACKIE BARTLEY

The Midnight Tech's Meditation

Here life's pure,
a monolayer of red
cells, a green blip
on a screen.

This one's delirious
in the warm
French-movie light
of ICU.

His blood's dark milk,
thick as it leaves
his arm

all these arms.

The nurse ran
to help
with the one who rose up
                              in bed.

"Patient refused procedure."

In 318, a blue-motel room
diabetic, listening
to Joni while he
told me
about his wildcatting days,

beyond his window, a panorama
of sky.

He'll die soon—
amputee

with creatinine
and blood urea nitrogen
off the charts.

His veins are hard rock
blue.

On 4-South, the thin
old woman

gravida 8, para 5

whose only palpable
veins
distend her feet.
Blue-black plug
of a hematoma
swells
the right foot's arch.

In ER, the aneurysm;
flood that breaks
the dam of the heart.
The man's eyes
gray-violet—wide
as a dog's
beneath the wheels
of the car it thought
to chase.

Death's Eyes.

I typed it *Stat,*
spun the tube,

the serum not yet
separate
from the clot,
stacked the units,
tore the segments off,
squeezed them
into saline, prepared
to check their match,

crossmatch.

Then a voice
that told me
I could stop.

Last week, a girl,
almost a woman,
became instead
"an acute lymphocytic,"

relinquished
her name in exchange
for her death's.

What lovely varied ghosts
her red cells
have become
in their purple
rain.

Marked anisocytosis,
poikilocytosis.

I compose their stories,
label their tubes,
line them up

in my rack like
a box of new crayons.
The orange and lemon serums
rise,
tornado skies
above red
prairie dirt.

Their mysteries numbered,
the wild, growing storm
of their deaths
given definition,

I extrapolate
from a teaspoon
of their blood
what I've been told
it takes
to fill the body.

A Waitress's Instructions on Tipping
or
Get the Cash Up and Don't Waste My Time

20% minimum as long as the waitress doesn't inflict bodily harm.
If you're two people at a four top, tip extra.
If you sit a long time, pay rent.
Double tips for special orders.
Always tip extra when using coupons.
Better yet, don't use coupons.
Never leave change instead of bills.
Never leave pennies at all.
Never hide a tip for fun.
Overtip, overtip, overtip.
Remember, I am somebody's mother or daughter.
Large parties *must* overtip, no separate piles of change.
If people in your party don't show up, tip *for* them.
Don't wait around for gratitude if you overtip.
Take a risk. Don't adjust your tip so your credit card total is even.
Don't ever, ever pull out a tipping guide in public.
If you leave 10% or less, eat at home.
If I call a taxi for you, tip me.
If I hang up your coat for you, tip me.
If I get cigarettes for you, tip me.
Better yet, do it yourself.
If you buy a $50 bottle of wine, pull out a $10.
If I serve you one cocktail, don't hand me $.35.
If you're just having coffee, leave a $5.
Don't fold a bill and hand it to me like you're a big shot.
Don't say, *There's a big tip in it for you if* . . .
Don't say, *I want to make sure you get this,* like a busboy would steal it.
Don't say, *Here, honey, this is for you* —ever.
Don't say, *I'll make it worth your while.*
If you're miserable, there's not enough money in the world.

JUDITH BERKE

Ms

This desk is an antique: it's dainty,
and has limbs, and boy are they shaky.
My boss is a woman, and luckily,
she got this really nifty desk for her office,
maybe to make up for something.
Today when I brought in coffee,
Mr. Tull was in the small chair, and
Mr. Royce on the desk, and then
Mr. Chagrew on the windowsill, you
know, like steps, so the big
boss just stood there and loomed
over them. I brought the messages in,
all folded up, like she likes them. The one I
wrote said: Maybe we should put a chair up
on the ceiling? That she kept stabbing at
like a shish kebab, maybe to keep
from laughing. Then she said, Violet,
get a more comfortable chair for Mr. Ruby
(he's the president), so I knew then
we had to put them in just
the right order, sort of like checkers
or musical chairs; and that's the way it is
here—everyone moves one over. Once I said
to my boss, Did you ever see the TV show
about the baboons? Actually my boss looks
like Jane Goodall—you know, delicate, except
of course she's part of the tribe now.
That's why she wears the jacket
with the shoulders. Sometimes we eat lunch
here in her office, and there she is,
her head back in the chair, swiveling,
and the jacket, like another person,
in back of her.

KAREN BRODINE

EXCERPTS FROM
Woman Sitting at the Machine, Thinking

1

she thinks about everything at once without making a mistake.
no one has figured out how to keep her from doing this thinking
while her hands and nerves also perform every delicate complex
function of the work. this is not automatic or deadening.
try it sometime. make your hands move quickly on the keys
fast as you can, while you are thinking about:

the layers, fossils. the idea that this machine she controls
is simply layers of human workhours frozen in steel, tangled
in tiny circuits, blinking out through lights like hot, red eyes.
the noise of the machine they all sometimes wig out to, giddy,
zinging through the shut-in space, blithering atoms;
everyone's hands paused mid-air above the keys
while Neil or Barbara solo, wrists telling every little thing,
feet blipping along, shoulders raggly.

she had always thought of money as solid, stopped.
but seeing it as moving labor, human hours, why that means
it comes back down to her hands on the keys, shoulder aching,
brain pushing words through fingers through keys, trooping
out crisp black ants on the galleys, work compressed into
instruments, slim computers, thin as mirrors, how could
numbers multiply or disappear, squeezed in sideways like that
but they could, they did, obedient and elegant, how amazing.
the woman whips out a compact, computes the cost,
her face shining back from the silver case
her fingers, sharp tacks, calling up the digits.

when she sits at the machine, rays from the cathode stream
directly into her chest. when she worked as a clerk, the rays
from the xerox angled upward, striking her under the chin.
when she waited tables the micro oven sat at stomach level.

when she typeset for Safeway, dipping her hands in processor
chemicals, her hands burned and peeled and her chest ached
from the fumes.
well we know who makes everything we use or can't use.
as the world piles itself up on the bones of the years,
so our labor gathers.

while we sell ourselves in fractions. they don't want us all
at once, but hour by hour, piece by piece. our hands mainly
and our backs. and chunks of our brains. and veiled expressions
on our faces, they buy. though they can't know what actual
thoughts stand behind our eyes.

then they toss the body out on the sidewalk at noon and at five.
then they spit the body out the door at sixty-five.

each morning:

fresh thermos of coffee at hand; for the slowing down, shift
gears, unscrew the lid of the orange thermos, pour out a whiff
of home, morning paper, early light. a tangible pleasure
against the unlively words.

funny, though. this set of codes slips through my hands, a
loose grid of shadows with big gaps my own thoughts sneak
through . . .

call format o five. Reports, Disc 2, quad left
return. name of town, address, zip. quad left
return. rollalong and there you are.
done with this one. start the next.

call format o five. my day so silent yet taken up with words.
floating through the currents and cords of my wrists
into the screen and drifting to land, beached pollywogs.
all this language handled yet the room is so silent.
everyone absorbed in feeding words through the machines.

enter file execute.

call file Oceana. name of town, Pacifica. name of street, Arbor.
thinking about lovemaking last night, how it's another land,
another set of sounds, the surface of the water, submerged,
then floating free, the delicate fabric of motion and touch
knit with listening and humming and soaring.
never a clear separation of power because it is both our power
at once. hers to speak deep in her body and voice to her own
rhythms. mine to ride those rhythms out and my own,
and call them out even more. a speaking together from body
to mouth to voice.

replace file Oceana.
call file Island.

scroll up . . . . scroll down.
what is there to justify?

the words gliding on the screen like the seal at the aquarium,
funny whiskers, old man seal, zooming by upside down
smirking at the crowd, mocking us
and his friends the dolphins, each sharp black and cream marking
streamlined as the water

huh. ugh, they want this over and over:
MAY 1 MAY 1 MAY 1 MAY 1 MAY 1 enough?
MAY 1 MAY 1

3

once I have typeset all the pages, I run the job out on tape
and clip it to the videosetter to be punched out.
then I swing out the door to get another job.

down the stairs into the cramped room where Mary and Rosie
and Agnes sit in the limp draft of one fan.
"must be 95 in here." "yeah, and freezing in the other room."
"got to keep the computers cool, you know."

back up the stairs past management barricaded
behind their big desks on the way to everything.
on the way to the candy machine.
on the way to the bathroom.
on the way to lunch.
I pretend they are invisible.
I pretend they have great big elephant ears.

and because they must think we are stupid in order
to push us around, *they* become stupid.
knowing "something's going on," peering like moles.
how can they know the quirk of an eyebrow behind their back?
they suspect we hate them because they know
what they are doing to us—but we are only
stupid Blacks or crazy Puerto Ricans, or dumb blonds.

we are their allergy, their bad dream.
they need us too much, with their talk of
"carrying us" on the payroll.
we carry them, loads of heavy, dull metal,
outmoded and dusty.
they try to control us, building partitions,
and taking the faces off the phones.
they talk to us slow and loud,

HOW ARE YOU TODAY? HERE'S A CHECK FOR YOU.
as if it were a gift.

we say—even if they stretched tape
across our mouths
we could still speak to one another
with our eyebrows.

4

2 hours till lunch.
1 hour till lunch.
43 minutes till lunch.
13 minutes till lunch.
LUNCH.

they write you up if you're three minutes late.
three write-ups and you're out.

I rush back from lunch, short-cut
through the hall to the door
locked like the face of a boss.

I tug at the door, definitely locked.
peer in through the glass, watery and dark,
see two supervisors standing 25 yards in,
talking, faces turned away.
oh good, I think, they'll let me in.
I knock on the glass, cold to my fist.
not too loud, just enough to let them know.
they glance at me, continue talking.
I knock again, louder.
one man looks right at me, turns his back.
I am furious, let me in!
and knock again, my fist white where it is
clenched. BAM BAM BAM pause
BAM BAM BAM BAM BAM
they don't even look up.
I knock harder and harder, the glass
shaking in its frame.
I imagine my hand smashing through the pane,
shaking their collars, bloody but triumphant.

5

Sleepy afternoon . . . halfway through typing a long page
about building specifications, lost, wandering
through strange buildings, wide deep fields at dusk,
trying to find the way home.

I reach a deserted building, a warehouse, fenced off.
people hurry to work, not stopping to talk.
a low-level murmur hovers below the surface, like the
slight draft that makes the hair on your arm lift.
birds clot on the aerials, the light out of whack.

we notice a tightness right below the hollow of the neck
gathering to a deep chestpain, slowmoving and thick.
we notice it like smog, waking up each morning
short-breathed and headachy. the officials say nothing's wrong,
any slippage is small, no measurable effects gather.

none of us talk outloud about this to anyone.

now though, crowds begin to pool, huddling together.
I hurry to a circle of women, where a girl dodges cops.
she is agile, darting back and forth, panting,
slippery as soap, her hair damp and glistening.
they lunge, she skips, twists, breaks from the circle
and runs. we race after her in a tumbling crowd,
she is at my ear, whispering, "money . . . burning . . . tell . . .
say . . . shout."

we are afraid, locked in a windowless building, guarded.
the pain is still here the way summer heat insists.
I repeat the words which are about the phony soap
the guards have handed us, sickly sweet,
"will it wash it will it wash it away" and another
woman joins me, "soap fake soap," and another

and now all of us are chanting and the ones guarding us
look uncertain, scared, as if they too wonder
and we are all chanting and shouting now,
"fake soap, will it wash it won't it wash it away."

6

Line corrections
Interview with Leola S.
Typesetter: Karen B.

Born in Shreveport, Leola
independence is important, she
one of fourteen children, her
housecleaning in San Mateo
divorced now, she lives alone in
serving dinner from 4–5 pm every
starting pay 1.53 per
h o u r

she and some co-workers
today more than ever in U.S.
h i s t o r y

posed to discrimination by sex,
race, color, religious or national
o r i g i n

more women go to work in

enter the labor
0 percent of the average wage
Black women lowest paid of
to organize the continuing fight
determined to be heard
plaints against unfair policies
something worth fighting for
sector of the working class
w o m e n

Rivera's mural, the women, rows of them
similar, yet each unique, their hands
the focus of the art
bodies solid, leaning forward, these women,
facing the voices, knowledge running through them

language the most basic of industry
to gather our food
to record exchange
to give warning and call for help
to praise courage
it flows through our hands and into metal
they think it doesn't touch us

a typesetter changes man to person
will they catch her?
She files one job under union,
another under lagoon,
another under cash

what if you could send anything in and call it out again?
I file jobs under words I like—red, buzz, fury
search for tiger, execute
the words stream up the screen till tiger trips the halt
search for seal   search for strike
search for the names of women

we could circle our words around the world
like dolphins streaking through water their radar
if the screens were really in the hands of experts: us.
think of it—our ideas whipping through the air
everything stored in an eyeflash
our whole history, ready and waiting.

8

at night switching off the machines one by one
each degree of quiet a growing pleasure
we swallow the silence after hours of steady noise
the last machine harrumphs off and it is so visibly quiet
switch off the fluorescent lights and it is so quietly dark

I say, goodby, see you tomorrow, and relax down the stairs
into the cavernous shop where the paper is stored
near the presses, huge cardboard cylinders of newsprint
stacked up ceiling high.

I curve toward the door in the shadows
smells sweet like a big barn
calm snowbanks these spools, or tree trunks
in the light sifting through the glazed windows

walking tired through the resting plant
past huge breathing rolls of paper
waiting to be used

DAVID BUDBILL

Jeanie

My life is a wreck.
I'm 27 years old and I feel like my life is over.
What am I going to do?
Am I going to spend the rest of my life
waiting tables at Matia's?

Matia's is nice and all that and it's not a bad place to work,
the pay's okay and the tips are pretty good—
a lot better than when I waited table in that
veggie-reggie-hippy-dippy restaurant.
Jeeze! All those left-wing, power-to-the-people types
are the tightest fisted, holier-than-thou crabs I ever met.

Matia's isn't like that.
The folks are friendly and the tips are good.
I mean, workers look after workers, don't you think?
It's not all up here, in the head, like it was
with those other types. The ones who come into Matia's
aren't that way. For them, it's in the stomach . . .
where it counts.

I like it there. I do. But . . . I mean . . . it's a diner!
How am I gonna meet a guy in a place like that?
Not that there's anything wrong with the guys that come in,
but, . . . you know . . . it's . . . a diner!

And when I get off work I stink.
I mean, waiting table is heavy work.
Anybody who's done it knows!
Ditch diggers, jack hammer operators and waitresses—
they're all the same. And on top of all of that
the grease and all that cigarette smoke is in my clothes and hair.

So I come home, take a bath, wash my hair,
sprinkle myself with powder and put on some nice, clean clothes.
I feel better. I feel good. I smell good. I like myself that way,
all clean and sweet and my clothes pressed and smelling good.

So then what do I do?
I go down stairs and have dinner with Mom.
And then the rest of the evening I watch TV—with Mom.

I mean, Holy Kripes,
I'm 27 years old and I'm workin' in a diner
and I'm still livin' at home . . . with Mom!

I actually look forward to comin' to work!
At least it gets me out of the house.
At least it's something different.
At least it gets me away from Mom!

Every time I step out the door,
when it's not to work, I mean,
Mom wants to know where I'm goin'.
I can't go out with a guy—not that I get that many chances—
without her asking all kinds of questions.
It's like I'm 12 years old, like I'm in jail!

I ought to get my own place. I know I should.
I would too, but . . .
What would she do without me?
She can't get along without me.
She'd fall apart without me.

I'm 27 years old and all I do with my life
is work at a diner and watch TV at home with Mom.

Is that all there is to life?
Matia's every day, come home, a bath,
then dinner and TV with Mom?
Is that all there is?

Isn't there something more to life?
What am I going to do?

Hove

for Leon Daniel

You know me. And don't. You wouldn't recognize me
In the street, though I have stopped you there
Dead in your tracks. Outside a cafe maybe

In Des Moines—a greasy spoon, say—on a morning
Like any other. You put your two bits in the box,
Reached for a paper, and froze: our boys are napalming

Kids now instead of Vietcong. Can't place me?
From Adam? Try this: *In order to save the village,*
The colonel said, we had to destroy it.

It was said. I have the notes, after all
These years. And my rival Peter got it, too.
Word for word. The kind of quote you think

God made to stick in our skull. Did you hear that?
I asked Peter, knowing we did, knowing we would
Cable it from Saigon. The colonel was caught up

In the count—bodies laid out for us like mats—
But we were stunned. The war, for once, made sense:
To save Vietnam, we would have to destroy it.

That was long ago. I am where I like to be,
Near water, waiting for something to surface.
Atomic submarine, finally making a port call.

Years. Imagine living so long near sea-bottom?
Women on board, too! The stories that have to abound.
Husbands and wives all around me, happy as clams,

Waiting to become triangles. Toddlers about to meet
Dad for the first time. Know how you hate a neighbor?
Try living like a sardine with one for thirty months.

Enemies, getting a break. But today I think of myself.
I am getting a chance to write something joyful,
A phrase that has jangled in my mind since Jakarta,

Where I was when that tidal wave cleaned East Pakistan.
You don't remember it, but you should. Who cares about
Asia anyway? One hundred thousand people washed to sea,

A wave fifteen feet high that swept over miles of paddies
And took everyone who wasn't two flights up. Not many
Buildings that high in Bangladesh, the name now

For that place. Place of death. One hundred thousand
People—more than half of Des Moines, god damn it—
And you didn't give a diddly. Let bygones be.

They pay me to tell you, not to make you think.
Leave that for the poets! This is what I want to write,
To cap a story you would clip and save like a stamp:

And the ship hove into port. Sure, we're talking
Submarine. But you get one chance: *And the sub
Hove into port.* Not bad. The desk may let it by,

And out it would fly on tickertape of your hometown
Newspaper. Make the eggs go down easier at that
Greasy spoon. Why does it mean so much? Why

Would I even want to tell you? Maybe you think
I've a little romantic in me. War correspondent.
Trenchcoat, Casablanca. I'm a backwoods boy

Out of Tennessee, a box of a man with no neck
For a raincoat. Pop-bottle glasses that make
My eyes too big and blue for my ruddy skin

And cheeky face. But you would tell me
Your life story. Ask the colonel. Ask Peter,
The competition. We didn't cover the half of it.

When you cable for bets on the body count at Da Nang,
They bring you home. Things happen. Say a reporter
Like Kate gets lost in the tropical forest and collapses

In your arms twenty-five days after the funeral.
We thought she was dead. We gave her desk to a rookie
From New York. She stumbled into the bureau

Scraggly, mosquito-bit, barely able to punch
Her story. But we let her, waiting, waiting
For the last click of the keys, for the last

Syllable to clear the continent. Kate Webb.
You don't remember her, but I do. She had
A phrase and she got to use it: *It was like*

A butcher shop in Eden, beautiful but ghastly.
That would have gone over big in Des Moines.
That was romance. That was foreign corresponding.

This isn't. This is busy work before they ship me
To Tel Aviv or Beirut. But a nuclear sub is news
When you see it: beautiful, ghastly. Dock it

In Mobile, and Alabama becomes a dangerous place.
You wouldn't know it the way the women in front of me
Stare at the ocean, awaiting their beloved.

Yearningly. Now there's a word! Women have
Waited at ports for millennia. They have courage,
All right. But you can't pin it with a medal.

Once a woman showed me where her breast had been.
Can you imagine that? I was between tours
And making the rounds, handshaking with publishers

And doing a local exclusive for the greasy spoon.
It was news then. Betty Ford just went through it.
A mother in Virginia had the operation and wanted

To talk. I'm a man, after all. What do you say?
Do you feel any pain? Do you cry in the night?
Does your husband love you the same way?

I'll never forget. That wonderful, wise,
Elegant lady looked at me square and asked,
As if she knew me a lifetime—no, more than that—

A *millenium,* "Would you like to see?
Would you like me to take off my blouse?"
All I could do was nod. She unbuttoned it

Slowly, tenderly almost as a lover might
Share the intricate wounds of the heart.
"Now you know," she said. "You can write about it."

I am thinking of her now. Also of Kate.
I do whenever the story seems bigger than me.
And the sub hove into port. I feel good about it.

The desk will let it by. Here it comes, Kate,
I am getting the chance. People are cheering,
And a band behind me is playing the Navy song

About anchors and ships. But what comes is a black
Pod of a vessel making its way into easy water.
"Hove" isn't right. A half-truth. A submarine "glides."

And the sub glided into port. Now that's bad.
The desk will ask what I am drinking.
What about you in Des Moines? Would you care

If a submarine "hove" a little on the front page?
I never lied before. Ask the colonel. Ask Kate.
Ask the woman who showed me where a breast had been.

Today the calm waters of Mobile, Alabama, are going to get
Rougher on the tickertape. I take it in, the slow dock
Of a submarine that can do more damage than a tidal wave,

The sailors and spouses eager again or wary,
An ensign refusing to smile for the cameras,
A toddler who struggles in the arms of a stranger.

I leave to make the call. Someone new is at the desk
In New York. Mike, out of college. He asks,
Who is this again? He doesn't know me from Adam.

But the voice is right, the way I dictate
Logo and dateline. He's ready now for the story.
Go ahead, he says. *And the sub hove into port.*

I continue from my notes, but he interrupts.
Flowery, he says. Can't use it. Just tell me
What it was like. *It was like a butcher shop*

In Eden, beautiful but ghastly. Pause.
He's got his hand over the phone and mumbles
Something. Something is mumbled back, and now

The editor is on the line. Hove, I tell him.
Not many people know it is the past tense of heave.
He wants to know, then, why we are using it.

I clear my throat. I want them to understand.
Every now and then, I say, there is a phrase
Somebody in Des Moines needs to hear. Today

It is, *And a sub hove into port.*
I wish it were a ship. I wish it had sails
That ruffled like a silk blouse, opening.

DEB CASEY

ZOOOOOOOM
A Familiar Story: Drop-off/Pick-up Panic

ZOOOM: morning frenzy, the held-breath beginning to each work day. (Zip past the entire get-up, dress-feed-comb/brush-assemble struggle, the tension between adults as to who is doing what, and who isn't.) **BEGIN** at the car: load, fasten, dash back for forgotten items. Check watch: two minutes past the sure parking spot. Accelerate. Stay calm. Sing, babble, wiggle, jounce, offer a finger to chew, look at the *"Look"* commands: back, sideways; **DRIVE.** Five miles to campus. **Park.** (First spot easy.) Unbelt, gather children (*stay close!* to the oldest), deliver one: sign in, situate, converse with Lead Teacher (casual mother), glance to clock, *Ooops!: Got to go* . . . Be thankful: almost past the tearful goodbyes with this daughter. **Re-situate:** baby into seat (again), kiss the sweet lips, eager eyes (careful not to bend legs backward in haste). Turn around. Now the real struggle. Twenty minutes gone in that drop-off (and the center opens no earlier). Circle. Lot after lot. Seeth. No parking. No options—no *good* options. Give up. **Park** on the fringe. Prepare for the hike. Gather bags, umbrella, baby stuff, books. Adjust Baby in the front pack, distribute weight. **Stride!** (And be thankful the umbrella isn't necessary, no hand left.) Trudge. **DELIVER** baby to grad-student in father's office. (Take advantage of his morning-empty space.) Whisk out the baby decor: padded play place, fur, jump-seat, chewables. Nurse. Insistently: here. Now. Greet care taker. Make fast small-talk. Say goodbyes. Breathe—no, not yet. Ignore the sudden squawk, tears, of a baby who wants you. No, don't: acknowledge the uneasiness. **Return.** Console. Promise. Leave again. NOW breathe. Find a bathroom—forget it: late. Run. (Forget, too, figuring how on earth you'll regroup bodies with the car, where it is compared to all three of our stations. **Skip** the logistics of breastfeeding connections and so on. Get to the day's close.) **DEPARTURE:** Get edgy as meeting runs late. **Fidget.** Lose all train of thought. Try not to be obvious as you pack-up, already overdue. Dash across the quad, and up three flights (fast!), present the breast, **FEED,** hear her contented warble, relax, sooth her moist cheek, soft fontanel, **marvel** again: how wide her *feed-me*-bird-mouth glomps around the nipple (See: we working mothers are not oblivious), keep her attached as you try to move smoothly, quickly (the easy minute up), **gather** her pieces. Sweater her snug, hug closely as you run to the car, urging all the bulk of you to advance a bit faster, imagining you'll find your older daughter parked on the curb: *"her time was up."* Don't exaggerate. No guilt: you called apologizing, think no more of it. Get to the car. Strap Baby in. Try to hush her yelps. Promise (again): *soon* . . . Remember what you should have brought home from the office. Try not to catch your mind sliding forward, backward. Don't think what you'd like is a drink. A moment . . . Watch the road, **shift, sing, juggle, jiggle,** finger-rub the baby's gums. Zoom. Grab Baby (gently!): up and over (watch the head). Find Older Daughter. Apologize to Lead Teacher. Concentrate on this reunion time: **focus** —while urging Daughter toward her cubby and out of the action. (And don't wrinkle the painting.) Keep Baby from the breast position temptation. **Give up:** sling Baby over hip, guide to nipple, button Older Daughter's sweater, one-handed, gather other drawings, praise (sincerely), pat, burp, sign-out (Don't forget!), get them out and loaded (again) into the car and belted and grinning, or grumbling (whatever), **DRIVE.** Sing. (What's in the fridge?) Shift.

Motherwork II: Consumption/Production Talk

mouth latching on to nipple
nipple stiffening
breast milk-hard
ready to be emptied
refilled   emptied   refilled   *ceaseless   relentless*
The night after night after day after hour minute every second
availability   attachment
joyterror bristling and steaming
leaking and loving
8 glasses of milk/water (no coffee, no spices) returned
transformed transferred: a liquid flow. Exchange rate undetermined.
Two daughters; 20 months plus 25: say four years of every X# hours
—maybe 20 or 40 minutes/hr. the first 3–6 months
with two to four hour intervals as breaks for sleep
then maybe 12 months at four hour intervals with say 6 to sleep,
on good nights, 3–4 more typically. (Some scold
I should have insisted otherwise, lengthening
these short shifts. *Sure, tell me.*) This
followed by 8–12 months of meal-time
connections plus any jet take-offs or landings
or moments of insecurity. Or pleasure.
And that's with X loads of wash/day × 365 days/year
× 8 years (so add 2 days for leap years)—maybe 2–3 loads at the beginning,
dropping to 1–2 loads per day as the bedding and spit-up changes decline.
Plus lumping the lint—to save for the stuffing.
Arriving, then at these sleepers and sewing each seam, head
to neck, sleeve to thumbed fist, stitch by stitch, needle picking
at my right index callous, and all the moments in between
to keep the milk or lint flowing. What measurements could possibly
by any known quantitative scale acknowledge the multiple dimensions,
could fluctuate with adequate sensitivity to accurately quantify value?
Because the drinking and sucking and wash cycles and stuffing
all might be simultaneous one moment,
adjacent the next, and now, again, shattered into isolated actions
fragments, shards with sharp edges, chunks too bulky

to manage, lumps that are a tactile handful,
pieces, cracking up.
Ceaselessly.   Incessantly.   And with reverence,
we connect. Empty. (Re)Fill. And try now to establish
value.   So you tell me
in cents per square inch or $/hour or ounce, what's the rate?
Simply a flat fee, maybe? An honorarium,
so to speak, admitting the lack of fit of this sort of making—mothering—
into what we call our business
or life.

One Flesh We Stretch

Pretend you're a mama with milk in your nipples.
Pretend I'm a baby with milk on my lips.

Full breast.
The baby cries. I remember
she opens her mouth like a hole to the center of earth.

Her mother's breasts ache. They pulse and tingle, throb
and tighten—I mean *my* breasts: blue
balls the child cranes
to reach (magnetic attraction, stiffening
fibers) breasts that contract
within the momentary muffled grope
as mouth and nipple nearly
connect, small
shivers as the reflex hits—milk-
damp (dribbles) nibbled attachment inten-
sified to gulps (to meet the steady stream) and shifts: two hearts
knocking toward one rhythmic slurping
cadence ease to one consuming hum. And when
the milk is gone, and the baby gurgles,
and the breasts sag slack,
the child—

(blue milky pool beyond her lips), open-
mouthed child, (how everything zeros
into that O, how everything falls
away from the hunger, even
the body pivoting on its nipple fulcrum
fades)—purrs. We're fed:
one flesh we stretch
ourselves into this moment small
and round and warm and whole.

73

A Seven-Day Diary

first line from Alan Dugan

Oh, I got up and went to work
cleared the lab bench,
unhooked a UV monitor, a fraction collector,
a microtiter plate reader
and loaded consumable labware onto a cart—
boxes of 50 ml centrifuge tubes,
disposable pipettes and petri dishes—
everything we won't need right away
I hauled down to the unfinished new lab.

Then I cleaned out the fume hood
removing radioactive waste.
Triple gloved, I shed a new layer
with each bag of waste I packaged
and hauled down to the Rad Waste Room.

And then I came home from work
and took a shower
and wolfed down my dinner
and drove forty-five miles to class
and thought about Charles Brockden Brown
and *Wieland*
and the meaning of the word "romantic"
and drove back home again
and kissed my wife and went to sleep.

Then I got up and went to work.
I borrowed an integrator and a fluorimeter
and wired them into the HPLC controller
and hooked the gradient delay input cable
and the inject hold cable
from the autosampler to the controller
and wrote the gradient control program
so all components could be in communication.

I checked on orders—
Fisher is out of Acetonitrile,
the guard columns haven't arrived
and the consultant forgot to mention
a half-dozen reagents we will need
for the assay he has come to show us—
so I pushed paperwork and harassed Purchasing.

Then I came back home
and played Legos with my daughter
building a house with doors
for her green and pink toy worms.
After dinner I thought about
"narrator reliability" in *Wieland.*
My wife read *Winnie-the-Pooh,*
chapter V "In Which Piglet Meets a Heffalump"
and I sang "Over the River" and "The Gypsy Rover"
and our daughter fell asleep.

Then I got up and went to work
and the "B" pump on the HPLC blew
when the consultant started it up.
We took it apart
and checked the inlet check valve
and the sapphire piston
and worried about the pressure transducer
and the pump motor gear box . . .

And then I called the service rep
who came and replaced a circuit board
and everything was fine.

So I took the bones of nine dogs
from the minus 70 freezer
and sawed them on a bandsaw,
extruding and discarding the marrow.

When I dropped them in liquid nitrogen
to make them brittle for pulverization
they tinkled like a wind chime
or broken pieces of fine china.

Ground down in a Wiley mill
to the consistency of sugar
they will be a source
of the bone collagen crosslinkers
that we are studying.

At five o'clock, I left the consultant
who hinted I should stay
but I came back home from work
and skipped dinner
and drove forty-five miles
and thought about how much room
a sonnet has to make its single argument
and maybe suggest a few things
and come to a strong, but graceful close.
And I envied the room a sonnet has.

Then I drove back from class,
but stopped twenty miles out
for a take-out ham and cheese
and a cup of coffee.

And then I got up and went to work again
regretting that cup of coffee
and had two more cups at 8 A.M.
at the seminar on
"Preventing Sexual Harassment in the Workplace."
Nobody said it, but everyone was thinking
"the company's just protecting itself
from potential litigation,"
especially when John asked about

the promotion statistics
of women in upper management
and was told his question fell under
"sexual discrimination, a topic
that wouldn't be covered today."
Then we all signed
the mandatory attendance sheet
and went to lunch.

After lunch, I got out of attending
the afternoon debriefing session
on the eight day Montreal meeting.
We tried to get a signal
from the fluorimeter to the integrator
and failed. The consultant called the integrator
"a bloody fookin' piece of shit!"
and I thought he'd be all right
to work with for the next six weeks.

And we pored over the instrument manuals
and borrowed a voltmeter
to check cable continuity
and I called Pete who came down
and found the bad contact.

And then I came home from work
and ate steak and corn from the garden
and played with my daughter
while my wife went to business statistics class.
Then I put our daughter to bed
and my wife came home
and we talked money
and got discouraged, but I know
the topic only comes up
because it triggers strong frustration
and makes us real to one another

when we've been out of touch too long.
We drifted off to bed, made love,
and fell asleep.

Then it was Friday, Friday, Friday
the most hopeful day of the week.
With the exception of a solvent leak
at a zero dead volume union
in the stainless steel LC tubing
which we fixed with a turn of a wrench,
the HPLC ran perfectly.
We injected dog urine
separating its components,
identifying the collagen crosslinks
that come from bone.
We injected the two purified standards
and the recording pen
traced out two sharp peaks.

Then I came home from work
and agreed with Grabo that Clara's
pat interpretation of Carwin's guilt
at the end of *Wieland*
was problematic and thought
she must be projecting
her survivor's ontological guilt
onto Carwin and finished a paper for class.

I remembered a dream—
walking down streets with my mother
the day after a rainstorm,
stopping to peel back a leaf
pressed to the grey slate sidewalk
just to see the dark, moist silhouette.

And someone's hopscotch game
chalked in orange
with a piece of broken flowerpot,
its numbers in ruins
half washed away by rain.

And a list of rules
kept running through my head—
never walk in front of swings,
duck your head when you play under the table,
don't tell people you don't like them,
remember to flush the toilet,
it's not nice to hit,
and don't throw stones at cars.

Thirty years, a child of my own,
a dream of my mother
and my own unexpressed gratitude
I must make time for.
Then Saturday was gone.

And Sunday vanished too—
a little pick-up around the house,
a drive to school to use the library and read
and one more fragment from my dream—

    Yesterday it rained
    and today it is warm.
    There are puddles I could jump in
    but I am being good.
    I am walking to the park with my mother
    under a sky that is longer than
    the longest car ride I have ever taken.
    She tells me the sky is really not a ceiling—
    it just goes higher and higher
    and is blue

and invisible at the same time
and at night there are stars in it
and in the day white clouds
which the winds blow
further and further away
but new ones keep coming . . .

And then Sunday was completely gone.

Talking to Patsy Cline

"Crazy"

Me with a steady job
and the post office won't take a check.
I have to talk to the man
through a hole in the glass.

I do interviews for a living,
phone surveyor,
I say to the man's lips.
His hands dart out under the glass,
snake heads
seeing if the hawk is out.

He's not listening.
Hands are deaf and spade-head as a cottonmouth.
I wave at the hole in the glass.

For the interviews,
I have to get Momma's smokehouse
and back-door trot
out of my voice.
I can do it too.
People think they're talking to someone
from Show-Me or Buckeye.

Where are you,
people sometimes ask?
I say it doesn't matter,
Sir or Ma'am.
If we could continue.

We all have our three walls.
I've got Patsy Cline pinned up
and hum "Crazy"

before someone answers.
No one has caught me yet.

I ask a lot.
Age? Race? Marital status?
How many times per week
do you go to the grocery store?
Are you more likely to go
in the morning or evening?

We don't get to ask why.
That's the only one.
Sometimes I say it in my head
after everything they say.
Why? Why? Why?
Like a kid that's just found the word.

Would you marry a man with one leg?
Would you let a snake on you?
Do you think God knows
about the back of the bus?
Well, what do you say?
I ask them in my head.
They don't know me or the questions
I don't ask.

Some questions come out of the blue.
Are there multiple births in your family?
Have you ever traveled outside the country?
Where? How long did you stay?
Given the chance,
Would you go back?

We aren't supposed to show a preference.
A preference will get you fired.

I don't show anything,
I just ask.

The post office man won't come out
from behind his frosted glass.
These have to go I say.
They're ends that have to be tied.
He won't take a check.
I go outside with my handful.
Now, I'm thinking, now
I've got to go home with these.

"I Fall to Pieces"

The day Patsy Cline died
in an airplane crash
"I Fall to Pieces" was number one
on the charts.

That's what I was thinking
when the woman picked up
and said, "Can't talk;
I'm alt'a pieces."
I heard the screen-door slap
in her voice.
She was from somewhere
I grew up.

It spooked me.
I had to go out to the picnic table
and take deep breaths.

Patsy's poster is a black and white,
which I guess was all they had,
but they've colored it.

Gave her a red hat
and rouged her cheeks.

She looks like a corpse, Melinda says.
But she's on my side.
When a woman answers,
I look up and talk to Patsy.

We don't get to pick our numbers.
The computer dials
and when we hang up,
it goes on.

So, I couldn't call back
to see if I could help.
I'd offer to keep her kids
or bring over something
or we could go drink beer
and play Ernest Tubb.

We wear headsets,
so the person answers
inside your head.
All day people say "Hello."
Sometimes, they pick up
before it rings.
Then we're waiting
like we're going to hear a secret.

At home,
I've dialed Momma's number,
and after the recording
about the number being disconnected
I listen to the hum
like it's a coincidence—

we picked up at the same time
and in a second she'll say "Hello?"

"Faded Love"

Momma talked to Patsy Cline one time.
Patsy was doing an interview
on a call-in radio show,
and you could ask her anything.

Patsy was talking to people
like they were kin.
All of a sudden
there was Momma with Patsy
in the green plastic box
on the kitchen cabinet.

"If the only way people could see you
was by your voice,
what would you look like?"
That took Patsy a minute.
It got quiet.
You could hear her breathe.
"Trouble and honey," she said.
"Trouble and honey."

Momma wouldn't look at the picture
they printed in the paper when she died.
"I know what Patsy looks like," she said.

I told that story
at the picnic table during lunch.
"You OK?" Melinda asked me
right in front of everybody.

"It takes a year or two to get over," she said.
Melinda watches too many talk shows.

On the way to work,
I saw a guy talking on the phone in his car.
I started wondering if we ever get them.
That would be a hoot.
He don't know where we are.
We don't know where he is.
Everybody's talking out of nowhere.

DAVID CITINO

Basic Writing, Marion Correctional

I come each day through fields
furrowed with corn, bean, and barbed wire
overseen by moonlighting farmers
perched in watchtowers, cheeks pink,
shotguns cocked to cultivate their order.
In the Visitors' Lounge the women
wait, weary from the bus ride
from Cleveland or Toledo, skirts slit
over best hose over legs new-shaven,
lips forcing smiles cold
as institutional porcelain.
In the corner a couple entwines,
his leg between hers, his hands
working beneath her blouse,
their children trying not to see.
The guard who frisks me jokes the same
each day: *You got anything in there*
but poems, Doc? I walk past The Hole
and see men come out, eyes wild
with crazy static. In the Job Readiness Room
they're all in jeans and work shirts
like my English-major classmates
at Ohio U in 1969. All chain smoke
but the Muslims. They want to know
about my wife. *What color hair?*
She make you happy? You got a picture?
I tell them about comma faults.
Delivery-van doors slam gunshot-loud outside,
jerk them from their seats.
The loudspeaker thunders above my words:
C Block, Chow. Work Call: Yard Gang,
Shop Gang, Laundry Gang, Sanitation Gang.
It was coke, speed, horse
that put us here, they write, bad crowds
we ran with, bad men that hustled
our mothers, The Man who jerked us around.

I help them with their letters.
O my precious lady I ache
for the righteous mysteries of your thighs.
Dear Honey I got something I been saving up
for you. Dear Most Gracious Ladies and Gentlemen
of the Parole Board: I've changed my life.
With their pencils they want to shake
the Governor. I'm magic as a preacher,
they believe, because of words,
because each night I sleep beside a woman
and each day I've leave to touch
a son's cheeks soft as petals
of a courtyard rose rising beyond
shadows of all four walls.
They yearn to soar above cinder blocks
of each lethal year, hearts constricting
in barred cells of the breast,
hands into fists. This makes nothing
better, all admit. We're waiting
for the bell, summons from a purer world.
Time's the law, the hell men do.

JAN CLAUSEN

Sestina, Winchell's Donut House

Watching the black hours through to morning
I'd set out each successive tray of grease-
cooked donuts on the rack, chocolate and pink-
frosted, to harden beneath the fluorescent light,
talk to crazy Harry, count the change,
listen to top-forty radio. Mostly, I was alone.

Every stranger's suspect when you're alone.
A woman was beaten badly early one morning
by a man who sneaked in the back while she made change,
so I'd rehearse scenarios of scooping grease,
flinging it at the assailant's face, cooking the light
or dark flesh to curl away at the impact, angry pink.

The cab drivers came in every night, faces polished pink
and boyish, arriving in pairs or alone.
Their cabs clotted like moths at the building's light.
They were outlaws and brothers, despised men who rise
                         in the morning.
They'd swagger, still dapper, if fattened on sweets and grease,
call me sugar and honey. I smiled. I kept the change.

Often I was too busy to see the darkness change,
flush from black to blue to early pink.
At four o'clock, my face smeared with congealed grease,
I think I was happiest, although most alone.
The harder hours were those of fullblown morning,
fighting depression, sleeping alone in the light.

Linda came in at six, awash with light,
businesslike, making sure there'd be enough change
to get her through the rigors of the morning.
She had a hundred uniforms; I remember pink.
Sometimes she'd cheat, leave me to work alone,
sneak out to flirt in parked cars, fleeing lifetimes
                         of grease.

89

I can see her cranking the hopper, measuring grease,
indefatigable, wired on coffee, just stopping to light
her cigarettes. She didn't want to be alone.
It was only my fantasy that she could change,
stop wearing that silly, becoming pink,
burn free of the accidents, husband and children,
                              some morning.

I remember walking home those mornings, smelling of grease,
amazed in summer's most delicate pink early light,
to shower, change, and sleep out the hot day alone.

RICHARD COLE

Waiting for Money

We sleep late in the morning and make
love quietly in the middle of the day.
We're waiting for the phone to ring.
Someone somewhere in California
is reading our script. They'll let us know
next week, they say. My wife says
it's like waiting for your dream
date to ask you to the prom.

We're mainly living on credit cards.
Each week, I can feel the easy trigger
tighten as I sign for cash.
We're optimistic. In New York
the air is filled with impossible money.
For the first time in months,
we have all day to be with each other.
We read or go to the Natural History Museum
on Wednesday nights when it's almost empty.
We study the natural defenses
of the sponge. We learn
where the dinosaurs went wrong and follow
the recorded spells of moody shamans.

When we get home, the answering machine
is silent. We'll watch
the late show like students
or insomniacs, and I'll fall asleep
remembering the dark museum
and the wolves racing
through the moonlit forest, racing
all night through the deep blue snow.

The Business Life

I'm leading the business life these days
in my gray business suit,
walking the morning sidewalks
littered with papers and broken trash bags
to catch a cab for the airport.
Overhead, the London plane-tree branches
soften in a haze of tiny new leaves,
light green and delicate.
The skies are clear. I'm leaving for Florida.

In '84, we had just arrived, had just met,
and our life was a movie.
We were going to make one in fact,
about ourselves making a movie,
and we knew the money would appear
like coal sliding down a chute.
We fell in love with an image
of ourselves in a modest,
three-story Village brownstone.
Each morning we would write
for love, then money. We'd escape
to the islands six months a year,
walking with our babies on the beach
in white flannel clothing, tanned
and confident, easy to love . . .
But our plots were boring. Nothing
happened. Then nothing happened.
Our vague millionaire stopped returning
our calls, and each day I ran off
to my terminal job feeling
conned, hating the woman
I loved with her anxious
reassurances and loud ideas,
the both of us picking fights
with strangers on the subway,
screaming at cabs. I would lie awake

listening to the couple downstairs
arguing and smashing. He sounded pathetic,
like a man drowning, like a man
going under. At the end of four years
we were broke, exhausted, and married.

There's not much to see in Florida
on a business trip. I saw palm trees
the last time and a blue inch of ocean
from my hotel window. I can't say
what will happen next—I trust my wife.
We lost the ambitions we needed to lose,
and I don't know what movie we're
living now, though it's not the one
where we drank champagne on the freezing roof
on New Year's Eve, watching the fireworks
melt and explode into darkness
overlooking the cold, brilliant city.

Success Stories

I

I'm still addicted to the *New York Times*.
On Saturday nights, I walk down Flatbush Avenue
for the Sunday edition. Vertical Manhattan
glitters in the distance, all "threats and diamonds."

I reach for the Arts and Leisure section,
the Book Review next, irritated with myself
for knowing all the latest about
those famous artists and intellectuals,
the ones with massive, dramatically carved heads
and powerful hair.

I sometimes see them on the street
avoiding eye contact or leaning on a young,
delighted companion. They look exhausted,
but in the papers they sit back
self-assured for the interview, attractively potent
and laughing with large, yellowed teeth.

I wonder what they're really like:
the fabulously affluent painter with his soft,
Virginia manners and ice cream suits,
the sculptor in his spartan loft, gesturing
wildly with a blow torch as he makes his point,
or the East Village novelist brooding at the camera,
slightly impatient, pressed for time, thoughts
flashing from her lowered brow.

I imagine their light, sure fingers
playing on the singing cables of Manhattan.
They have it made, I tell myself.
They work for themselves. They can write
their own ticket.

II

"We're not the geniuses we thought we were,"
my wife says, and of course, she's right.
Self-pity only goes so far, so every morning
I go to work on the F train, briefcase packed
with wandering journals, Whitman and Rilke,
minor notes to myself, and lunch.

"Ninety-nine percent of poetry
is in the living," Dr. Williams said.
So where do the poets in America belong?
That is to say, what do they do
for a living?

I work in an ad agency, writing
sales brochures for computer systems.
Each night, I go home to Brooklyn,
hang up my coat, say hello to my wife.
I'm an old hand at the office now,
and others are promoted past me, but that's OK.
I'm left alone to think, and I do.
I shut my office door each morning,
remembering how I used to storm to work
along Park Avenue, hating my wife, my obligations,
no time to write, repeating Rembrandt's motto:
"Concedo Nulli!" Yield to No One!

I thought I was drowning. Now, I have a scenic
view of the Hudson River from my window.
I can watch the Circle Line Tour ships
slowly backing away from the pier, tiny arms waving.

III

I wanted to vanish into the woods
and re-emerge with something wonderful,
a white light cradled in my hands.
I wanted to astonish.

Monday rush. 8 A.M. It's raining.
On the subway, we smell like big, wet dogs
hunched together in our raincoats, umbrellas
dripping on our shoes. My little book says,
"Surrender your will. Only then can the rest
of your life begin." We slowly emerge
from the ground and pause at an elevated station.

The doors open. For a moment, I can feel
the cool morning air on my face. Miles
of low, gray buildings, overcast skies . . .
And seagulls! The cries of seagulls
circling somewhere in the fog overhead.
Then the doors squeeze shut, and we're
rumbling down into the earth again, toward
Manhattan, wealth, and our steady jobs.

Working Late

Only a few of us left, working late.
Last month, the stock market fell
over 500 points, and the aftershocks
travel through all of us
one by one. In the corner office
behind oak doors, I hear angry shouting,
a filing cabinet slammed shut.
Then the door opens with a terrible silence.

The permanent cleaning woman
is working her way
down the hall toward my office,
emptying the trash. She turns
off a light, and Manhattan
leaps out behind her in the dark windows,
black and glittering.

My phone rings: another writer,
a quiet, older man who was fired
two years ago.

We talk about business for a moment,
the usual things: who's in, who's out.
He mentions his divorce again,
his daughter's bat mitzvah,
and he starts to describe a project
we could freelance together.

Next door the cleaning woman
thumps a wastepaper basket
twice on the side of her cart.
I look at the clock.
I tell him I'm under deadline
and he understands. He says
we can help each other. He says
let's keep in touch.

Business Class

The flight attendants maneuver their way
down the darkened aisles, bending and smiling,
checking our condition. After three good
bourbons, I glance around. I'm surrounded
by people in business suits who look
like me, the older ones reading,
the younger ones pointing out bonus
rewards in their sales catalogs.
"Have a nice day," the recorded message
at the airport urges in all sincerity,
and we've tried, in all sincerity.
We've tried to make money, for ourselves
and our homes and expensive families.
We're doing the best we can, living
out of briefcases filled with reports
and PERT charts, rental car tickets,
stock quotes, Maalox, cigarettes, and gum.
On the seat beside me, a senior man
is already asleep, a finance review
resting on his stomach, his mouth half open.
Each year I tell myself that I'm leaving
in the next few years. A writer can't
live like this, can't think, and yet
if I had the perfect leisure to think,
with endless mornings and a solid desk
overlooking the ocean, perhaps I would
think of nothing at all, or a little
less each year, more baffled and secure
than I already am. No, I have my heavy
bills to pay, like every other poet
on this plane. So tell me this isn't
a life or a living. Tell me that it all
doesn't count.

Dignity

So at last I've finished
writing this sales
flyer on mid-sized business
computer solutions,
right on dead-
line (from the chalk
lines around POW
camps in the Civil War,
if a prisoner crossed it
they shot to kill), the way
it's done in the business
world, so I treat myself
to a cab, go bombing
up Third Avenue
to visit Client, and just
for today, I'm feeling
on top of this city,
and the afternoon is autumn
glorious, brilliant
with the smell of leaves
and Chinese
restaurants. I get
chills as the driver
dodges, darts around
the buses like a bicycle
messenger, and we even pass
poetry in the street,
barricades set up,
city workers in orange
day-glo jackets, dragging
jackhammers, shovels,
teaspoons, and whatever
else they need to repair
the state of the art (assuming
that's what this city needs).
And we're passing other

cabs and even an ambulance
late for Bellevue, making
record time to mid-town,
and I tip the driver in English
and head inside, floating
up in the gold elevator
to confer with Client
who reads the copy
with a worried expression

and loves it! Happiness! And I do
my little reassurance dance,
and we hug, we kiss,
friends forever as far as that
goes, and what the hell,
I take another cab and
God, the city is looking
better than before,
and I've got a check,
got a check for twelve hundred dollars
and I'm going to the bank
and I'll make a deposit
for the rent and groceries
and a few days of peace
to write all this down,
and I'll look that teller
right in the eye and sign my name
with dignity.

Recession, 1992

The Nikkei's dropped over 30%
this month alone. World stocks
flutter, unable to recover
momentum as we search
for the leveraged cash engines
that drove us straight
through the arrogant Eighties.
I twist and turn in the triple
mirrors at Brooks Brothers,
feeling reckless as I'm fitted
for a lucrative suit that says
I'm a man who hopes to be taken
seriously. Cool analysts say
the layoffs are a "wake up call"
for an unrealistic economy
but when two young writers
were suddenly let go last week,
we who were left still
needed to believe that somehow—
it was their own damn fault,
that the black spot was slowly
darkening on their foreheads
all along. With a wife
and baby at home, I'm grateful
to work longer hours
and catch the early train
each morning. In the dim bedroom,
I review the day as I prep
for my office role: fresh shirt
and muted tie, Italian belt,
gold watch. But who is the boy
who dresses this man? I open my wallet—
two palms of credit cards—like a dad.
My son's still asleep. I stroke

his face, reluctant to leave,
trying not to wake him
as I say goodbye.

Drone

i am a clerk
i am a medical billing clerk
i sit here all day and type
the same type of things all day long
insurance claim forms
for people who suffer chronic renal failure
fortunately these people i rarely see
these are hardcore cases
most of them are poor, black, or latin
they are cases most other doctors refuse
they are problem cases
some of them have complications like heroin abuse
some of them are very young
most of them have brief charts
which means they died within a year of beginning treatment
sometimes a patient gets worried about his or her
coverage and calls the office
i refer them to the dialysis unit caseworker
a few of the patients do bad things. for instance
some of them might refuse treatment as scheduled
sometimes they get drunk and call up
the nurses or attendants and curse them out
sometimes they try to fight the attendants
because they feel neglected/afraid
sometimes they wait until the last minute
to show up and it is the last minute
most of the patients, good patients,
quietly expire
i retire their charts to the inactive file
a few more claims i won't be typing up anymore
they are quickly replaced by others black, latin, or poor
i make out crisp new charts
and the process starts all over again
the cash flows and flows and flows
so that the doctors can feed their racehorses
and play tennis and pay the captains of their yachts

and keep up their children's college tuition and
trusts and maintain their luxury cars
for this service i am paid a subsistence salary
i come in here each morning
and bill the government for the people by the people
for these patients
i sit here and type
is what i do and that's very important
day after day/adrift in the river of forms
that flows between my desk and the computer that
prints out the checks
there are few problems here. i am a very good clerk
i sit here all day and type
i am a medical billing clerk
i am a clerk
i clerk

Bad

night at the taco house
he came in to rob the place
the waitresses were flush fear and tears
the guys sat around yammering
what he was doing caused some kind of disruption
he beckoned. i went over to his corner
he put the gun to my head, said
"empty the register"
the kiss deep hard cold against my temple
there was a click sound
if i move sudden i'm dead, i thought
and if i hesitate this clown might off me
and so i said, "shoot motherfucka or quit wasting my time"
there was surprised silence
then everyone broke into strained laughter
"it's a joke," he said, "you didn't cry like the other girls"
and there were slaps on the back and
cracks about my ice cool
and from that day till the day i quit
everybody kept their distance

Job Hunter

ridin' the newsprint want-ad range
i head to town, work up courage for the showdown
long as they think i'm safe to have 'round
can corral that pay check

but i leave the interview disappointed
he said nothing except, "we'll let you know"
my exit haste/confusion/struck out again
what's it about me that frightens these dough-flesh
desk-riders? something outlaw

wig hat, earringed & platform shod, i prowl
the badlands/corporate territory
downtown & dare ambush—another interview

i sport my purse a six-shooter & bullets
instead of a potpourri of feminalities
her eyes meet mine, register fear, and hurry past
she tells her boss man
his smile approaches and calls me "kid"

"you can come in now"

it's high noon
the sheriff is an IBM executive
it shoots 120 words per secretary
i reach for the white-out
it's too fast for me
i'm blown to blazes

it's the new west, Durango
the sun never sets
and death is an elevator on its way
down to the lobby

Casting Call

snow in the blood. my lover's coo

the maroon man in the black stingy brim smokes camels
tells me i'm a honorary member of the camera crew
one of the chosen chosen
he hands me a nip of concord grape, paws my thigh
requests my zodiac sign and floor plan
slips me twenty to cover expenses

stars twinkle twinkle in asphalt—one looks down not up

at the unemployment office i await sign-up
for stipend. we've been in a slump since reconstruction
the casting director asks me to strip, looks over
my appointments. tells me my figures don't fill the bill
but he can always use a good secretary

the haitian photographer displays a composite of seductees
at two hundred dinars i can join his line-up
he takes my vital statistics down to ring size
measures my tongue
determines i'm vitamin-M deficient and there's
little hope for cure and less for a part

we don't do black on black

the seersucker film producer doubles as clairvoyant
attempts to decipher my mind-set. decides i'm
just the item he'd like to market. alack it's too late
my kliegs are blown
i'm lost in the parking mall, unable to locate my car
unable to remember my name

on hiatus

Office Politics

the white boss

stops at my desk to see how i'm doing. it's something, what a
good strong work horse i am. nothing like those lazy mexicans
and them power hungry jews can't be trusted
who knows what's on the oriental mind
but we negroes understand what the white man is about
we understand that his best interest is ours
that's why we've always made such fine employees

the jewish foreman

stops at my desk to say how's it going. we are soul mates
after all we have much more in common than other races
my slavery and his death camp. not like those greasy mexicans
or clannish orientals. there are jews in the NAACP
and Harlem was once a jewish ghetto
if it weren't for jews the negroes would be
worse off

the white feminist co-worker

brands men subhuman. as her black "sister" don't i understand
our oppression is the same? what is the difference
between being lynched and being man-handled?
and didn't white female abolitionists play a major role
in our emancipation? and black men are
the same as white men. they are men aren't they?

the mexican co-worker

confides outrage. the white boy's days are numbered
california & texas will be spanish-speaking again and soon
we will not allow the red herring of jobs
to set us at each other's throats. the white boy and

the jew can only buy the illusion of loyalty from us
never the reality

the japanese accountant

passes by my desk to his
does not say a word
when everyone else
is out of the office
save me and him
he goes into his attaché case
for the flask of scotch
and bottoms up
without offering me
a sip

my black co-worker

comes over to my desk. looks deep
into my eyes. opens his mouth. moans
shakes his head
and goes back to work

Office

for Fred Pollack

there the time clock's feverish ticks
there the bulging files full of static information
awaiting application
there the sturdy metal desk, upon it the word processor
with computer terminal and disc storage compartment
multiple metal filing trays, reference books
a pencil sharpener, pen & pencil holder, calendar
stapler, ashtray full of knick-knacks & paper clips
in-and-out trays, an anti-glare desk lamp
transcriber/dictator machine with special lite-wear
earphones, a box of snotkins, a half-eaten
chewy caramel nut bar, a cold cup of coffee grown over
with bacteria

a monster has eaten the secretary in this picture

intense focus on small things
keeps sane

Unfinished Ghost Story (2)

this used to be her office.

it's chilly in here.

they've taken out some of the equipment and moved it over to the new building.

what was she like?

quiet. a good worker, actually. but a loner—kind of eccentric.

how so?

she was an odd dresser—head wraps, flashy jewelry—that kind of thing. she wasn't very good at small talk. not a gofer. it was her independent attitude, unsuited to this kind of job.

what's that odor?

some cheap perfume. she always kept a bottle of it there in the upper right hand drawer.

i've heard noises in here in the late afternoon. sometimes the word processor clicks on by itself and begins typing.

yes. others have made the same complaint.

and Lopez, the security guard has seen her going in and out of the ladies' restrooms. he's tried to catch her, but she turns a corner and disappears.

yes. the boys in the mail room have bitched to administration that she appears at 8 A.M. every Thursday and deposits invisible mail into the slots.

what are they going to do about it?

corporate exorcism.

isn't that dangerous business?

routine, these days.

STEPHEN COREY

Domestic Life: Nurse and Poet

for Mary

We talk tonight as if tomorrow will be the same,
as if we'll rise at six to get the children off,
then work the day—I with words and students,
you with the sick, the dying, and their desperate families—
until we come home at five to unleash the dog
and feed the children. We expect we'll read to them,
shush them resisting off to bed, sit here on the couch
to talk once more. We are thirty-three, but the world
mistakes you always for six or seven less.
Tonight you smile—nobody died today.
Beneath your eyes only inches away,
I catch for the first time tiny marks,
hairbreadth engravings of a stylus on copper.
On another they would be lines,
but on you, tonight, while we consider tomorrow
and who can hurry home to meet the plumber,
they are the tightening muscles in my gut,
the faults in the deepest beds of rock.

Patty's Charcoal Drive-in

First job. In tight black shorts
and a white bowling shirt, red lipstick
and bouncing pony tail, I present
each overflowing tray as if it were a banquet.
I'm sixteen and college-bound,
this job's temporary as the summer sun,
but right now, it's the boundaries of my life.
After the first few nights of mixed orders
and missing cars, the work goes easily.
I take out the silver trays and hook them to the windows,
inhale the mingled smells of seared meat patties,
salty ketchup, rich sweet malteds.
The lure of grease drifts through the thick night air.
And it's always summer at Patty's Charcoal Drive-In—
carloads of blonde-and-tan girls
pull up next to red convertibles,
boys in black tee shirts and slick hair.
Everyone knows what they want.
And I wait on them, hoping for tips,
loose pieces of silver
flung carelessly as the stars.
Doo-wop music streams from the jukebox
and each night repeats itself,
faithful as a steady date.
Towards 10 P.M., traffic dwindles.
We police the lot, pick up wrappers.
The dark pours down, sticky as Coke,
but the light from the kitchen
gleams like a beacon.
A breeze comes up, chasing papers
in the far corners of the darkened lot,
as if suddenly a cold wind had started to blow
straight at me from the future—
I read that in a Doris Lessing book—
but right now, purse fat with tips,

the moon sitting like a cheeseburger on a flat black grill,
this is enough.
Your order please.

JIM DANIELS

Short-Order Cook

An average joe comes in
and orders thirty cheeseburgers and thirty fries.

I wait for him to pay before I start cooking.
He pays.
He ain't no average joe.

The grill is just big enough for ten rows of three.
I slap the burgers down
throw two buckets of fries in the deep frier
and they pop pop spit spit . . .
psss . . .
The counter girls laugh.
I concentrate.
It is the crucial point—
they are ready for the cheese:
my fingers shake as I tear off slices
toss them on the burgers/fries done/dump/
refill buckets/burgers ready/flip into buns/
beat that melting cheese/wrap burgers in plastic/
into paper bags/fries done/dump/fill thirty bags/
bring them to the counter/wipe sweat on sleeve
and smile at the counter girls.
I puff my chest out and bellow:
"Thirty cheeseburgers, thirty fries!"
They look at me funny.
I grab a handful of ice, toss it in my mouth
do a little dance and walk back to the grill.
Pressure; responsibility, success,
thirty cheeseburgers, thirty fries.

Places Everyone

"There's a place for everyone in our organization."

The best-looking women
work in bedding.
The fat, wholesome women who smell like cookies
work in kitchen.
In china and silver
the women are fragile, elegant, middle-aged.
In men's
hen-pecked grandfathers
with their pasty smiles
suck ass to sell suits.
The healthy bastards
with sons who have failed them
work in sporting goods.
All the angry people
work downstairs in the stockroom
heaving boxes in and out of trucks.
That's where all the blacks work.
I work down there
tossing boxes with them
not even trying
to match their anger.

For People Who Can't Open Their Hoods

Some fat lady in a mink
storms in
says her car won't start
left her lights on
got her son outside with cables
but they don't know how
to open the hood.

Because I'm head stockboy
because she's a good customer
they send me out to help her.
I grin at the two of them
son fat as mother
shaking pink cheeks in the cold
cables dangling from his gloved hands.
He hands them to me
like they're dead snakes.

I pop open the hood
of the mother's new Grand Prix.
They stand aside yapping
not even looking at me.
I start up the son's Cadillac
and sit behind the wheel for a while.
They look at the mother's packages
that I carried out minutes before
without getting a tip.

I rev it up, my foot to the floor
while I check out the plush interior
stereo tape deck, digital clock, cruise control
power everything.
I beep the horn.
They stand in the cold
suddenly looking at me.
I put the car in reverse

118

and back out to move in position
for the jump.
I put it in drive and grip the wheel
and for one long moment
they think   I think
I will drive away.

Night Janitor, McMahon Oil

for J. P.

No one working late tonight.
I mean, except us, but some say
we don't work here, we just clean.

Warm spring. Door ajar.
Freshen up these stale donuts.
Tonight, no radio.

Air freshener stinks up the tiny men's room where lawyers
miss, piss on the floor. Jeff vacuums *spot theory*—
he's done in minutes. I make all the steel shine.

I know a few faces, the late-nighters
with their tired smiles. What are they
doing to celebrate this spring evening?

We're going fishing. I grab a roll of toilet paper
for home. Gravel crunches under us
in the empty lot. We spin out. For the hell of it.

Along the banks of the Pine River
near the Center Street Bridge. No bass or pike tonight.
We catch bluegills, throw them back.

The company brought in Red Adair once,
the famous oil-fire fighter. Everyone wore hard hats
and got their picture taken with Red to hang on office walls.

There's no pictures with guys holding cleanser
posed around a toilet, but I'd like to see one of those.
I'd like to see one of those guys piss straight.

Jeff lost his CETA job working with deaf workers
because there is no CETA anymore. He has taught me
some. *I love this,* he signs.

It's nice that he doesn't have to speak.
Jeff gets letters about his loans. They burn like any paper.
I rest my head in my hands and smell cleanser.

Friends passed this job on to us, a couple
who got better jobs and moved on. This job
not enough to live on. We both work days

minimum wage. *Every three months*
steal one can of coffee, our friends said.
We will leave this job as soon as

something comes up. That's a wish. Something
to come up. Tonight I wish my hands smelled
like the river. I let them drag in cold water

but it's not enough. If I catch enough fish
and let them go, my hands will smell like fish.
That's the deal I make tonight. Or maybe just my wish.

The fish slide out of my hand and flop back
into the dark river. If I am a fish I am a bluegill.
If you've ever fished, you've caught a bluegill.

And if it was your first fish, maybe someone let you
keep it if it was big enough. Most likely
you threw it back. If it didn't swallow the hook.

It's my goal never to swallow the hook.
Jeff has to leave soon because a woman loves him
and he loves her. She has long blonde hair

and paints black canvases. She tends bar
at the Pine Knot and slides us a pitcher or two.
I would like to be in love tonight

but I will settle for my hands smelling like hands.
I will settle for a new roll of toilet paper,
the soft kind, my bonus to myself.

Instead of a cleaning service
they settled for us. We work cheap. Settle too easily,
I think. The office keys rattle in my pocket.

They're alright, the ones I've met,
sweating over figures. Tonight I want
to be generous like the river and let things be.

We stand for a moment and listen to water
rushing past below us before we get in the car.
My hands smell a little like fish, a little like cleanser.

I cup them against my face while Jeff drives.
You praying again? he says.
It's a joke because he's never seen me pray.

Yeah, I say. I want to make a joke
but I just say *yeah.*

Busboy and Waitress: Cashing Out

I sip my free drink with Karen,
my uniform stained with slop
from scraped plates, a rancid buffet.
I close my eyes and try to sigh
deep enough. I hear her splash
change onto the counter,
rustle her bills.

My face is tired, she says.
Her own stains: a businessman's
crude remark, the visual undressing,
some old ladies who stayed forever
then stiffed her. I wait
for her to shove a little money my way,
nodding, listening—part
of what I'm paid for.

Hacking It

"If you can't hack it, get a job as a dishwasher."
—Ernie (the Cat) Ladd

for Gary Ostanski

Never eat in a place
with Salisbury Steak on the menu,
a cook tells me while preparing some.
I believe that more than I believe
the poet who writes: *How much longer*
will I be able to inhabit the divine Sepulcher . . .
or another poem about Icarus or Ulysses.
How can we believe in gods
when our bosses are ready to hammer us?

In the clatter of silver and plates
my hands wrinkle and redden
among those named Cyclops, Clutter.
Who knows what it takes,
how to define *hacking it,*
working for minimum wage
in Detroit, Michigan? My friend
from Yugoslavia says *Dishwasher here*
work like slave. We two stooches
to be here.

What gods there are live among us
with homemade tattoos and homemade potions
with permanent limps and taped glasses
with stained uniforms and rusting cars
hacking it the best they can
against those who sign their checks
and cannot pronounce their names.

Tenured Guy

I have smiled
and said hello in the hallways
I have lost sleep over brief exchanges
I have changed pants
just to pick up my mail
and I have gotten tenure.

I have kept my one good pair of shoes
and my corduroy sportcoat in my office
just in case. I have nodded
at the names of authors
I have not and will never read
and I have gotten tenure.

I have kept my nose clean
literally, I have sipped my wine
at department parties and receptions
staying just long enough.
I have sat in the back at lectures
far enough away to really not hear
and I have nodded astutely
I have never asked a question
or disagreed with anyone
in any of the long
Meetings of the Living Dead
and I have gotten tenure.

I have served on committees
with a smile, oh, always
with a smile. I have blended
into the beige paint
I have become the beige paint
subtlely, so subtlely
that I'm not quite sure
where the paint stops and I begin.

I have gotten tenure
and it's my own fault.

Even as I write this
I am not sure anyone will ever see it.
But why should I care
now that I have gotten tenure?
I am so used to caring
I don't know if I can stop.

I have rounded off my grades upward
to avoid the student complaint
and I have gotten tenure.
I have been a nice guy in class
to students majoring in whining
and I have gotten tenure.

I have published bad work
and I have gotten tenure.
I have padded my vitae—
what I used to call my resumé—
and I have gotten tenure.

I don't have a skilled trade.
I have been paid to do one thing
most of my adult life.

My friend Tom quit teaching
and became a waiter
only to get his jaw busted after work
by an unknown assailant. He once said
the ideal job would be to teach half the time
and haul garbage the other half.
He's teaching again now.

I have kept secrets, I have covered up
I have been bored to death
I have been attacked by unknown assailants
behind my back, I have started to grit my teeth
grind my teeth I am wearing them down
the fangs are dulling
but I have tenure.

Half my friends hate me for getting tenure.
They think I am lucky or that I sold out.
Maybe they're just jealous or maybe
I'm just paranoid. I would like workman's comp
for paranoia I have been injured on the job
I have been injured on the way to tenure
I have gotten lost on the way to tenure
I am still waiting for the official letter
I am still waiting for the map
I am still waiting to find my way home.

I have cut back on my contractions
cut back on my *ain'ts* and *yeahs*
I have discussed my work in an intellectual fashion
I have talked about my place in American literature
I have talked about breaking new ground
I have ranked myself very highly
the Dean said *top ten* so I have said
top ten.

I once said all I wanted to do was teach and write.
A Full Professor laughed at that.
How naive, I'm sure she was thinking.
Maybe someday I'll be a Full Guy
and I'll be able to sit
with the other Full Guys and Full Gals
and have a Full Meeting. Oh I have a hard on
just thinking about it.

I have tenure, did I tell you that?
I explain it to my family and they nod:
You can never be fired, great. Oh,
I am in the club now, my referees
have blown their whistles in my support,
I am studying the secret handshakes and codes
I am growing a beard so I can stroke it wisely
while I vote on another person's fate.

When you see me walking down the hall, say
Hey, there's the tenured guy! And I will give you
my little tenured wave, not too exuberant—
just so long, so high.

The Former Miner Returns from His First Day as a Service Worker

at McDonald's—somewhere in Appalachia

All day he crushed the spongy buns, pawed at
The lids of burger boxes and kiddie pacs
as if they were chinese puzzles.

All day his hands ticked, ready to latch on
Or heave or curl around a tool
Heavier than a spatula.

All day he rubbed his eyes in the crisp light.
All day the blue tile, the polished chrome, said
Be nimble, be jolly, be quick.

All day he grinned while the public, with bland
Or befuddled faces, scowled over his head
And mumbled, whispered, snarled, and snapped.

All day his co-workers, pink and scrubbed,
Prattled and glided and skipped while he,
All bulk and balk, rumbled and banged.

Near shift's end he daydreamed—of the clang
Of rock on steel, the skreel
Of a conveyor belt, the rattling whine
Of the man-trip, the miner's growl of gears
As it gnarled, toothing at the seam.

He makes his slow way home, shadow among
Roadside shadows, groping back in himself
For that deep, sheltering dark.
He has never been so tired.
His hands have never been so clean.

EXCERPT FROM
Natural Birth

Delivery

i was in the delivery room. PUT YOUR
FEET UP IN THE STIRRUPS. i put them up, obedient
still humbled, though the spirit was growing larger
in me, that black woman was in my throat, her thin
song, high pitched like a lark, and all the muscles
were starting to constrict around her.
i tried to push just a little. it
didn't hurt. i tried a little more.

ROLL UP, guzzo said. he wanted to give me
a spinal. NO. I DON'T WANT A SPINAL. (same
doctor as ax handle up my butt, same as shaft
of split wood, doctor spike, driving the
head home where my soft animal cowed and prayed and
cried for his mother.)

or was the baby
part of this
whole damn
conspiracy,
in on it with
guzzo,
the two of them
wanting to shoot
the wood
up me for
nothing,

for playing
music to him
in the dark
for singing
to my round

clasped
belly
for filling
up with
pizza on a cold
night, dough
warm.

maybe
he
wanted
out,
was saying
give her
a needle
and let me/the hell/
out of here
who cares
what she
wants
put her
to sleep.

(my baby
pushing off
with his black
feet
from the dark
shore, heading
out, not
knowing
which way and trusting,
oarless and eyeless, so
hopeless
it didn't matter.)

131

no. not
my baby.
this
loved
thing
in/and of
myself

so i balled up
and let him
try to
stick it in.
          maybe
something was
wrong

     ROLL UP
he said
     ROLL UP
but i don't want it
     ROLL UP ROLL UP
but it doesn't hurt

we all stood,
nurses, round the white
light
hands
hanging
empty at our sides
     ROLL UP IN A BALL
all of us not
knowing
how
or if
in such a world without

false promises
we could say
anything
but, *yes,*
yes.
come take it
and be quick.

i put my belly in my hand
gave him that
thin side
of my back
the bones
intruding on the air
in little knobs
in joints
he might
crack
down my spine
his knuckles
rap
each twisted
symmetry
put me on
the rack,
each
nerve
bright
and stretched
like canvas.

he couldn't get it in!
three times, he tried
ROLL UP, he cried, ROLL UP
three times
he couldn't get it in!

133

dr. y (the head obstetrician)
came in

"what are you
doing, guzzo,
i thought she
wanted
natural . . .

(to me) *do*
you want
a shot . . . no? well,

PUT YOUR LEGS UP,
GIRL, AND
PUSH!"

and suddenly, the light
went out
the nurses
laughed
and nothing
mattered
in this 10
A.M. sun
shiny morning
we were well
the nurses and the
doctors cheering
that girl
combing hair
all in one
direction
shining
bright as water.

                    i

grew deep
in me
like fist and i
grew deep
in me
like death
and i
grew deep
in me
like hiding in the sea and
i was
over me
like
sun and i
was under
me
like sky and i
could look
into myself
like one
dark eye.
        i was her
and she was me
and we were
scattered round
like light
        nurses
        doctors
cheering

                                such waves

my face
contorted,

never
wore
such mask, so
rigid
and so dark
        so
bright, un-
compromising
brave
no turning
back/no
no's.

i was so
beautiful. i
could look
up in the
light and
see my huge-
ness,
arc,
electric,
heavy, fleshy, living
light.

no wonder they
praised me,
a gesture
one makes
helpless and
urgent, praising
what goes on
without our praise.

when there
was nowhere

i could go, when i
was so deep
in myself
so large
i had to
let it out
they said
    drop back. i

dropped back
on the table
panting,
they moved
the head, swiveled
it correctly

    but i

    i

    was
    loosing
    her. something
        a head
    coming through
    the door.
    NAME PLEASE/
    PLEASE / NAME / whose

    head / i
    don't know / some /
        disconnection

        NAME PLEASE /

137

and i
am not ready:
the sudden visibility—
his body,
his curly wet hair,
his arms
abandoned in that air,
an arching, squiggling thing,
his skin must be
so cold,
but there is nothing
i can do
to warm him,
his body clutches
in a wretched
spineless way.

they expect me
to sing
joy   joy
a son is born,
child is given.
tongue
curled in my head
tears, cheeks
stringy with
damp hair.

this lump
of flesh,
lump of steamy
viscera.
            who

is this
child

who

is his father

      a child
      never having
      been seen
      before,
      without
      credentials
      credit cards without
      employee
      reference or
      high school grades or
      anything
      to make him
      human make
      him mine but
      skein of
      pain to
      chop off
      at the navel.

           while they could
           they held him down and
           chopped him, held him up
           my little fish, my blueness
           swallowed in the air
           turned pink
           and wailed.

                no more. enough.
                i lay back, speechless, looking
                for something

to say to myself.

after you have
touched the brain,
that squirmy
lust of maggots,
after you have
pumped the heart,
that thief,
that comic, you
throw her in the trash.

and the little one
in a case
of glass . . .

> *he is not i*
> *i am not him*
> *he is not i*

. . . the stranger . . .

blue
air
protects us from each other.

here.
here is the note he brings.
it says, *"mother."*

but i do not even know
this man.

Gratitude

I'm here
        to tell you
                an old story.
                This
Appears to be
        my work.
                I live
                in the world,
Walk
    the streets
                of New York,
                this
Dear city.
        I want
            to tell you
            I'm 36
Years old,
        I have lived
                in and against
                my blood.
I want to tell you
                I am grateful,
                        because,
                        (after all),
I am a black,
        American poet!
                I'm 36,
                and no one
Has to tell me
        about luck.
                I mean:
                after a reading
Someone asked me
                once:
                If
                you weren't

141

Doing this,
          what
               (if anything)
               would you be doing?
And I didn't say
          what we both
                    understood.
                         I'm
A black, American male.
                    I own
                         this particular story
                         on this particular street
At this particular moment.
                    This appears
                                   to be
                                   my work.
I'm 36 years old,
               and all I have to do
                              is repeat
                              what I notice
Over
     and over,
               all I have to do
               is remember.
And to the famous poet
                    who thinks
                                   literature holds
                                   no small musics:
Love.
     And to the publishers
                         who believe
                         in their marrow
There's no profit
               on the fringes:
                              Love.
                              And to those

142

Who need
        the promise of wind,
                        the sound of branches
                        stirring
Beneath the line:
            here's
                another environment
                poised
To open.
        Everyone reminds me
                        what an amazing
                        Odyssey
I'm undertaking,
            as well they should.
                            After all,
                            I'm a black,
American poet,
            and my greatest weakness
                            is an inability
                            to sustain rage.
Who knows
        what'll happen next?
                            This appears to be one
                            for the books,
If you
    train your ears
                for what's
                unstated
Beneath the congratulations(!)
                        That silence
                                is my story,
                                the pure celebration
(And shock)
        of my face
                defying
                its gravity,

So to speak.
        I claim
                this tiny glee
                not just
For myself,
        but for my parents,
                        who shook their heads.
                        I'm older now
Than my father was
                when he had me,
                        which is no big deal,
                        except
I have personal knowledge
                of the wind
                        that tilts the head back.
                        And I claim
This loose-seed-in-the-air glee
                    on behalf of the
                    social studies teacher
I had in the tenth grade,
                a real bastard
                      who took me aside
                      after class
The afternoon
        he heard I was leaving
                    for a private school,
                    just to let me know
He expected me
        to drown out there,
                      that I held the knowledge
                    of the drowned man,
The regret
        of ruined flesh
                in my eyes;
                which was fair enough,
Except

144

I believe I've been teaching
far longer now
            than he had that day,
And I know
        the blessing
                of a
                narrow escape.
And I claim
        this rooster-pull-down-morning glee
                            on behalf of anyone
                            who saw me coming.
And said yes,
            even
                when I was loud, cocky,
                insecure,
Even
    when all they could have seen
                            was the promise of a germ,
                            even
When it meant
            yielding ground.
                    I am a bit older
                    than they were
When I walked
            into that room,
                    or class
                    or party,
And I understand the value
                of the unstated push.
                            A lucky man
                            gets to sing
his name.
        I have survived
                long enough
                to tell a bit
Of an old story.

145

And to those
who defend poetry
against all foreign tongues:
Love.
And to those who believe
a dropped clause
signifies encroachment:
Love.
And to the bullies who need
the musty air of
the clubhouse
All to themselves:
I am a brick in a house
that is being built
around your house.
I'm 36 years old,
a black, American poet.
Nearly all the things
that weren't supposed to occur
Have happened, (anyway),
and I have
a natural inability
to sustain rage,
Despite
the evidence.
I have proof,
and a job that comes
As simple to me
as breathing.

Why Do So Few Blacks Study Creative Writing?

Always the same, sweet hurt,
The understanding that settles in the eyes
Sooner or later, at the end of class,
In the silence cooling in the room.
Sooner or later it comes to this,

You stand face to face with your
Younger face and you have to answer
A student, a young woman this time,

And you're alone in the classroom
Or in your office, a day or so later,
And she has to know, if all music
Begins equal, why this poem of hers
Needed a passport, a glossary,

A disclaimer. *It was as if I were . . .*
What? Talking for the first time?
Giving yourself up? Away?
There are worlds, and there are worlds,
She reminds you. She needs to know
What's wrong with me? and you want

To crowbar or spade her hurt
To the air. You want photosynthesis
To break it down to an organic language.
You want to shake *I hear you*
Into her ear, armor her life

With permission. Really, what
Can I say? That if she chooses
To remain here the term
Neighborhood will always have
A foreign stress, that there
Will always be the moment

147

The small, hard details
Of your life will be made
To circle their wagons?

"Who Looks After Your Kids?"

"Who looks after your kids when you work?"
"Who does the housework?"
"How do you manage working those long hours with a family?"
"How do you manage with the kids?"

Well, there's their father, and a nanny and a day care centre
but they don't really hear, the people who ask.
They don't want to know about it.

What they want to hear is:

Who does the housework? My henpecked worm of a husband. Me,
until four in the morning. A Jamaican wetback whom we blackmail
into slaving for peanuts. Nobody, we all live in a huge tattered
ball of blankets like a squirrel's nest.

Who bakes the bread? Never touch it. Mac's Bakery. The pixies.
A little old Irishwoman named Kirsten Emmott comes in every week.

How do you manage with the kids? I don't. I neglect them.
I'm on the verge of a nervous breakdown, please help me.
I'm drinking heavily. I don't give a damn about the kids,
let them go to hell their own way.

Who looks after the kids? Nobody, I tie them to a tree in
the back yard every day. My senile old grandmother. The
Wicked Witch of the West.

No Fear of Blood

I

I have to be careful about suede or canvas shoes,
for once you get blood on them it's hard to get it out.
Even in scrub boots you can't always protect your feet
from the cascade of blood that follows the birth of the placenta
or worse, at Caesarean section, the opening of the uterus
and the blood and amniotic fluid pour down her side
and onto your shoes
especially if you are standing on the assistant's side
to which the belly is always tilted:
Anyway, you can't very well say to the shoe salesman,
Something suitable for wading in blood, please.

Taking the newborn child on your lap
results in a wet and sometimes bloody lap.
Manual removal of a placenta
means a bright red glove of blood.
Cutting the cord, which is under pressure between the clamps,
results in a spray of blood, right in your eye if you're not careful.

You have to clean up pretty carefully before leaving the delivery room,
lest the next tour of pregnant couples
peering about the delivery suite
get a shock at the sight of you.

II

The blood of birth, which is normal, which nature builds up slowly
in generous amounts over nine months, ready to be harmlessly shed,
is beautiful.

It's the most beautiful red there is.
And the hot red blood smells good, it's a strange animal smell,
odd the first time you notice it.

150

Most people think it's crazy
to have no fear of blood and its smell
of women and their lively flavours
but not me.

I love the smell of labouring women, the amniotic fluid that
soaks the bed, their earthy beauty.

GAIL RUDD ENTREKIN

The Business Man

The company, like a small herd of brilliant sheep
who have inadvertently grazed all morning on marijuana,
staggers toward its highly technical goals.
Worker sheep wander off in all directions
and you are the sheepdog, the *pro* whose rented brain
holds the final destination and inherent true shape
of the herd. Your special skill, like that of any whore
or genius, becomes depleted, sucked away.
You circle the perimeter, hushing the bleating panic here,
signaling danger there, as the herd swerves just in time
to avoid falling into the abyss.

                        You are good, all right,
and well worth the exorbitant rates they pay.
What's left at the end of the day
pushes open the front door like a spent alcoholic
puffy-eyed, necktie hanging like a noose.

When there is not too much sticky on the floor
too many broken lawn chairs in the yard
too much fighting or weeping in the children's rooms,
I feed you, take you in where it's hot and sweet
and there is nothing to remember but the way
the current takes you, slides you back, pulls you in again.

Jorge the Church Janitor Finally Quits

Cambridge, Massachusetts, 1989

No one asks
where I am from,
I must be
from the country of janitors,
I have always mopped this floor.
Honduras, you are a squatter's camp
outside the city
of their understanding.

No one can speak
my name,
I host the fiesta
of the bathroom,
stirring the toilet
like a punchbowl.
The Spanish music of my name
is lost
when the guests complain
about toilet paper.

What they say
must be true:
I am smart,
but I have a bad attitude.

No one knows
that I quit tonight,
maybe the mop
will push on without me,
sniffing along the floor
like a crazy squid
with stringy gray tentacles.
They will call it Jorge.

Green and Red, Verde y Rojo

for Jacobo Mena

At night, when Beacon Hill
is a private army
of antique gas lamps
glowing in single file,
Jacobo vacuum-cleans
the law office of Adams and Blinn,
established 1856, with the founder's
wire-rimmed Protestant face
still supervising the labor,
a restored photograph in the window.

Jacobo's face
is indio-guatemalteco,
bored as the work,
round as worry,
heavy as waiting.
Guatemala is green and red,
green volcanoes, red birds,
green like rivers in rain,
red like coffee beans at harvest,
the river-green and quetzal bird-red
of his paintings,
perfiles del silencio.

Testimony of death-squad threats
by telephone, shrilled in the dark,
the flash of fear's adrenaline,
and family stolen with the military's greed
for bodies, all recorded by stenographers,
then dismissed:
Guatemala leaves no proof,
and immigration judges are suspicious
only of the witnesses, who stagger and crawl
through America. Asylum denied,
appeal pending.

As he waits, Jacobo paints
in green and red, verde y rojo,
and at night he cleans the office
of Adams and Blinn,
where Guatemala cannot be felt
by the arrogant handshake of lawyers,
where there is no green or red,
only his shadow blending
with the other shadows in the room,
and all the hours of the night
to picture the executioners.

Watch Me Swing

I was the fifth man hired
for the city welfare cleaning crew
at the old Paterson Street ballpark,
Class A minor leagues.
Opening Day was over,
and we raked the wooden benches
for the droppings of the crowd:
wrappers, spilled cups, scorecards,
popcorn cartons, chewed and spit hot dogs,
a whiskey bottle, a condom dried on newspaper.

We swung our brooms,
pausing to watch home runs sail
through April imagination
over the stone fence three hundred feet away,
baseball cracking off the paint factory sign
across Washington Street.
We shuffled and kicked,
plowed and pushed
through the clinging garbage,
savoring our minimum wages.

When the sweeping was done,
and the grandstand benches
clean as Sunday morning pews,
the team business manager
inspected the aisles,
reviewed the cleaning crew
standing like broomstick cadets
and said:
"We only need four."
I was the fifth man hired.

As the business manager
strode across the outfield
back to his office,

I wanted to leap the railing,
crouch at home plate
and swing my broom,
aiming a smacked baseball
for the back of his head,
yelling, "watch me swing, boss,
watch me swing."

City of Coughing and Dead Radiators

—Chelsea, Massachusetts

I cannot evict them
from my insomniac nights,
tenants in the city of coughing
and dead radiators.
They bang the radiators
like cold hollow marimbas;
they cry out
to unseen creatures
skittering across their feet
in darkness;
they fold hands over plates
to protect food
from ceilings black with roaches.

And they answer the call
of the list,
all evictions in court,
brays the clerk.
Quiet and dutiful
as spectral troops returning,
they file into the courtroom,
crowding the gallery:
the patient one from El Salvador,
shoemaker's union refugee,
slapping his neck
to show where that vampire
of an army bullet
pierced his uncle's windpipe;
the red-haired woman
with no electricity
but the drug's heat
swimming in the pools
of her blue bruises,
whiteskinned as the candles
she lives by,

who will move this afternoon
for a hundred dollars;
the prostitute swollen
with pregnancy and sobbing
as the landlady
sneers miscarriage
before a judge
poking his broken hearing aid;
the girl surrounded by a pleading carousel
of children, in Spanish bewilderment,
sleepless and rat-vigilant,
who wins reluctant extermination
but loses the youngest,
lead paint retarded;
the man alcohol-puffed,
graph of scars
stretching across his belly,
locked out, shirt stolen,
arrested at the hearing
for the rampage
of his detox hallucinations;
the Guatemalan boy, who listens
through the wall
for his father's landlord-defiant staccato,
jolted awake
by flashes of the landlord
floating over the bed,
parade balloon
waving a kitchen knife.

For all those sprawled down stairs
with the work boot's crusted map
printed on the back,
the creases of the judge's face
collapse into a fist.
As we shut files

159

and click briefcases
to leave,
a loud-faced man
trumpets from the gallery:
Death to Legal Aid.

LYN FERLO

Billy

Billy came through the office today.
EVERYONE was wishing they had worn a skirt.
We ran our fingers through our hair
and tried to keep our eyes
from running out of control
over his
fine
blue
denim.

It was his eyes (I think)
we liked the most.
His hands . . .
he could probably do a lot of things with his hands.

It was good he came
to fix the air conditioner.
It's a lot cooler in here now.

Fictions of the Feminine: Quasi-Carnal Creatures from the Cloud Decks of Venus

I. The Cocktail Waitress

Before work, I practice Bo-Peep put-offs under veils
of Maybelline, pop two No-Doz, and stop
at church. I pray
for the creeps with bucks
to burn, for those receptacles,
the dancers, who throw their legs
over strangers' shoulders, rolling
their heads and tongues in scorn-
ful seizure; pray to escape this low-class pain, become a flight
attendant. Sometimes I'm the only decent female

in the place. A magenta spotlight,
a glitzy reptilian globe, dyes flesh
the winking livid pink
of badly tuned TVs.
Stone freaks, diddlers, Raincoat
Charlies stare at the strut-
way through three-dollar beers
or scan the racked fantasies
in back: ersatz nuns
with bewildered German Shepherds, condoms
stamped with El Greco's
"View of Toledo." Above me,

women spiked with hard-
ware strip down to garters
full of dollars. It gets in my head,
bothers my mind to see
their breasts cemented by silicone, unmoved
whether they laugh or cry, faces so puffy
they have to sleep upright
to keep the stuff from slipping.
I hate them

for the way they hurt themselves, working
this place like a purgatorial
gyno ward, letting hope live
in their smiles like a tic, thinking some Sugar
Daddy will save their lives
in Vegas, a vested broker wive them,
the way Aztec victims thought
they'd go to heaven and be reborn as hummingbirds
or goddamned butterflies.

II. The Paralyzed Client

To replace thought with sensation, that's why
I come. To see pouty flowers

squirm in mimeo-
violet light, three floors of XX fun.

As a kid, XX stood for kisses:
now, of course, it's different. They swivel down the ramp,

germ-sinuous, diseaseable as
scavenger eels eating up dead

rivers, the swash and backwash
of their strip, their looping moves, powerful

and crass as propaganda. "Showgirls."
What a sham! Only shiftless

idiotheads would work this gig.
I have a certain objectivity. As a kid, I saw

slides of atrophied muscle,
my own, I bet, magnified 1000×:

gauzy as cheesecloth, a fine plaid lilac.
Dad was a pathologist. I have his

scientific eye. I hate
the other patrons with their static

can-do vanity, hate the haggling
glances of these pancaked tramps.

164

Last week, blunt as a judge,
one offered me a real sex rub. Took me

for a sucker, another fool
for oogling, but I knew her gaff

game: the knockout
drops in liquor, the stacked

quarters—they'll clip you.
I've ordered a power-

driven chair. Then I'll be able
to travel with the lightning

menace of a centipede, a gladiator
in fetters. I'll come armed

with shellcrackers, live
ammo, do some damage to the situation,

put a stagger in their struts.
As a kid, I'd find human

limbs in the fridge.
I've always been like this.

III. The Stripper

"100 Pounds of Passion
from London's Mousetrap Lounge!"
The histories they invent for me . . .
I'd like to enter shrink-wrapped in lead
sheeting, leopard skin, tinsel, and an orthopedic shoe.
"A Fiction of the Feminine, a Quasi-Carnal Creature
from the Cloud Decks of
                Venus," I could be. Elevated
        feeling's always rhythmic. I dance
    to gutbucket jazz, to fragments of myself hung-
up in mirrors across the room, swiveling
with the current like a body in a river. A good strip
depends on intricate, smooth moves, a thrust for every nut:
            the hook and eye
        and switch and mince, the wrench
    kicks, heavy-duty ratchet
dips, the chops, the hits, each detail planned and weighed
like a successful suicide. At the end I pick up
        the moltings, go backstage.
            The dressing rooms of skin boutiques smell
        haunted—decades of burnt sweat, I guess.
Once, doing breastercises with a pair of brass fire
hose nozzles, I saw this antique spangled tarantella
of a burly queen, showing her fangs
and laughing at me, the flabby old vamp.
            Most dancers here are lesbians.
        The creeps that patronize are sick. I say
    they have fiberfill for minds, icicles for dicks.
They think they're special, though, the dimwits.
When they ask, I say I'm quitting to work with autistic kids.
        Some girls go
    horizontal, do floorwork,
        some clubs have touch, but I never get on

166

eye level. I make the dumb fucks look
up. Last night they rolled a wheelchair
at me like a bowling ball. "Farther!" he yells,
tears running from his eyes, mouth, nose.
> They come to drool
> > at us marooned in black and white,
> > in either/or, virgin/whore.
The spotlight, the darkness,
shields them like the polished visors of riot
police. Appetites like this are dangerous, growing
> > on what they can't quite handle.
> But I prefer that to any
> > vis-à-vis. I'm a modest person by nature.
To tell the truth, I do this now through force
of habit. One night, for a hoot, I'll put pasties,
gown, mask, wig and boa over a rented skeleton suit.
> > Moving slowly, I'll pose, give
> > looks, then what a show! I'll come bumping
> through their heads stripped down to a string
> of glowing bones: the ultimate
in unpeeled flesh.

I Stop Writing the Poem

to fold the clothes. No matter who lives
or who dies, I'm still a woman.
I'll always have plenty to do.
I bring the arms of his shirt
together. Nothing can stop
our tenderness. I'll get back
to the poem. I'll get back to being
a woman. But for now
there's a shirt, a giant shirt
in my hands, and somewhere a small girl
standing next to her mother
watching to see how it's done.

Trying to Catch Up

I'm coaching the Warsaw baseball team,
thirty-five guys who throw—excuse me—like girls.
They are trying to catch up on something
they don't even know they've missed: all those
springs and summers, those long days of stepping out
and following through, of firing over and over
into the sun, into a skinny or fat
buddy's oiled mitt until they can't quit
this thing, this motion, this smooth overhand wave
taking in Koufax and Kaline and Mays, taking in
as darkness comes on, all the stars
and taking them home, night after night
the perfect plays wrapped in a glove
strapped to a bike's handlebars
or tucked in a rear pocket like glorious cash
that can't be given for anything ordinary—
night after night of keeping
their tails down and scooping up
dream grounders, tossing the fleetest
runners out by half a step, by inches, by those
whiskers that won't appear for years yet, and maybe,
if they're good enough, if they can make it up there
where it's always summer, never . . .
But here in Warsaw, in February, in a frigid
gym we use weekend afternoons, plus Wednesday
for an hour, I've got thirty-five guys already shaving
and throwing—OK, strong as bulls—
but looking as if they're about to fall over.

Ravens

We do wind sprints, we play catch
and pepper, but we do not chatter—
it's so quiet we could be in church
when I shut up, or on the street
like all those silent Poles in line
for lemons, leeks, and toilet paper.
"George, baseball players *talk*.
They razz and praise each other,
they're like ravens, man, they haw
and quack and keep their heads up—
listen, your guy's pitching
you say come on baby blow it
past this ugly cripple he can't hit
kielbasa come baby smoke it
hum it Jacek humbabe humbabe
swing batter *swing,* and if
he does and misses give the needle
to him, Georgie, croon like you just got a
kiss off Miss Polonia in her underwear . . . "
"Coach, I think I couldn't think
on baseball." "Right, Georgie, pay
attention, your guy's up to bat now
you say good eye Andrzej good eye
baby pick the cherry pick the plum
hey pitcher this one's coming back
between your jollies buddy
this one's on the grits it's all she wrote
hey pitcher pitcher this one's
going going this one's going—
where's it going, George?"
"It's going over the fence, Coach."
"Hell, George, give it a ride, baby,
pound it over the tallest joint in town."
"It's going over the Palace of Culture, Coach."
"All *right,* all the way to Moscow boom boom
and landing on Lenin's tomb."

A Mouse

Yesterday at batting practice
Froggy got a mouse—
he watched, dead still,
as one of Piotr's fastballs came
and caught him in the face.
A straight, no fooling thud.
                              At once
Piotr ran and kissed him
where the mouse would be, crooning Polish.
Froggy is a car mechanic, his big
meaty hands are nicked all over,
half the nails are blue.
He put an arm around Piotr,
crooning back. The pitcher
gave him three or four more kisses,
loud smacks across the knuckles,
then they laughed.
                        I tried to picture
something like this in the States.
Maybe at a nursery school you'd see it,
where people have good manners, love,
and other things to teach—
but not on any fields that I knew of.

In Cheever Country

Half an hour north of Grand Central
the country opens up. Through the rattling
grime-streaked windows of the coach, streams appear,
pine trees gather into woods, and the leaf-swept yards
grow large enough to seem picturesque.

Farther off smooth parkways curve along the rivers,
trimmed by well-kept trees, and the County Airport
now boasts seven lines, but to know this country
see it from a train—even this crowded local
jogging home half an hour before dark

smelling of smoke and rain-damp shoes
on an afternoon of dodging sun and showers.

One trip without a book or paper
will show enough to understand
this landscape no one takes too seriously.

The architecture of each station still preserves
its fantasy beside the sordid tracks—
defiant pergolas, a shuttered summer lodge,
a shadowy pavilion framed by high-arched windows
in this land of northern sun and lingering winter.

The town names stenciled on the platform signs—
Clear Haven, Bullet Park, and Shady Hill—
show that developers at least believe in poetry
if only as a talisman against the commonplace.
There always seems so much to guard against.

The sunset broadens for a moment, and the passengers
standing on the platform turn strangely luminous
in the light streaming from the palisades across the river.
Some board the train. Others greet their arrivals
shaking hands and embracing in the dusk.

If there is an afterlife, let it be a small town
gentle as this spot at just this instant.
But the car doors close, and the bright crowd,
unaware of its election, disperses to the small
pleasures of the evening. The platform falls behind.

The train gathers speed. Stations are farther apart.
Marble staircases climb the hills where derelict estates
glimmer in the river-brightened dusk.
Some are convents now, some orphanages,
these palaces the Robber Barons gave to God.
And some are merely left to rot where now
broken stone lions guard a roofless colonnade,
a half-collapsed gazebo bursts with tires,
and each detail warns it is not so difficult
to make a fortune as to pass it on.

But splendor in ruins is splendor still,
even glimpsed from a passing train,
and it is wonderful to imagine standing
in the balustraded gardens above the river
where barges still ply their distant commerce.

Somewhere upstate huge factories melt ore,
mills weave fabric on enormous looms,
and sweeping combines glean the cash-green fields.
Fortunes are made. Careers advance like armies.
But here so little happens that is obvious.

Here in the odd light of a rainy afternoon
a ledger is balanced and put away,
a houseguest knots his tie beside a bed,
and a hermit thrush sings in the unsold lot
next to the tracks the train comes hurtling down.

Finally it's dark outside. Through the freight houses
and oil tanks the train begins to slow
approaching the station where rows of travel posters
and empty benches wait along the platform.
Outside a few cars idle in the sudden shower.

And this at last is home, this ordinary town
where the lights on the hill gleaming in the rain
are the lights that children bathe by, and it is time
to go home now—to drinks, to love, to supper,
to the modest places which contain our lives.

The Man in the Open Doorway

This is the world in which he lives:
Four walls, a desk, a swivel chair,
A doorway with no door to close,
Vents to bring in air.

There are two well-marked calendars,
Some pencils, and a telephone
The women at the front desk answer
Leaving him alone.

There is a clock he hardly sees
Beside the window on the wall.
It moves in only one direction,
Never stops at all.

Outside the February wind
Scrapes up against the windowpane,
And a blue-green land is fading,
Scarred by streaks of rain.

The phones go off. The files are locked.
But the doorway still is lit at night
Like the tall window of a church
Bleached in winter light.

Sometimes the shadow of his hand
Falls from his desk onto the wall
And is the only thing that moves
Anywhere at all.

Or else he will drive back at night
To walk along the corridor
And, thinking of the day's success,
Trace his steps once more,

Then pause in a darkened stairway
Until the sounds of his steps have ceased
And stroke the wall as if it were
Some attendant beast.

Elbee Novelty Company Inc.

1985

For I have seen Louie Berkie in his warehouse rows of plastic
Dog Poo, rubber chickens, Beagle-Puss glasses and snap cigarettes,
the boneyard and revival ward of 1947's Party Vomit,
Fool 'Em bon-bons, Squirting "Fountain" Pens and X-ray Specs,
while the whole 6th floor of the Calcasieu Building trembles
like the angels' own Joy Buzzer, at the metallic and bronchial hack
of the wooden nickel machine "and I print both sides" "and
orders come in from New Mexico even" "and charities half-price." And
the elevator of the Calcasieu Building smells of piss, of real human
piss, not Eau de Toilet "give-em-a-wiff." but the compiled
untended accidents and sacrileges of 1947 to date, that can't be
bought or later laughed away, but must be only witnessed
after the fact, transparent uric-yellow ghosts,
as the cage wheezes open and Louie Berkie greets you in
his Pop-Out Eyes, "just look wherever you want, hey Rosie
give this guy a bag, just fill the bag, who wants these anyway,
when I die they can put a hundred thousand goddam
squirt carnations on my grave." For I have filled my bag.
For the matchbook snaps, and the chewing gum snaps,
and the dribble glass works like a wonder. And the employees of
the Elbee Novelty Company Inc. work wonders no less.
For the man without teeth stacks Chattering Teeth in what could be
Hieronymus Bosch's Walk-up School of Dentistry supply room,
and the boy without a work permit or English is filing bogus
permits—Fishing, Fucking, Bullshitting, Parking, Mooching—by
a personal system of color and width-of-animated-astonishment in
the eyes and leaping buttocks of the figures depicted thereon, and
Rosie—Rosie who hasn't saved a penny has tended these nickels
stamped with the logos of wholesale faucet distributors and furriers
since 1947, Rosie No-Last-Name, Our Lady By Now Of A Million
Wooden Bucks. And Louie Berkie can show you exploding
cigars all day and not tire. And Louie Berkie can light up his nose.
"Here look at the classic, the universal Palm Shocker, always good
for a *Ha!!*" And his real eyes light really up.
"We all need a gag" and "we all want guffaws" and "I live alone,

177

one thousand Suction Zulu Dancers, I like to make everyone happy but
tell me who the hell wants to inherit a wall of Suction Zulu Dancers?"
For dice can electrify. For fly-in-the-icecube won't
melt, fly or fail. And the street in front of the Calcasieu Building,
200-something Broadway, San Antonio, Texas, smells like, yes and is,
the afternoon's true introduction to the Calcasieu Building elevator, and is
the Elbee Novelty Company Inc.'s world of Original Forms where the puddle
of vomit in front of Europe Deli and News is real and the scars
won't peel off and be folded away. "I started a clown, and then I woke up
one morning and said, 'Sell things, let everybody be a clown.'" And
the liver spots on Louie Berkie's hands will not unstick for slipping
back in a cellophane wrapper, nor his tremor come unplugged. "Hoo, I love
when the first twinkle shows in their eyes." For I have rummaged the
dust-&-clutter of sneezing powder, itching powder, Bird Doo in such quantity
a Jackson Pollock action mural pales in scope, and Snake-in-a-Can.
For Bald Wig, Bum Wig, Beatnik Wig and Bozo Wig are tête-à-tête
in emptiness forever. And in 1947 Louis Berkowitz was 30,
stocking shelves here for the first time, maybe running his hands
in grandeur down a catalogue's columns, Laffs-a-Lot's, the way somebody
else might turn in bed and for the first time
trace a naked spine. And lettering the street signs
for his 6th floor city of yuks—Adult Goods, Party Favors, Gags . . .
For I have filled my bag with Mouse-in-the-Camera, Fake-O bedbugs,
latex worms, The Forehead Faucet, limp forks, smoking spoons.
For Rosie will make change out of a tree all day and drink herself real
shitdrunk all real night. And this is the Louie Berkie Happyrama 1947
Calendar pinned to a wall. "And this is my sister. She
died. It happens. You know? It happens." And
this is the leatherette Turkish Harem Peepbook
"with the best snapper in the business." Louie Berkie is in the business,
is in the funny stuff business and I know well, for I have seen him
walking his rows in the darkness, talking funny talk to 38 years and thousands
of the loveliest best snappers, cocked in expectation,
wasted maybe, beautiful to the right eyes maybe, here on the 6th floor,
"I'm 68," "I only wanted some laughter should fill up
the silence, right? I know, I live alone. Here, shake my hand on it.
. . . HA!!"

The Women's Committee

two men come to our meeting,
they are only middle-management,
but still we are delighted, whisper

to each other, *at last*
they are taking us seriously.
our fingers gush with reports
and statistics. we eat up
their advice, they tell us
what we are doing wrong.
at coffee break we flock to talk
to them, thank them for
coming. our smiles stretch across
our faces like rubber bands, snap
back when they are gone and
nothing is on the table except
papers, the flat hunger
of type.

Waiting

after the meeting the women go to lunch.
the waitress watches, awkward on her high heels
like some odd hoofed animal, while we decide.
a smile is stapled on her face like part
of the menu. small puckers of burns
are splattered part-way up one arm. she is
all of us, our first lurch into the working
world, learning to sell service, it is
where we begin, before we become
the women who go to meetings, the ones
who are never satisfied, we are pains
in the management ass, we're as tired of it
as they are, but still we keep asking,
saying, 64% is not enough, the waitress
is still who we are, coins rattle
their judgments in her pocket.
when she brings us our bill she asks
is there anything more that we want.

Cavities

> If there is no face in the mirror, marry.
> If there is no shadow on the ground,
> have a child. These are the conventions
> the will consents to. But there is a face.
> There is a shadow. They are simply
> unsuitable.
> —Jane Rule, *Desert of the Heart*

sometimes I have a daughter.
she is 15 now, I worry
about her friends, is she taking drugs.
but I raised her well, I am sure of that,
I am a mother, it is
my name.

sometimes I have a daughter,
when I am alone in my office
at night, off-guard, a headache
a crack across my temples, the day's

perspiration hardening like wax into
my pores, my briefcase swollen
with work. she is the choice I think
would have saved me
from being here now, my life full
the way a file cabinet is full,
the way a tooth is filled
but ticking still with that faint pain
no pill can work away.

November

it starts when you do it again after they
said no, it starts when you say Wc and
know who you mean, and each day you
mean one more.
                          —Marge Piercy

it has always happened somewhere else,
somewhere in history before
they knew better, or somewhere south
where politics means guns
and electrodes on the skull.
if it got closer we just
moved away, there was
always another country, another
province. this time
there is no leaving it
to someone else, someone who is
a better revolutionary.
we have lived here too long
to pretend we are still
tourists taking
notes for a book,
with somewhere safe to go home to.
this time it is ourselves
on the picket lines,
we are cold and frightened and
tired, and changed in a way
we will never forgive.

JUDY GRAHN

The Common Woman Poems

I. Helen, at 9 A.M., at Noon, at 5:15

Her ambition is to be more shiny
and metallic, black and purple as
a thief at midday; trying to make it
in a male form, she's become as
stiff as possible.
Wearing trim suits and spike heels,
she says "bust" instead of breast;
somewhere underneath she
misses love and trust, but she feels
that spite and malice are the
prices of success. She doesn't realize
yet, that she's missed success, also,
so her smile is sometimes still
genuine. After a while she'll be a real
killer, bitter and more wily, better at
pitting the men against each other
and getting the other women fired.
She constantly conspires.
Her grief expresses itself in fits of fury
over details, details take the place of meaning,
money takes the place of life.
She believes that people are lice
who eat her, so she bites first; her
thirst increases year by year and by the time
the sheen has disappeared from her black hair,
and tension makes her features unmistakably
ugly, she'll go mad. No one in particular
will care. As anyone who's had her for a boss
will know
the common woman is as common
as the common crow.

II. Ella, in a Square Apron, along Highway 80

She's a copperheaded waitress,
tired and sharp-worded, she hides
her bad brown tooth behind a wicked
smile, and flicks her ass
out of habit, to fend off the pass
that passes for affection.
She keeps her mind the way men
keep a knife—keen to strip the game
down to her size. She has a thin spine,
swallows her eggs cold, and tells lies.
She slaps a wet rag at the truck drivers
if they should complain. She understands
the necessity for pain, turns away
the smaller tips, out of pride, and
keeps a flask under the counter. Once,
she shot a lover who misused her child.
Before she got out of jail, the courts had pounced
and given the child away. Like some isolated lake,
her flat blue eyes take care of their own stark
bottoms. Her hands are nervous, curled, ready
to scrape.
The common woman is as common
as a rattlesnake.

SHARON HASHIMOTO

Four Weeks Unemployed: I Fail the Water Department's Lift and Carry Exam

My cheek feels the rough touch—
burlap hugged close in my arms.
A man repeats the warning:
Lift with your legs, not your back.

Burlap hugged close in my arms,
I raise 30 pounds of soil to the table,
lifting with my legs, not my back.
The shifting sack has no bottom.

How to raise 40 pounds of soil to a table?
I balance the weight on my hip.
The shifting sack shapes a bottom
on the ledge of bone. I stumble—

unbalanced. The weight on my hip
wants to return to the earth, spill
over the ledge of bone. Stumbling,
my breath collapses like skins of small balloons

wanting to return to the earth, spilled
of their air. At 50 pounds, my body knows its limits.
My breath collapses like skins of small balloons
holding everything together. But I can't escape

beyond a body's limits.
I want a job, a secure position
to hold everything together. I can't escape
the words of my mother and father:

You need a job, they say, *a secure position.*
Late nights, I fell asleep listening
to the words of my mother and father.
When did they let go of their dreams?

Late nights, did they fall asleep listening
to each drop of rain breaking against the roof,
remember how the sky let go of its dreams?
I pulled the illusion of warmth close to my body,

folded myself into rain breaking against the roof:
My cheek feels the rough touch
of burlap. *Two minutes to finish,*
a man repeats the warning.

Eleven A.M. on My Day Off, My Sister Phones
Desperate for a Babysitter

Sitting in sunlight, the child
I sometimes pretend is my own
fingers the green weave of the rug
while the small shadow of her head falls over
a part of my lap and bent knee. At three,
she could be that younger part of myself, just beginning
to remember how the dusty warmth feels on her back.
"Are you hungry?" I ask. Together we open
the door of the refrigerator. One apple sits
in the vegetable bin but she gives it to me,
repeating her true mother's words "to share."
Turning the round fruit under the faucet,
the afternoon bright in my face, I look down
at a smile in the half moons of her eyes
and for a moment, I'm seven, looking up
at my childless aunt in Hawaii,
her hands and the long knife peeling
the mango I picked off the tree, rubbing my arms
from the stretch on the back porch
to an overhead branch. Plump
with the island's humidity, it tasted tart
like the heavy clatter of rain on a June Sunday.
"Careful," my niece warns as I slice the apple sideways
to show her the star in the middle.
She eats the core but saves the seeds
to plant in the soft earth of my yard.

LAURIE HENRY

A Former Dispatcher's Comment

To the Editor:

I had a problem which I needed to straighten out.
I wanted a sick day to get my thoughts in order.
I am thankful for your calls, which have been constant.

After working six years, giving notice was sad to think about.
The sheriff phoned my home and threatened Father.
I had a problem which I needed to straighten out.

I violated FCC rules with personal calls for only a moment
but harassing reprimands appeared in my folder.
I am thankful for your calls, which have been constant.

I used the emergency line to order a root-beer float.
(I can't use the Coke machine, due to my disorder.)
I had a problem which I needed to straighten out.

Sheriff said, "If I fired you, I'd never hear the end of it,"
but because of his harassment I have no future.
I am thankful for your calls, which have been constant.

I have not given up on finding other employment.
I have always done my best; as stated earlier,
I had a problem which I needed to straighten out.
I am thankful for your calls, which have been constant.

EDWARD HIRSCH

Commuters

It's that vague feeling of panic
That sweeps over you
Stepping out of the #7 train
At dusk, thinking, *This isn't me*
Crossing a platform with the other
Commuters in the worried half-light
Of evening, *that must be*

Someone else with a newspaper
Rolled tightly under his arm
Crossing the stiff, iron tracks
Behind the train, thinking, *This
Can't be me* stepping over the tracks
With the other commuters, slowly crossing
The parking lot at the deepest
Moment of the day, wishing

That I were someone else, wishing
I were anyone else but a man
Looking out at himself as if
From a great distance,
Turning the key in his car, starting
His car and swinging it out of the lot,

Watching himself grinding uphill
In a slow fog, climbing past the other
Cars parked on the side of the road,
The cars which seem ominously empty
And strange,
         and suddenly thinking
With a new wave of nausea
This isn't me sitting in this car
Feeling as if I were about to drown

In the blue air, *that must be*
Someone else driving home to his

189

Wife and children on an ordinary day
Which ends, like other days,
With a man buckled into a steel box,
Steering himself home and trying
Not to panic

In the last moments of nightfall
When the trees and the red-brick houses
Seem to float under green water
And the streets fill up with sea lights.

JONATHAN HOLDEN

The Crash

October, 1987, Wall Street

1. Tuesday, 10/6/87

Passion was supposed to be great fun,
like a roller-coaster ride, scary,
but you never risk your life, he thinks.
No one talks about the other side
of being "in love," the work it is,
the obligations of adultery,
like holding down a second full-time job.
Moonlighting, he thinks, as he shaves, pleased
with the turn this turn of phrase has taken.
All summer, Tuesdays and Thursdays, as if
to attend some special seminar
on schedule at noon sharp, he emerges
from the tinted glass mirroring panoply
of the brokerage. The Fifth-Avenue bus
comes swinging in, brakes sneezing, he swings
aboard. Clenched secretly inside,
like a man straddling a knife-blade,
he's borne uptown to her basement apartment.
He'll lock the door, turn to her.
They'll welcome each other with a hug,
and now a kiss (the kind of kiss that opens
gradually like a fissure,
swallows us.) And so, without more fuss,
they'll strip and efficiently every-
which-way slip into each other.

"Habit of production," Aristotle
called art, "according to right method."
Six months of doing it, and they
can ply their trade
deftly as a pair of licensed plumbers,
or like two potters, both professionals,

191

wedging and centering the clay
without a fuss. They can do it
with maximum insinuation or with
tenderness. They can do it with sudden, passionate squalls
with sobs, or laughter. With whispers. This
is serious play. Adult play. Adultery.
After much practice, they begin
to call their different lunch-hours "poems."
They rate them afterward.
"That was one of our best poems," he murmurs
two hours later on the phone. "Yes,"
she breathes. Then silence
as they think about their "poem,"
though he's not a poet. He has contempt
for poetry, he only likes the *word* (her word).

He likes the idea of what he thinks
it is. Something about flowers. Birds.
And bees. A kind of pink decorum. For him
the real poetry is money,
and in a way he's right. Money *is*
a kind of poetry. But he wouldn't call it that.
What Coleridge called "that willing
suspension of disbelief that is poetic faith,"
he'd call "leverage," he'd call it "credit."
"Yes," she sighs, "it was a lovely poem.
It left me sleepy." She sighs again.
It's October six. It's 2:30 in the afternoon.
The poetry of money is being read out.
The Dow Jones Industrial is hovering at 2640,
a new high. The prime lending rate is 8.75.
His attention wanders from the tickertape.
His every surface is so freshly painted
he can sense its glistening, it's not dry yet,
he's coated with her sex, his hands
so sticky with it that, surreptitiously,

he touches his fingers to his lips, tastes
his own skin to catch a whiff of her.
It's siesta time. Sitting upright,
he seems to doze awake.
The bond market is steady at this hour.
AT&T is flirting with an all-time high
near thirty-seven. He'd like a jelly doughnut.
He wonders what his wife will cook for supper.

2. 10/19/87, Black Monday

Noon. The bus comes swinging in, doors
wheeze open. He enters blindly. The weather's
pretty, yet (He can't quite put
his finger on it) false.
Ever since that Wednesday, October 7,
when the Fed jacked up the prime
a full half point, sending the Dow stumbling
ninety points downstairs,
to close at 2516,
the market's been subject to odd moods.
Down 34 that Friday, even further down
last Friday—down 57 points—
and it's headed down today. He needs
something to relax him.
She strips efficiently, he fumbles at his belt.
He checks his watch. She notices
how compulsively he checks his watch.
He doesn't take it off. No one could possibly
know his whereabouts right now, yet he acts
as if at any second the telephone is going to ring
for him. "Are you okay?" she asks. "Sure."
She draws the curtains closed.
But, flopped on the waterbed, one arm flung
limply over her flank, he finds himself unable

to make the usual "poem." He's imagining
instead his office telephone ringing
three quarters of a mile away and ringing,
and ringing. Money, like a screaming
infant, requiring attention immediately, *this*
instant, while he lies here, helpless, pitying
his poor, distracted penis. It's like the market.
Neither will go up.
Outside the midday sun shines uninterrupted
in a major key. The sky is blue, without a blemish.
The real world seems not the least aware
of this other weather, an exotic weather only he
can see, The Market—told only in the barometer.
That she is real—her tongue and teeth real
as raw oysters on the half-shell—
should reassure him. And that she is here
while billions of dollars are ceasing to exist.
They're not going up in smoke or steam. They're
not going anywhere. There is no "where" for money.
No "here." Or "there." *Honey,*
are you okay? He cannot answer her.
Because he's neither here nor there.

LYNDA HULL

Night Waitress

Reflected in the plate glass, the pies
look like clouds drifting off my shoulder.
I'm telling myself my face has character,
not beauty. It's my mother's Slavic face.
She washed the floor on hands and knees
below the Black Madonna, praying
to her god of sorrows and visions
who's not here tonight when I lay out the plates,
small planets, the cups and moons of saucers.
At this hour the men all look
as if they'd never had mothers.
They do not see me. I bring the cups.
I bring the silver. There's the man
who leans over the jukebox nightly
pressing the combinations
of numbers. I would not stop him
if he touched me, but it's only songs
of risky love he leans into. The cook sings
with the jukebox, a moan and sizzle
into the grill. On his forehead
a tattooed cross furrows,
diminished when he frowns. He sings words
dragged up from the bottom of his lungs.
I want a song that rolls
through the night like a big Cadillac
past factories to the refineries
squatting on the bay, round and shiny
as the coffee urn warming my palm.
Sometimes when coffee cruises my mind
visiting the most remote way stations,
I think of my room as a calm arrival,
each book and lamp in its place. The calendar
on my wall predicts no disaster
only another white square waiting
to be filled like the desire that fills
jail cells, the old arrest

that makes me stare out the window or want
to try every bar down the street.
When I walk out of here in the morning
my mouth is bitter with sleeplessness.
Men surge to the factories and I'm too tired
to look. Fingers grip lunch box handles,
belt buckles gleam, wind riffles my uniform
and it's not romantic when the sun unlids
the end of the avenue. I'm fading
in the morning's insinuations
collecting in the crevices of buildings,
in wrinkles, in every fault
of this frail machinery.

DAVID IGNATOW

Sales Talk

Better than to kill each other off
with our extra energy is to run after the bus,
though another be right behind. To run
and to explain to ourselves we have no time
to waste, when it is time that hangs
dangerously on our hands, so that the faster
we run the quicker the breezes rushing by
take time away.
                    For comfort we must work
this way, because in the end we find
fume-filled streets and murder headlines:
one out of insanity breaks loose:
he could not make that extra effort
to keep connected with us. Loneliness
like a wheeling condor was attracted
to the particle that had strayed apart.
The brief case we carry, the pressed trousers,
the knotted tie under a white collar add up
to unity and morale.

The Business Life

When someone hangs up, having said
to you, "Don't come around again,"
and you have never heard the phone
banged down with such violence
nor the voice vibrate with such venom,
pick up your receiver gently and dial
again, get the same reply; and dial
again, until he threatens. You will
then get used to it, be sick only
instead of shocked. You will live,
and have a pattern to go by, familiar
to your ear, your senses and your dignity.

Keep Time Away

On some mornings she calls him up just as lunchtime begins, and croons into the phone, "Sweetheart. Yes, darling. Take it easy. Don't worry yourself, we'll manage," while she leans across the boss's desk, using his phone. He chews on a sandwich savagely, a glass of milk at his side. How he would like to fling her out of his office for using a business phone for such petty talk, but he needs her experience at the job. She croons a little longer, then hangs up gently so as not to give an impression of impatience at the other end. She is kind and good, fearful that a man can walk out on you, independent and haughty at having to be supported, suspecting contempt or belittlement from the other. She must be gentle with the last vestiges of love—that makes her arms go up and down at the gangstitcher, that makes her walk and talk buoyantly during lunch, that keeps her hair dyed brown and false teeth bright in her mouth, that makes her look toward the next day and say, "We'll manage."

And this boss, as she hangs up—he is chewing his sardine sandwich—says, with a full mouth, jaws clumping up and down, "Must you call up every day, and every day get calls back—from relatives too?" Poor man, he is anxious only for any business missed through her call, lacking the business that would let him eat in peace. As she thinks of a sharp answer, her face white and puffy, she restrains herself by clutching a handkerchief. She turns back into the shop to read the newspaper about the troubles of other people. The tears of her reddening eyes shine for a second in one last look at the boss. At her age, at fifty, to be told what to do and what not to do: to be denied or rebuked. At her age, when persons like herself have spent their energies to get some peace. For what else had all the fuss in her youth been but to assure her of that peace? At her age, still to be talked to like the worker she had been thirty years ago, except at that time she could understand it from an older person to a young girl. Still to face a young girl's havoc at her age, but without the strength or will to withstand it or to build upon it as youth does. Still, as if to stumble upon a rolling log upon a river, with no other safety or support but that rolling log. At her age of varicose veins, of great, burdensome breasts, of thick thighs and ponderous buttocks to be agile upon a log in the middle of a neverending rapid river. Her tears shine for a moment, dry up under the anger of the boss chewing sardines and sipping milk.

During lunch, all is quiet in the bindery. She sits beside the gangstitcher and reads with steel-rimmed glasses of what other people say and do that reminds her of her own circumstances. There is murder; there is insanity; sports to keep time away. Perversion, stag parties, robberies, and suicides. She reads and finds solace in that her case is not news enough to be printed: solace in knowing her predicament not yet that drastic.

Sound of a tiny bell brings the workers back from the corners of the bindery where they had sat eating, and the gangstitcher starts up again. With one last look at the boss through the open door of the office, she wonders if the day will go by without another word from him.

At home sits darling, brooding over his wife working to support him. How can she convince him that it is love and only love that keeps her here away from him?

Emergency Clinic II

Your eyes were bulging behind thick horn-rimmed glasses
and you smelled of liquor, staring at me speechlessly
above wet, protruberant lips. You kept up your head
with difficulty, slowly slipping down the chair.
I heard you mutter God, once, and turn your head

to stare silently and dazedly at the side wall.
I kept addressing you, seeking answers
to my questions about your child, ill
of pneumonia in the waiting room, its mother
at its side. Why drunk at such a time?
But I assumed you drank regularly and heavily.
I typed the answers as you gave them,
after repeated questioning and waiting.
Your eyes dropped and closed, then struggled open
on a blank face.
                    You had some learning,
from the neat clipped speech and complete sentences
you did manage to speak. You got to your feet,
after bracing yourself on the arms of the chair,
then sighing with the effort to stand left
without another word or glance, still struggling
to keep your head from falling between your shoulders.
I forgot about you, relieved as you left,
taking the fumes with you. I admitted another
patient and slipped into the lobby with my records
to take an elevator to the wards. Your wife
was there waiting too, with the child in her arms,
as you stood swaying beside her,
and she swayed, hers the bleary face
of a heavy drinker too
who looked at me blankly
as if waiting for a comment on your lives.

White, White Collars

We work in this building and we are hideous
in the fluorescent light, you know our clothes
woke up this morning and swallowed us like jewels
and ride up and down the elevators, filled with us,
turning and returning like the spray of light that goes
around dance-halls among the dancing fools.
My office smells like a theory, but here one weeps
to see the goodness of the world laid bare
and rising with the government on its lips,
the alphabet congealing in the air
around our heads. But in my belly's flames
someone is dancing, calling me by many names
that are secret and filled with light and rise
and break, and I see my previous lives.

Any and All

You draw nearer to see her more closely
the blind woman by the bronze doors

of the old Merchants Bank, her mouth
wide open as if in a silent roar,

several dollars stuffed in the pockets
of her mink coat. She is easy to forget

a few days later when you think of her
—not long. The phone is ringing.

You put Byrdman on hold. Polen
wants you in his office immediately.

The lawyers from Mars and the bankers
from Switzerland have arrived to close the deal,

the money in their heads articulated
to the debt of the state of Bolivia.

How much later the Croatian woman
who empties the wastebaskets laughs

when you answer you've been better
and you've been worse. How much sooner

you're told not to tell anyone Byrdman's
grandfather was a Jew. How much No. 54

Wall Street, emblematic reality of extreme
speculations and final effects.

The other evening at a party in the West Sixties
you say as much. None of them knows

what any of it is worth, you say to yourself
later, spitting into an unexpected breeze.

Yellow moons of street lamps on Ninth Avenue
obscured by atmospheric soot and fog,

in the Twenties empty windows of butcher shops,
factories and warehouses without names,

no taxis, the green light behind the window
of a corner bar. A young man sporting muscles,

a woman he might own on his arm, clearly
doesn't like the way you look or look at him,

lets his leash out enough for his wolfdog
to just nip your leg. Another day

you contemplate your strategy:
think about how they think about you

thinking about them and the look on your face
to prove you have the proper attitude.

Let no laughter reveal moods. Let
Charlotte Stone reveal that her father

over the weekend purchased a peninsula in Rhode Island
for Harry and her, let her teeth

be too large and too gray: there is blood
and there is blood-letting; this is not your blood.

Shut the door and wait. Someone else's father
forgives you when you know not what you do,

reminds you, "He's a weasel but he's my friend."
You're a monkey and you work for him,

decide for him whether his clauses should be restrictive,
whether to replace every "any" with "all."

Restaurant

for Lilah Kan

The main cook lies sick on a banquette, and his assistant
has cut his thumb. So the quiche cook takes
their places at the eight-burner range, and you and I
get to roll out twenty-three rounds of pie
dough and break a hundred eggs, four at a crack,
and sift out shell with a China cap, pack
spinach in the steel sink, squish and squeeze
the water out, and grate a full moon of cheese.
Pam, the pastry chef, who is baking Choco-
late Globs (once called Mulattos) complains about the disco,
which Lewis, the salad man, turns up louder out of spite.
"Black so called musician." "Broads. Whites."
The porters, who speak French, from the Ivory Coast,
sweep up droppings and wash the pans without soap.
We won't be out of here until three A.M. In this basement,
I lose my size. I am a bent-over
child, Gretel or Jill, and I can
lift a pot as big as a tub with both hands.
Using a pitchfork, you stoke the broccoli and bacon.
Then I find you in the freezer, taking
a nibble of a slab of chocolate as big as a table.
We put the quiches in the oven, then we are able
to stick our heads up out of the sidewalk into the night
and wonder at the clean diners behind glass in candlelight.

Meeting at Different Conventions in the Same City

To arrive there took decades, luck, thousands
of dollars. And determination, however
subconscious. But there I stood proudly
in my beige suit, bearing my brief case,
loads of budgetary decisions, memos,
personnel problems, the underside of paper-
weights. An only child, an odd girl, I
never knew until that unexpected moment of moving
through a distant hotel lobby, how much in me
so-called equality had set free, all for one
historic instance of patriarchal approval.
How far I'd come for such conventions. Ready
to see, however unexpectedly, one silver-
haired v.p. (a.k.a. Daddy), but more clearly
to have him see me. After all, I knew
the muse refuses measurable success, the cutting
edges of science and business. So when that
old executive perspective recognized me in that split-
second, born of our separate itineraries, I stood
apart his daughter and a part, his own identity.

EDWARD KLEINSCHMIDT

University of Iowa Hospital, 1976

The last time I walked into
Ward C-22 I was stoned,
It was evening, I was picking
Up my final paycheck:

Where to begin in this never
Ending blasted field of corpses.
Men looking like they had been
Attacked repeatedly by a succession

Of wild animals, throats half gone,
Eyes bleeding, raw meat heaped
In piles. One walks around
Sniffing through his long tubes.

A woman in a private room lies
Curled like a Cro-Magnon mummy
In the museum. Where are the doctors
Of love, love apples,

The supervisors of love, love
Administrators? Pain is a steady
Fall from a high place, one with
No view, no vision outside

Itself. Pain is a weed more
Vivid to look at than
The room of flowers next to it.
It lasts through no rain,

Resists scissors, takes over.
Last Christmas in the back room
An intern sat putting a black
Jigsaw puzzle together, one thousand

Pieces, one very long night. I
Took a boy who had shot his face
Off six months earlier on a walk
Around the hospital grounds. He

Was still uninterested after all
That damage. Another showed me 200
Miles of scars, sixty years of making
That road. I know fifty people who are

Now dead. One I watched die, his blood
Pressure dove to nothing, and I had
To stuff him with cotton, tie a
String around his penis, glue a label

On his forehead. I became extremely
Careful driving home each day, I ate
Good foods, slept the right amount,
Lived the short life of convalescence.

Father

Theodore Briggs Kooser
May 19, 1902–December 31, 1979

You spent fifty-five years
walking the hard floors
of the retail business,
first, as a boy playing store

in your grandmother's barn,
sewing feathers on hats
that the neighbors threw out,
then stepping out onto

the smooth pine planks
of your uncle's grocery—
SALADA TEA in gold leaf
over the door, your uncle

and father still young then
in handlebar mustaches,
white aprons with dusters
tucked into their sashes—

then to the varnished oak
of a dry goods store—
music to your ears,
that bumpety-bump

of bolts of bright cloth
on the counter tops,
the small rattle of buttons,
the bell in the register—

then on to the cold tile
of a bigger store, and then one
still bigger—gray carpet,
wide aisles, a new town

210

to get used to—then into
retirement, a few sales
in your own garage,
the concrete under your feet.

You had good legs, Dad,
and a good storekeeper's eye:
asked once if you remembered
a teacher of mine,

you said, "I certainly do;
size ten, a little something
in blue." How you loved
what you'd done with your life!

Now you're gone, and the clerks
are lazy, the glass cases
smudged, the sale sweaters
pulled off on the floor.

But what good times we had
before it was over:
after those stores had closed,
you posing as customers,

strutting in big flowered hats,
those aisles like a stage,
the pale manikins watching;
we laughed till we cried.

The Salesman

Today he's wearing his vinyl shoes,
shiny and white as little Karmann Ghias
fresh from the body shop, and as he moves
in his door-to-door glide, these shoes fly round
each other, honking the horns of their soles.
His hose are black and ribbed and tight, as thin
as an old umbrella or the wing of a bat.
(They leave a pucker when he pulls them off.)
He's got on his double-knit leisure suit
in a pond-scum green, with a tight white belt
that matches his shoes but suffers with cracks
at the golden buckle. His shirt is brown
and green, like a pile of leaves, and it opens
onto the neck at a Brillo pad
of graying hair which tosses a cross and chain
as he walks. The collar is splayed out over
the jacket's lapels yet leaves a lodge pin
taking the sun like a silver spike.
He's swinging a briefcase full of the things
of this world, a leather cornucopia
heavy with promise. Through those dark lenses,
each of the doors along your sunny street
looks slightly ajar, and in your quiet house
the dog of your willpower cowers and growls,
then crawls in under the basement steps,
making the jingle of coin with its tags.

The Goldfish Floats to the Top of His Life

The goldfish floats to the top of his life
and turns over, a shaving from somebody's hobby.
So it is that men die at the whims of great companies,
their neckties pulling them speechless into machines,
their wives finding them slumped in the shower,
their hearts blown open like boiler doors.
In the night, again and again these men float
to the tops of their dreams to drift back
to their desks in the morning. If you ask them,
they all would prefer to have died in their sleep.

They Had Torn Off My Face at the Office

They had torn off my face at the office.
The night that I finally noticed
that it was not growing back, I decided
to slit my wrists. Nothing ran out;
I was empty. Both of my hands fell off
shortly thereafter. Now at my job
they allow me to type with the stumps.
It pleases them to have helped me,
and I gain in speed and confidence.

A Death at the Office

The news goes desk to desk
like a memo: *Initial*
and pass on. Each of us marks
Surprised or *Sorry.*

The management came early
and buried her nameplate
deep in her desk. They have boxed up
the Midol and Lip-Ice,

the snapshots from home,
wherever it was—nephews
and nieces, a strange, blurred cat
with fiery, flashbulb eyes

as if it grieved. But who grieves here?
We have her ballpoints back,
her bud vase. One of us tears
the scribbles from her calendar.

Carrie

"There's never an end to dust
and dusting," my aunt would say
as her rag, like a thunderhead,
scudded across the yellow oak
of her little house. There she lived
seventy years with a ball
of compulsion closed in her fist,
and an elbow that creaked and popped
like a branch in a storm. Now dust
is her hands and dust her heart.
There is never an end to it.

MARILYN KRYSL

Quadriplegic: The Bath

"You'll feel like
new," I said, keeping things
breezy, as though we all know
how getting clean feels
good, no one in their
right mind
would refuse it, because he looked
like he just might file
a dissenting opinion. Which he could

do. Though he couldn't
get up and go—*bye, sugar buns,*
I'm walkin' out on you—which is
what he'd have

liked to do. He leaned
back then, the old stinker, like Caesar
in his chariot, and let me see his
penis, that loose fold
of flag that would not
fly again,
and said, "M'am, you seem to have
the wrong man. I don't require either your services
or your opinions." I could see

how indeed
neither service nor opinion
would be of the slightest
use to him. "O.K., all
right," I said, hand across
forehead, in mock
shock, letting him know the sharpness of the male
was in him still. "O.K.," I said, "I get
the picture." And I turned and was
going, leaving him the privacy
he had once, like a general,

commanded. "Aw
shit," he said, and with a wide sweep
drew me in. "You'll catch hell
if you don't do me. Anyway,
I stink. Come on with your
scrub brush."

So I knelt beside the water
the orderlies had set him in
and began to bathe him.

The Other

When I watched them clip away the bandages
and unwrap the burned man, I envied them,
as he must have, their motion, bending
and snipping, turning and rehooking a tube

as they talked to him. Though he could not speak
and did not move, except when they moved
a part of him, one lifting a leg while another
clipped away gauze, there was a moment's

pause when his right hand opened, palm up,
quivering, he raised his right hand, as though
reaching for something just out of reach.
Now she'll take it in hers, I thought, the one

beside him, because she'd laid
her scissors aside. I watched her
stand and watch his hand fall back.
Though they spoke kindly, they were cheerfully

matter of fact, as though unpacking
supplies, as though soon he would rise, leave them
to the rest of the inventory. Oh they are wise,
I thought, these women, to wash him, to wrap him

but not to become too attached to him,
the other. For he will indeed leave them,
just as they imagine. He will leave them
alone, a changed man, one way or another.

Sunshine Acres Living Center

The first thing you see up ahead is Mr.
Polanski, wedged in the
arched doorway, like he means absolutely
to stay there, he who shouldn't
be here in the first place, put in here
by mistake, courtesy of that grandson
who thinks himself a hotshot, and too busy
raking in the dough to find time for an old
man. If Polanski had anyplace
to go, he'd be out
instantly, if he had any

money. Which he doesn't, but he does have
a sharp eye, and intends to stay in that
doorway, not missing
a thing, and waiting
for trouble. Which of course
will come. And could be
you—you're handy, you look
likely, you have

the authority. And
you're new here, another young
whippersnapper, doesn't know
ass from elbow, but has been given
the keys. Well he's

ready, Polanski. *Mr. Polanski, good
morning*—you say it in Polish,
which you learned a little of
when you were little, and your grandmother
taught you a little song about lambs, frisking
in a pen, and you danced a silly little dance
with your grandmother, while the two of you
sang. So you sing it

220

for him, here in the dim, institutional
light of the hallway, light which even you
find insupportable, because even those who just
work here, and can leave when their
shift ends, deserve light to
see by, and because it reminds you
of the light in the hallway
outside the room
where, when your grandmother
died, you were three thousand miles

away. So that you're singing the little song
and remembering the silly little dance
to console yourself, and to pay your grandmother
tribute, and to try to charm Polanski,

which you do: you sing, and Mr. Polanski,
he who had set himself against the doorjamb
to resist you, he who had made of himself
a fist, Mr. Polanski,
contentious, often
combative and always
and finally
inconsolable

hears that you know
the song. And he steps out
from the battlement
of the doorway, and begins to
shuffle

and sing along.

There Is No Such Thing as the Moment of Death

I work nights, and he was awake.
When he saw me, he said, "I'm not going to
make it." Well when they say that
they know. People can tell. You don't

argue with an expert. I wet the cloth
and bathed his face, but it didn't do him
good. So I took his hands in my two
and we held on. No one

was alone in that motion. The way water
is a part of itself, we were the going
until his hands went slack in mine.
Still I held on, some final acknowledgment

beginning its climb out of the body,
his skin resilient still, that shine
across a taut thing—then I saw it sag
and go flat. His body had a clearness

about it then, the clean weightlessness
of a crucible completely empty,
in which you hear the air ticking
against the glaze. Then I heard another

sound, like when you're a kid, holding
a shell to your ear, hearing
the ocean. I held on, and then I understood:
it was the sound of my own blood.

Midwife

Though I seem to wait
    I'm moving at the speed of light

Though I seem to stand by
    I'm running easily over the windswept grasslands
    to where the river divides the plains from the mountains

Though I seem to stand by
    I'm gathering the sweet and the bitter herbs
    in shade and in sunlight
    I'm digging out the bones of the lost animals
    embedded in the lakes of tar

Though I seem idle
    I'm releasing the father's fear into the wind,
    watching the wind disperse it

Though I seem idle
    I'm sending the mother the energy of the waves of the deep
    and of the shallow waters

Though I seem idle
    I'm traveling by night and by day, over earth and over sea
    to meet the new being

When I time the contractions
    I'm counting the sheeves of grain gathered in the mother's
    harvest

When I measure the opening
    I'm calculating the number of followers in the mother's
    fields

And when I touch the father's shoulder
> I'm singing the many names of the ancestors who overcame
> fear

When I seem to pause
> I send light to the father, to the mother, to the older
> sister

When I seem to pause
> I send light to those who will wash and wrap the new being

When I listen to the heartbeat of the new being coming
> I hear the thud of the rapids upriver

When I listen to the heartbeat of the mother
> I hear the tumbling of water down a great falls

When I lean forward, hands cupped for the head
> I'm dividing the wind in the four directions

When I lean forward, hands cupped for the head
> I'm gathering together the rain and the desert heat

And when at last I hold the head in my hands
> I've hoisted the sun to the pinnacle of the heavens

When I hold the new being in my hands
> I've brought the mother, father, and child to the center
> of the eleven sacred circles

And when I lay the new being on the mother's breast
> I'm sending the flocks of goats out to graze on the hillside
> and in the valleys

I'm setting the fish loose at the headwaters of the rivers
I'm letting the birds go upward and out into the great
migrations

When I clamp the cord in two places
I'm saying the child's two names,
one from the mother, one from the father

When I give the father the tool to cut the cord
I'm binding three people together
until the death of the last of the three

When I take the print of the new being's foot
I'm writing in the ancient alphabet the word just uttered

When I wait for the placenta
I'm spreading bleached linen on all the mattresses of
darkness

And when it comes, when I examine the placenta
I'm sorting the particles and waves in the spectrum of light

And when my work is finished and I go from the place of birth
I walk out across the fields of the planets
into the spaces between the furthest stars

BRAD LEITHAUSER

EXCERPT FROM

Two Summer Jobs

II. *Law Clerk, 1979*

My fingers having checked and re-checked my tie,
I'm at ease—or nearly so. We're lunching high
over Manhattan, a hundred floors above
streets new to me still. He asks whether I

find the work "exciting." Behind him a buffet
tastefully boasting shrimp, squid salad, paté,
beef, chicken, cheeses, and some good marinated
mushrooms, calls me to come boyishly away

and fill my plate a second time. And I'd love
another beer. I think he thinks that one's enough.
"Exciting? Very"—which is not untrue.
"Best of all"—I'm speaking off the (starchy) cuff—

"I liked the document search in Tennessee."
Indeed, I did. How strange, how fine to be
a someone someone flies a thousand miles
to analyze ancient business files! Now he—

but who is he? A *partner,* first of all,
by which is meant no confederate or pal
of mine, but a star in the firm's firmament.
He's kind, though, funny, and lunch is going well

enough—the conversation light, the view vast
beyond my farthest hopes. The kid's arrived at last:
not just New York, but New York at the top.
Just think of all the noontime views that passed

into the void because I wasn't here! Think
of the elevated wines I never drank

in this very room! The tortes I failed to eat!
—Lunch here is money in the memory bank.

Why, then, wishing I were somewhere else? Why
does my glance drift sidelongingly, my mind stray
from his fatherly banter? When will I shake
this shakiness? It's worse at night. I sometimes stay

late at the office. The place starts thinning out
by six; cleaning women, outfitted to fight
their bosses' daily disarray, marshal vacuums,
trashbins, brooms. Their leaving leaves me free to write,

or to try, as the city underfoot
starts breathing visibly, bubbles of light,
hundreds and hundreds, a champagne glitter
promising love and—more—a distant, delicate

loveliness. *Here* is inspiration. Yet the clock
clicks; my mind does not. Could this be "writer's block,"
nothing but that ailment which, like tennis elbow,
raises its victim's status? Yet it's no joke,

this scooped-out feeling, a sense that language
will never span the gap within. The Brooklyn Bridge,
trafficking in cars and literary ghosts,
shimmers mockingly below. I can't budge

the block; thwarted, I inch instead toward parody,
Keats' "On the Grasshopper and Cricket" to be
wittily urbanized as "The Snowplow
and the Lawnmower"; I'll set "The poetry

of earth is never dead" upon its head.
And yet, though I have the title, and the thread

of a joke as a starter's cord, "Snowplow" will not
start: some mechanical failure under the hood.

In a later, hopeless project Shakespeare
writes in a fancy bar—"To beer or not to beer"
and "The Singapore Slings and Sombreros
cost an outrageous fortune." I'm going nowhere . . .

Most nights, the air's sticky. Too hot to jog,
I take myself out for a walk, like a dog,
once round the block. Inside, endlessly, my
electric fan rustles like a paper bag;

and armed with a borrowed book called *Parodies,*
I rifle my old English 10 anthologies
in search of targets. It seemed this would be simple
but it's not. And I'm hot. And the nights pass

slowly. Then: a new month: still stuck, parodies lost,
when, wolfing lamb at lunch, I find I've crossed
Cinderella's fable (a cleaning woman swept
like me into moneyed worlds) with— Robert Frost.

"Whose shoe this is I need to know.
Throughout the countryside I'll go
In search of one whose gaze is clear,
Whose royal skin is white as snow."

Now *this* is simple, stanzas dropping into place,
and while I couldn't say precisely what it is
I'd like to say, just writing quickly is enough.
And the last stanza is, I think, quite nice:

"And if she's lost, I'll settle cheap—
A helpmate from the common heap,

Some kitchenmaid or chimneysweep,
Some kitchenmaid or chimneysweep."

What now?—next? Will the impasse pass? After work,
I'm roundabouting home through Central Park
when a voice cuts short all questions. *"Bradford."*
It sounds like someone I hope it isn't. " . . . Mark."

He's wearing jeans and a work-shirt with a rip
in the neck, whereas I'm caught in the trap-
pings of a Wall Street lawyer. As we lob our
pleasantries across the Sartorial Gap

he studies me. Mark's a poet too, if you take
the thought for the deed—but who am I to talk?
At Harvard, hardly friends, we were nonetheless
drawn together by a fiercely sophomoric

contest: my-potential's-bigger-than-yours.
He's just in for the day, he quickly offers,
as if this were a kind of feat. City living
taints the artist's soul—he's suggesting of course—

which is his old, still tiresome refrain. So why
do I yet feel some need to justify
myself to him, who, he tells me, moved to a farm,
makes pots (a bad sign) and (I'm sure) lives high

on Daddy's bucks. His dad makes pots and pots
of money in securities—but let's
not hear me griping at the rich while wearing
one of my two two-hundred-dollar suits.

Mark draws from a knapsack the books he's bought—
Pound, Lawrence, Durrell (I thought he was out),

Smart and Clare (safer choices, both being mad)
and a surprising, handsome *Rubaiyat.*

Mark asks about my job. He has me twice
repeat my salary, each time bulging his eyes
in sham barefaced amazement. Later, alone
and gleefully free to wage my wars in peace,

I derail a quatrain (striking at that band
of Harvard potters who'd "live off the land"
a summer or two before going on
for M.B.A.'s, just as the parents planned):

"A Book of Verses underneath the Bough,
A Jug of Wine, a Loaf of Bread, and Thou-
sands in the Bank; fleeting though Riches be,
And powerless, They comfort anyhow."

Yes . . . And all at once, summer's nearly through.
I return *Parodies,* a week overdue.
And I'm asked to join the firm, beginning next year,
with four months to decide . . . Oftener now

I linger at work, to watch how the setting sun
at once sharpens and softens the skyline;
sometimes—the better for being rare—the dusk-light's
perfect and, while occupied toy boats twine

the Hudson with long, unraveling wakes,
the sun buffs hundreds of windows, reglazes bricks,
ruddies a plane's belly like a robin's,
and seems to free us from billable time, from stocks

and bonds (both words a pun, ironically,
on hand-fetters), leases, estate taxes, proxy

fights, adverse parties, complainants, claimants,
motions to suppress, to enjoin, to quash, oxy-

moronic lengthy briefs, and the whole courtly game
of claim and counterclaim; seems to say we come
through drudgery to glory . . . Look—down there! Wall
Street's turned to gold at last! And there are some

silver nights of emptied offices, raindrops
washing out the glue on those envelopes
in which memories are sealed and the entire
cleared distances offered up, all the old hopes

intact, as if nothing's been mislaid. This obscure
sense that one's past is safely banked somewhere
finds confirmation each time the recumbent
city, touched by darkness, begins to stir

and with a sufferance that's nearly heartbreaking
undergoes a pane by pane awakening
until just as fresh, as sparklingly replete
as last night, or any night before: *not a thing*

is lost. The frail headlights drift, as white as snow
it's fair to say. I'll leave here soon, for good. I know
"for good" is for the better, in some ways, and know
I'll be ready to leave. Or nearly so.

Buying and Selling

All the way across the Bay Bridge I sang
to the cool winds buffeting my Ford,
for I was on my way to a life of buying
untouched drive shafts, universal joints,
perfect bearings so steeped in Cosmoline
they could endure a century and still retain
their purity of functional design, they
could outlast everything until like us
their usefulness became legend and they
were transformed into sculpture. At Benicia
or the Oakland Naval Yard or Alameda
I left the brilliant Western sun behind
to enter the wilderness of warehouses
with one sullen enlisted man as guide.
There under the blinking artificial light
I was allowed to unwrap a single sample,
to hack or saw my way with delicacy
through layer after layer of cardboard,
metallic paper, cloth webbing, wax
as hard as wood until the dulled steel
was revealed beneath. I read, if I could,
the maker's name, letters, numbers,
all of which translated into functions
and values known only to the old moguls
of the great international junk companies
of Chicago, Philadelphia, Brooklyn,
whose young emissary I was. I, who at
twenty had wept publicly in the Dexter-
Davison branch of the public library
over the death of Keats in the Colvin
biography and had prayed like him
to be among the immortals, now lived
at thirty by a code of figures so arcane
they passed from one side of the brain
to the other only in darkness. I, who
at twenty-six had abandoned several careers

in salesmanship—copper kitchenware,
Fuller brushes, American encyclopedias—
from door to unanswered door in the down
and out neighborhoods of Detroit, turning
in my sample cases like a general handing
over his side arms and swagger stick, I
now relayed the new gospels across mountains
and the Great Plains states to my waiting masters.
The news came back: Bid! And we did
and did so in secret. The bids were
awarded, so trucks were dispatched,
Mohawks, Tam O'Shanters, Iroquois.
In new Wellingtons, I stood to one side
while the fork lifts did their work,
entering only at the final moment to pay
both loaders and drivers their pittances
not to steal, to buy at last what could
not be bought. The day was closing down.
Even in California the afternoon skies
must turn from blue to a darker blue
and finally take the color of coal, and stars
—the same or similar ones—hidden so long
above the Chicago River or the IRT
to Brooklyn, emerge stubbornly not in ones
but in pairs, for there is safety in numbers.
Silent, alone, I would stand in the truck's
gray wake feeling something had passed,
was over, complete. The great metal doors
of the loading dock crashed down, and in
the sudden aftermath I inhaled a sadness
stronger than my Lucky Strike, stronger
than the sadness of these hills and valleys
with their secret ponds and streams unknown
even to children, or the sadness of children
themselves, who having been abandoned believe
their parents will return before dark.

233

JULIA LISELLA

Jean and Jules Work at the Queen of Peace Nursing Home

They never had more in common
in all their forty years.
Now they both take care of people
just a little older than themselves,
fry their eggs, wash their dishes.
My mother's wide peasant feet
tramp up and down that huge industrial kitchen
run by nuns. She is amazed
by her own power, the enormity
of the breakfasts she produces—
125 eggs cracked and fried
and stacks of pancakes towering over her.
She has to use a stool to reach
the shiny aluminum stove with its beaming burners.
My father's engineer's hands
slosh it up in the dishroom
once or twice a week where he
craftily slides plates
from soapy water to dryer
patiently explaining to his dishroom partner, Sonny,
there is a method.
On Christmas eve
they take us on a tour of the kitchen,
and introduce us to the nuns
who are stunned Jean and Jules
have such grown up children.
And then they introduce us to the old people
who fall asleep standing up
or drool staring at us.
It's a strange parade up and down
the antiseptic halls,
my mother leading, the brisk short walk
of a short woman determined not to finish last,
my father bringing up the rear,
the stern assertion
of a man who has triumphed.

Like My Father Waking Early

Even for an undertaker, it was odd.
My father always listened through the dark,
half-dreaming hours to a radio
that only played police and fire tunes.
Mornings, he was all the news of break-ins, hold-ups,
now and then a house gone up in flames
or a class of disorder he'd call, frowning,
a *Domestic.* They were dying in our sleep.
My father would sit with his coffee and disasters,
smoking his Luckies, reading the obits.
"I've buried boys who played with matches
or swam alone or chased balls into streets
or ate the candy that a stranger gave them . . . "
or so he told us as a form of caution.
When I grew older, the boys he buried toyed
with guns or drugs or drink or drove too fast
or ran with the wrong crowd headlong into peril.
One poor client hung himself from a basement rafter—
heartsick, as my father told it, for a girl.
By sixteen, I assisted with the bodies,
preparing them for burial in ways
that kept my dread of what had happened to them busy
with arteries and veins and chemistries—
a safe and scientific cousin, once removed
from the horror of movements they never made.
Nowadays I bury children on my own.
Last week two six-year-olds went through the ice
and bobbed up downstream where the river bends
through gravel and shallows too fast to freeze.
We have crib deaths and cancers, suicides,
deaths in fires, deaths in cars run into trees,
and now I understand my father better.
I've seen the size of graves the sexton digs
to bury futures in, to bury children.
Upstairs, my children thrive inside their sleep.

Downstairs, I'm tuning in the radio.
I do this like my father, waking early,
I have my coffee, cigarettes, and worry.

FRANCES McCUE

The Stenographer's Breakfast

I

Legs pinched together, I play the machine
sidesaddle, fingers bobbing from the keys like I'm pulling
laundry from a trough. History dictates
such wrong-headed order which I *digest,*
resuscitate as *skill, employ*—a wry design
to sit off-center and transcribe
roomfuls of men, their ties loosened,
interrogating the next of kin.

Aside: *To take dictation* means I watch each speak,
turn my face, read lips and leap—*space*—

from one to the other.
Today there are three of them.
Across the table, a widow props her body up,
answering as she can.
When they called me here
to conference table, stiff-backed chair,
I dedicated my serving them as a prayer
for this woman. I prepared

to be the voyeur, the silent ear,
the widow's distillery of truth and relay.
The government of such a room—
Never stop the proceedings. Speak when spoken to.—
prevents an active defense. What this group of men
delivers is some quest for accuracy,
but I know this technique
depends on the distance between man and paper,

chair and door, woman and her role.
All this talk might well have been
over a telegraph, the way the tap-tap clicks
and bounces back. The lawyers only call the widow in

so they may watch her eyes and face
to find, by chance, if she wished her husband dead.
In a skirt, ascot-necked and jacket
tight, I blend right into them, take my place and offer

Shorthand: a lack, understaffed, decoding and
recoding, carrying language to its core.

And more—the world of facts brought to bear
on whatever questions they ask of her.
Your husband, did he provide for you?
The day he died, what was it that he wore?
I'll revive it later, fill the gaps.
Umm hmm. Cough. Cough. included as the manual says.
Such faith I have in sounds not yet
formed as words, shy riddles and intrusions

into code. *Interruptions are difficult*
but essential to include in any transcript.

II

Clerk smart, each step parts my raincoat
as if I'm crossing through brambles
or over tracks. This is the walk from the office
when the keypunch and earphones
shinny down my bones, and patter skin.
Not long, and I can't distinguish between my own
footfall and the street, my eye from market
or kiosk—I can't help transcribing

everything. *The curb stiffens like a brow.*
Cars unscrew the pavement. Time releases
the tower's clock from its confines.
A back alley considers revealing some trauma,

my reason for clipping forward. And the walls,
what do they reflect, as wainscot and gargoyle
lift to frame my stroll?
Even these coordinates weaken to arcs,

tease my decoding mind—
flit of paper, twirl of can.
Today, taking dictation from the men,
word by word, I took the widow's life,
pushed its tiny pulse through the chords.
After the flush of pity, I could only be
stoic. And tomorrow, as I translate
those symbols, the marks like stray hairs

on the tickertape—they will spell out phrases:
I don't know. He just stopped breathing.
There's nothing else to say.
He turned blue.
And the pinched sobs, to chart as stage directions,
what the manual dictates as *the witness cries,*
or in some other case, *the witness gestures,*
the witness faints.

You know the joke: The Stenographer's Breakfast
is a cup of coffee and a Winston. On the bare stage

with table and placemat, the secretary
empties her life before she goes into work.
When I reach the stairs
and my rooms, even the absent-minded move,
a nod to the dog, flip of the light switch
is some calculated truth. I document the area,
and think how heaven must be some version
of a waiting room—the widow's husband

lingering on a cloud-swollen couch.
Here in my walk-up,
I can look out to a sky
blown into dome by breath
while somewhere overhead
Galileo milks the stars
one at a time.
Like my keys, his notes

test the pure relay of truth,
but the truth is quick and small
however bright. And in this time
when each place is earmarked
by hordes, purity frustrates me
as heaven does. How can I help
loving the chronological
seductions of file and box?
Imagine the alternative chaos.

My Corporate Life

10:30: Morning Break

"So Steve just wants to get ahead. Who don't?"
That's how Sam needled Jennifer that day.
It was Wednesday, the hump of every week.
Her luckless eyes remote, her manner gruff,
Poor Jenny spread her bagel with cream cheese
And sat up straight in a backless bucket chair
(the plastic back punched out). She wished for silence
But Sam was on a roll, the know-it-all.

"He wants to run a project, be a boss,
Do lunch with all the top dogs from New York,"
He says as Jenny lights a cigarette.
Sam sticks two fingers out and says "Me, too."
She pushes the pack across the particle board.

"I thought you quit," she says.
                                        Sam grimaces
And wreathes his face in conspiratorial smoke.
"You know, we oughtta trash this joint," he murmurs.

"That's swell," Jen says, and pushes back to go.

"Come on, sit down! Let's take another five.
No, wait! Is that a brown smudge on your nose?"

11:45: The Copy Center

"Not everybody runs a xerox well,"
Says Sam. He strokes his polyester sleeve
As Mimi tries to find an auditron.
"I'll look," he says, and drops down on his knees
To peek once up her dress. He talks too fast.
"This copier is tough—it's a *machine.*"

241

He hears in Mimi's voice the drone of work
As she replies
"That's right, it's a machine."
Then Zeke walks in. She feels her face turn red
And will not meet his eyes. She rushes off.
Zeke watches her tight ass, her hurried stride,
Then focuses on Sam's butt sticking out.

"Get up, you jerk," he barks.
                              Sam bumps his head
And tries to speak, but nothing clear breaks through.
"Oh, save it, dork," Zeke says. "Fifteen of this."
He bombs the xerox lid with a huge report.

"Tomorrow be ok?" Sam asks.
                              Zeke stares
As if Sam were a reeking garbage can.
"Try thirty minutes, son." Sam hates that sneer
But sags and quasimodos to his task
While Zeke turns crisply on a wingtipped heel
And quick-steps to his post inside the maze.
Anarchic Sam turns servile till quitting time.

                    1:00 P.M.

It's lonely in the Annex. Steve chews gum
While glancing over temporary walls.
In makeshift, shoebox offices the writers
Read clotted passages and scribble notes.
Steve watches as Kate doodles in green ink,
Then steps around her wall and says *Aha!*
She gasps and jumps a little in her chair.
Steve says he's sorry, sits down at her side
And thumbs through papers, messing up her desk.

"Please stop!" she says. "Which stem starts out best?"
And picking up a sheet she quickly reads:
So, *which of these perhaps most likely happens,*
Or *which of these most likely happens next?*

"Beats me," Steve says. "It's awful either way."

"That's great," Kate says. "It's aimed at seventh grade."

They see Jim enter, dragging toward his desk.
He sits down heavily and packs his case
As if he's in a trance, then tidies up
And stands as if deciding where to go.
He stops to say goodbye to Steve and Kate.

"They let me go," he says. "I finished up
My section of the project ahead of schedule."

"That's rotten," Kate declares.
                                        Steve checks his watch.
"That's tough luck, Bucko, but we've got to run."
Kate reprimands him with an acid look,
But Steve just smiles. "The meeting," he reminds her.
Jim knows the score. He nods and goes away
As Kate looks like she might break down and cry.
"A couple of doughnuts will pick you up," Steve says.

2:30: The Meeting

The conference room must flower with their thought
If their evil competition will be crushed—
Or so Director Sain (ironic name!)
Would have them believe. He builds them up at first,
Then defers to his ambitious underling
Who happily announces plans to cut

Their health insurance. Employees squirm a bit,
But take the news like children of defeat.
Steve sits up straight, attempting to impress,

As Kate's expression darkens like a bubble
Filled in sadly with a #2 pencil,
An untouched doughnut on a paper plate
In front of her. Zeke strokes his razor chin
And leers at Mimi, who holds a scream inside.
Sam sweats and fidgets, anxious for a smoke
While Jenny wonders why she needs this job.

The moment pre-arranged, Director Sain
Stands up, approachable as a Christmas ham;
His Friday, in a domineering voice,
Announces that the meeting is adjourned.
As Sain moves toward the door his workers part
Though some, like pets, are ecstatic if he deigns
To pause for a private word.
                                        Outside the compound
The Annex people slowly make their way
Back to their desks where all the products lay.
No glances are exchanged, nobody speaks,
Though all are chewing earnestly on this:
More benefits have just been swept away.
Back at their desks all eyes seek out the clocks;
The day is dying, but never fast enough.

After Five

Safe in his car Steve cranks the tapedeck up,
Fast-forwards to the track he really needs—
Sinatra crooning *My Way*. The tone is right
For gaining speed and getting on the highway.
Steve warms up the challenge, bearing down

As traffic thickens north around the bay.
He whips from lane to lane without concern;
The other drivers get out of his way.

"It's just the same at work," Steve tells himself,
And thinks of how his cohorts put in time
Without a master plan. Too bad for them.

I've traveled each and every . . .
                                        Enough of that.
Sinatra is ejected, and in his place
Another *My Way* screeches, covers him.
Sid Vicious leads, and Steve screams right along:

I killed a cat out in the driveway! . . .

In his garage Steve slowly comes back down,
And when the sweat he drove up in has cooled
He numbs himself with whiskey, sees the kids
(who seem more alien each grinding day),
And greets his wife with a waxy peck on the cheek.
The two exchange inconsequential news,
Then lapse into exhaustion's frosty silence—
Another evening anchored by TV.
Before he sleeps Steve fights the urge to doubt:
How might his life improve if he ever quit?
Quit what? Himself? His job or family?

"Fat chance," he tells himself, "and no regrets."

Politics

The chairman is washing his dirty hands again
and I am trapped here in the handicapped stall
as he palms a thin red liquid from the dispenser,
looking in the mirror at my shackled ankles.

And I am trapped here in the handicapped stall
while he works up a massive lather on his arms,
looking in the mirror at my shackled ankles,
wondering how long I can loiter on the toilet

while he works up a massive lather on his arms
and patiently rinses them in the gagging sink,
wondering how long I can loiter on the toilet.
The chairman brushes his fresh-bleached teeth

and patiently rinses them in the gagging sink.
How long can I sit here and feign this crap?
The chairman brushes his fresh-bleached teeth,
lets me gather enough paper to hang myself.

How long can I sit here and feign this crap?
He admires himself in the stainless fixtures,
lets me gather enough paper to hang myself.
As the chairman is combing his expensive hair

he admires himself in the stainless fixtures,
his comb whispers doom through black teeth.
As the chairman is combing his expensive hair
the fluorescent tubes wave a pale farewell,

his comb whispers doom through black teeth,
the tiles are an emptied graph of my life.
The fluorescent tubes wave a pale farewell:
I must peel myself from this cracked horseshoe.

The tiles are an emptied graph of my life:

I finally have to flush and take a stand,
I must peel myself from this cracked horseshoe.
I finger the whitewashed words and clear my throat.

I finally have to flush and take a stand!
As he palms a thin red liquid from the dispenser,
I finger the whitewashed words and clear my throat.
The chairman is washing his dirty hands again.

Capitalist Poem #5

I was at the 7-11.
I ate a burrito.
I drank a Slurpee.
I was tired.
It was late, after work—washing dishes.
The burrito was good.
I had another.

I did it every day for a week.
I did it every day for a month.

To cook a burrito you tear off the plastic wrapper.
You push button #3 on the microwave.
Burritos are large, small, or medium.
Red or green chili peppers.
Beef or bean or both.
There are 7-11's all across the nation.

On the way out I bought a quart of beer for $1.39.
I was aware of social injustice

in only the vaguest possible way.

DAVID McKAIN

Door to Door for a Tenant's Union

Six days in a row below zero,
we pamphlet through a sea-captain's house
broken to apartments.
In the hall through waterstains,
lead-base paint, and scaling plaster
we could see a sinking ship.
The mocha walls and brown linoleum,
they're colors from the bottom.

We climb stairs to a cell
under the widow's walk
where a woman eighty lives alone.
She can't climb stairs and has no phone
so when we knock, she clasps her hands
and sings it's Christmas.

Inside, listening to how cold it gets
at night, we sip coffee with our coats on:
a pan of water sits frozen by her bed.

She says she came from Ireland
without anybody—no mother, no father,
but like a pretty penny, found a job,
a live-in housekeeper for a doctor.
They kept her twenty years.
She says this, her eyes wide and shining.

Smiling, she says it doesn't matter.
She doesn't want the trouble we call help.

Found Poem #40: (Record out of Range)

```
FIND CHAN
NOFIND CHAN
FDIN CHAN
***SYNTAX ERROR***
CORRECT AND RETRY (Y/N?) N
FIND CHAN
NOFIND CHAN
INDEX STUALPHA
100 RECORDS INDEXED
200 RECORDS INDEXED
300 RECORDS INDEXED
305 RECORDS INDEXED
FIND CHAN

DISPLAY CHAN
0038 CHAN
FIND RECORD 0038
RECORD OUT OF RANGE
FIND RECORD 0038
RECORD OUT OF RANGE
FIND CHAN
NOFIND CHAN
```

STANLEY MARCUS

At the Office

You cannot find yourself in this calm.
    Nothing vibrates, and the blue-
tinted plate glass you occasionally
    stare through when the quartz
seconds relax is really the flat
    side of the building. You speak
casually about casual things,
    and if yesterday's sediment
is still stuck in your teeth, you excuse
    yourself mildly and spit. By ten
the flavor is gone. The raw umber
    morning from which you ascended,
irritable as air, your two feet
    two slippery eels
you've pinched into submission,
    your breath reeking of insolence,
neither blusters nor whispers but hangs
    inaudibly like an English
oil. The clouds lighten and darken
    and you are suspended between
the two points of departure and arrival,
    and you can insist on neither.
You say phrases that are not yours—
    you hear phrases that are not
theirs—not quite a victim but
    a shareholder in a kind
of confinement that, like a scab, hurts
    when it is rubbed. You squirm
in and out of sensations, but each
    week there are things that you must
say. You know yourself by the echoes,
    but here, where the flat meadows
are well-cropped and boxed in
    by hedgerows, valleys
are in bad taste. The lead ends
    of your legs are planted deeply

in the assigned turf under your shoes
    and you live vigorously
and with great effort in that small space.
    Neither neutral nor
committed, you bide time, either
    by work or at noon when consuming
becomes your sole means of expression.
    You are an insult to
yourself because you request that
    which you are unable to bare.
But you are forgiving, for what use
    is a great emotion? There
are times when the seedlings in you can smell
    the sun and you are sprouting
in four directions. And at moments in
    the afternoon, the dark
winter clouds incongruously
    stir you and your walkup
thoughts are like freckles that have never
    quite disappeared. You chuckle—
almost involuntarily—and the minutes
    are not tender or hard but
slide conclusively to an end.
    You have misplaced your
coordinates, but there is no
    reason for you to anguish—
the walls are padded and you are held
    together by your clothes.

Corporate Meeting

Not an oblong, as one would envision,
    nor deep grooves in the oak
where long ago sons of fierce families
    carved names in heraldic
script or whittled the day down
    to dusk, but rectilinear
and smooth like everyday streets
    that repeat and repeat and are numbered
neatly so even the dumb can finger
    their ways down tar and arrive
groomed and smiling on the burst of nine.
    There is no tradition here,
and none asked, for bobbing at
    twin ends of the economy
executives and the "team," as they like
    to address us, see
eye to eye only on
    the waxed surface of the wood,
and down below, among the struts
    and wedges, among the miter
joints and the mortises, the truth shuffles
    like Jim Crow in the back
of a bus. That we eat rare beef
    together and chitchat
in the holes between figures, that
    we accept commonality
to a variable level, seems almost
    to attest to a kind of humanness,
as if the mothers in us were bent
    deep together in an autumn
harvest, or the cock crowing in the mist
    predicted a sort of hope.
Yet there is nothing sacred here—
    not a hammer or word—not a clerk
ascending a tree—but a structure and order
    that are neither theories nor laws

nor syllogisms of a playful inventor
    but compel obedience by
their lack of insistence. It is something we know—
    that behavior replaces ritual—
that the bowels remain silent—that
    the weather in the seats
of our pants is tempered by protocol.
    Outside are the leaves
beckoning and a pink terrace
    is lit up like coral
in the August sun. Here there is nothing
    living but accommodation—
no mystery, no intent, no
    derivations—but the bald,
unfathomable hours that seem
    to glide from coffee to coffee.

Jimmy Allen at the Library of Congress

The folklore researchers, all Ph.D.'s,
dropped by to collect softball behavior,
part of the Lowell Folklife Project.
Dr. Tom began shooting in the hot, low sun
backlighting trees at Parker Field;
Dr. Doug and Dr. Dave taped the chatter:
"C'mon now, be a hitter! Dig in. Take a look.
Make the pitcher work. Good eye. Drive that ball!"

After the win, Dr. Tom set up a team portrait,
then everyone drove to the Civic Club
for a feast of popcorn, pizza, and beer.
Somebody kept yelling a cousin curse;
Dr. Tom made a note of the term.
Bird informed the bar regulars
that the folklore guys were "Congressmen,
right from the Library of Congress!"
Next, Bird and Dr. Dave sang "O, Canada"
while Dr. Tom took another team photo,
sort of a "before and wasted" situation.
That's when we called it a night.

Months later, Dr. Doug gave a lecture with slides
on Capitol Hill for the erudite, including
Smithsonian scholars and National Geographic Society.
He showed a Greek priest, Cambodian dancers,
kids on skateboards, a wine-maker,
and suddenly Jimmy Allen was on the mound
in his crimson Burgess Construction jersey,
as big as he'd want to be on screen,
throwing a strike for American folklife.

SUZANNE MATSON

The Regulars

Like a haunting we could predict them
more or less
and though they were annoying
we were more annoyed when they didn't show
to sit smugly with their "usuals," content
that here, at least,
it was someone's job to know exactly
what they needed.
Linda, whose pigmentless hair and watery eyes
could only come out after dark, her four
Sweet 'n Lows, half-coffee-half-hot-water,
dark bread only, heels if we had them.
Richard's daily pastry with which
he would sweeten unemployment,
and Brian at his writer's table in the corner, his rent
for five hours one large soup, one cherry
strudel, with endless decaf to be poured
whenever he was one-quarter inch down.
This to make sure he never felt a sense of progress
as he scribbled always in the middle of
his novel of twenty years.
They all tipped like the Depression,
as if their daily visits only served
to make them feel more homeless
no matter what their actual roof.
This was years ago.
I could still serve them to perfection,
remembering every stubborn taste like a harried mother,
and though I don't miss them I could make them happy,
knowing their happiness consisted of
not changing, ever.
All except one, the near-regular
whose name we never learned,
the young man who came once or twice a week
with his index cards
on which he had laboriously printed

everything he had done every day
since beginning rehabilitation from the accident.
He asked us what was good, took it
however it came, let it and his coffee cool
as he studied those cards, trying to see something
from the day before that might have happened to him.
A sweet guy and a good tipper.
Not a regular. He, nameless,
and without a pattern to follow,
who would give anything—thirty, forty percent—
to give up the chalky blackboards
on which could only be inscribed
what the single, solitary day had to offer.

Wifery

After the gentle click of the latch behind him
the house readjusts to a new order,
its details trembling on a string of lists:
walk to market, walk to cleaners, start stew.
She is testing a life as readymade for her
as love, how the shape of someone's
shoulders suddenly comes to mean *this much;*
this far and no farther. With utter
certainty she crushes the iced slush underfoot
in a morning as wide-open and delicate as
the mouth of a teacup: she must have
12 small white onions, she must have
bleeding cubes of stewing beef, and cream
of tartar for biscuits. The summer night they met
she said, I can't cook, I don't cook.
Now in winter the blade makes neat work
of her lie, quartering potatoes
glistening in their nudity, filling the simmering
pot to its fragrant hissing lip.

Deli

I

number 46 please

they appear like phantoms
one minute no customers
the next
there are four   eight   fourteen
they stand staring
clutch their pink numbers
as we deliver
  package after package after package
of meat loaf   salami   ham

the plexiglass doors open and shut
                           open and shut
the slicer spits it out

          spits it out
               spits it out
in a space four feet by twenty
with three women whirling
as the scale
sticks out its tongue
with the printed price
     black forest ham $2.94
into a bag
and seal

     number 47 please
     can I help you
     with or without garlic
     will that be all

no conversation
amongst ourselves
not allowed

no conversation
with the customers
no time

and the meat
    the meat
    the meat

    the meat

II

in slower moments I notice
the couples
as they stand before me
the showcase between

some
welcome me with their eyes
their clothes of comfort
show little shyness of colour

I hear what he likes   she likes
           kid likes   dog likes

others
the woman is pressed against the case
and with the same insistence
her thighs push against polyester pants
she orders me
her eye on the scale
as her husband
leans on the cheese cooler
arms folded   ankles crossed
and discovers the ceiling

then there is the couple
where the man looks me in the eye
the woman   stands slightly behind
picks at the stitching in her coat
he jokes
talks about the weather
tells me what he wants
as I fill his order
I feel
her lowered eyes

III

sometimes
when I'm pawing the meat ends
obliging
a taut lipped customer   who is pressed
against the deli case
their apologetic demands
set my jaw tight
indignation colours my cheeks
as I look for the not
too spicy
no rinds
only ham
no head cheese

        oh   and in three separate bags of 123 g

I imagine them
stark naked
hairy armpits
and a body marked
with the resentful red lines
of underwear

I smile
as I pass their package
over the case

                    IV

the doors are locked
the shearing sound of dropped blinds
in the muted light
the atmosphere breathes again

        pull tickets
        clean spoons
        windex case
        cover meats
        clean slicer
        cash out

a relief
to be able to
just   work

aprons are peeled off
hair let down
finally
we can talk

begin to serve

ourselves

Women Whose Lives Are Food, Men Whose Lives Are Money

Mid-morning Monday she is staring
peaceful as the rain in that shallow back yard
she wears flannel bedroom slippers
she is sipping coffee
she is thinking—
                              —gazing at the weedy bumpy yard
at the faces beginning to take shape
in the wavy mud
in the linoleum
where floorboards assert themselves

Women whose lives are food
breaking eggs with care
scraping garbage from the plates
unpacking groceries hand over hand

Wednesday evening: he takes the cans out front
tough plastic with detachable lids
Thursday morning: the garbage truck whining at 7
Friday the shopping mall open till 9
bags of groceries unpacked
hand over certain hand

Men whose lives are money
time-and-a-half Saturdays
the lunchbag folded with care and brought back home
unfolded Monday morning

Women whose lives are food
because they are not punch-carded
because they are not unclocked
sighing glad to be alone
staring into the yard, mid-morning
mid-week
by mid-afternoon everything is forgotten

There are long evenings
panel discussions on abortions, fashions, meaningful work
there are love scenes where people mouth passions
sprightly, handsome, silly, manic
in close-ups revealed ageless
the women whose lives are food
the men whose lives are money
fidget as these strangers embrace and weep and mis-
     understand and forgive and die and weep and embrace
and the viewers stare and fidget and sigh and
begin yawning around 10:30
never make it past midnight, even on Saturdays,
watching their brazen selves perform

Where are the promised revelations?
Why have they been shown so many times?
Long-limbed children a thousand miles to the west
hitch-hiking in spring, burnt bronze in summer
thumbs nagging
eyes pleading
Give us a ride, huh? Give us a ride?

and when they return nothing is changed
the linoleum looks older
the Hawaiian Chicken is new
the girls wash their hair more often
the boys skip over the puddles
in the GM parking lot
no one eyes them with envy

their mothers stoop
the oven doors settle with a thump
the dishes are rinsed and stacked and

by mid-morning the house is quiet
it is raining out back

or not raining
the relief of emptiness rains
simple, terrible, routine
at peace

ED OCHESTER

Working at the Wholesale
Curtain Showroom

"Can you type?" Jake said.
"Maybe ten words a minute."
"That's OK," Jake said, "we just get
a couple letters now and then,
what we need is a smart kid to be nice
to customers, you don't have to know nothin
about curtains, just be nice when people
come through the door, talk nice to the buyers
you don't have to know nothin about curtains,
just show them the way to the samples,
we got all the stuff, the styles, the prices,
printed on the cards. What we need is a nice
educated kid, like you, you'll do fine."

And I did, and this is in praise of Jake,
may he have prospered, who payed me for nothing,
and who knew the great secret of living:
"be nice," and who once sent me with roses
to the apartment of a female buyer
with the warning "this is a fine lady,
look around and tell me what the place
looks like, you can tell a lot about people
from the look of their place," and I came back
and said, "she's got a nice place, and she's really
pretty, and she's got a full set of the Yale Shakespeare
books in her living room," and Jake said, "oh shit,
I'll never get anywhere with her
if she's an intellectual."

Station

Coming in off the dock after writing,
I approached the house,
and saw your long grandee face
in the light of a lamp with a parchment shade
the color of flame.

An elegant hand on your beard. Your tapered
eyes found me on the lawn. You looked
as the lord looks down from a narrow window
and you are descended from lords. Calmly, with no
hint of shyness you examined me,
the wife who runs out on the dock to write
as soon as one child is in bed,
leaving the other to you.

            Your long
mouth, flexible as an archer's bow,
did not curve. We spent a long moment
in the truth of our situation, the poems
heavy as poached game hanging from my hands.

The Language of the Brag

I have wanted excellence in the knife-throw,
I have wanted to use my exceptionally strong and accurate arms
and my straight posture and quick electric muscles
to achieve something at the center of a crowd,
the blade piercing the bark deep,
the haft slowly and heavily vibrating like the cock.

I have wanted some epic use for my excellent body,
some heroism, some American achievement
beyond the ordinary for my extraordinary self,
magnetic and tensile, I have stood by the sandlot
and watched the boys play.

I have wanted courage, I have thought about fire
and the crossing of waterfalls, I have dragged around
my belly big with cowardice and safety,
my stool black with iron pills,
my huge breasts oozing mucus,
my legs swelling, my hands swelling,
my face swelling and darkening, my hair
falling out, my inner sex
stabbed again and again with terrible pain like a knife.
I have lain down.

I have lain down and sweated and shaken
and passed blood and feces and water and
slowly alone in the center of a circle I have
passed the new person out
and they have lifted the new person free of the act
and wiped the new person free of that
language of blood like praise all over the body.

I have done what you wanted to do, Walt Whitman,
Allen Ginsberg, I have done this thing,
I and the other women this exceptional
act with the exceptional heroic body,

this giving birth, this glistening verb,
and I am putting my proud American boast
right here with the others.

Seventh Birthday
of the First Child

The children were around my feet like dogs,
milling, nipping, wetting, slavering,
feed sieving from their chops like plankton.

I slid on their messes, I found their silky bodies
asleep in corners, paws fallen
north, south, east, west,
little sexes gleaming.

Ankle-deep in their smell, their noise,
their crisis, their noses cold and black
or going soft with fever, I waded, I slogged.

Crowding around my toes like tits,
they taught me to walk carefully,
to hold still to be sucked.
I worked my feet in them like mud
for the pleasure.

And suddenly there is a head at my breastbone
as if one of the litter had climbed
onto the branch of a dwarf tree
which overnight grew to here
bearing you up, daughter, with your dark
newborn eyes. You sit in the boughs,
blossoms breaking like porcelain cups around you.

The Talk

In the dark square wooden room at noon
the mother had a talk with her daughter.
The rudeness could not go on, the meanness
to her little brother, the selfishness.
The 8-year-old sat on the bed
in the corner of the room, her irises dark as
the last drops of something, her firm
face melting, reddening,
silver flashes in her eyes like distant
bodies of water glimpsed through woods.
She took it and took it and broke, crying out
I hate being a person! diving
into the mother
as if
into
a deep pond—and she cannot swim,
the child cannot swim.

Life with Sick Kids

One child coughs once
and is sick for eight weeks, then the other child coughs so
hard he nearly vomits, three weeks, and then
stops and then the first child coughs a first cough,
and then the other delicately and dryly begins to cough,
death taking them up and shaking them
as kids shake boxes at Christmas. So in bed on the
third day of the blood when it would be
almost safe to use nothing,
just a tiny door left open for a resourceful child,
I cannot see or feel or smell you, I keep
thinking I hear the unconceived one
cough a little introductory cough.

That Moment

It is almost too long ago to remember—
when I was a woman without children,
a person, really, like a figure standing in a field,
alone, dark against the pale crop.
The children were there, they were shadowy figures
outside the fence, indistinct as
distant blobs of faces at twilight.
I can't remember, anymore,
the moment I turned to take them, my heel
turning on the earth, grinding the heads of the
stalks of grain under my foot, my
body suddenly swinging around as the
flat figure on a weathervane will
swerve when the wind changes. I can't
remember the journey from the center of the field to the edge
or the cracking of the fence like the breaking down of the
borders of the world, or my stepping out of the
ploughed field altogether and
taking them in my arms as you'd take the
whites and yolks of eggs in your arms running
over you glutinous, streaked, slimy,
glazing you. I cannot remember that
instant when I gave my life to them
the way someone will suddenly give her life over to God
and I stood with them outside the universe
and then like a god I turned and brought them in.

ALICIA SUSKIN OSTRIKER

Taking the Shuttle with Franz

A search for metaphors to describe the thick
Pig faces and large torsos of businessmen.
I am encountering a fiendish wall
Of these on the Newark-Boston 9:35 shuttle flight.
My friend Franz Kafka has his nose in a book,
As ever, preparing his lecture notes, while I
Weave among the strangers, spindling and unspindling
My boarding pass, and am aghast with admiration for the cut
Of their suits, the fineness of their shirt
Fabrics, and the deep gloss of their shoe leather.

But what amazes me most is the vast expanse
Of clothing required fully to cover them,
So that one fancies a little mustached tailor
Unrolling hopefully bolt after bolt of excellent
Woolen stuff. How lucky they are, after all,
That stores sell jackets, trousers, etcetera,
In these palatial sizes.
What if they had to clothe their nakedness
With garments made for lesser men?
It would have to be in patches, possibly

Even with stretches of raw flesh showing.
As it is, they look good
Enough to ski on. And they talk
In firm but thoughtful voices, about money.
Only about money. It is not my aural delusion.
It is commodities, it is securities.
"Franz," I whisper, "take a look. What do you think?"
Of course I cannot consider them human, any
More than I would consider the marble columns
Of an Attic temple human. Franz agrees,

But sees them more as resembling something Chinese,
Perhaps the Great Wall. Similarly, they,
Although they speak of money,

Glance from their eye pouches at us, low
Of stature, ineffably shabby (we
Have dressed our best), with "Intellectual"
Scripted messily in ballpoint across our foreheads.
Now as they do so, the athletic heart
Throbs within them, under cashmere and cambric:
"Vermin," they think, imagining stamping us out.

Mother in Airport Parking Lot

This motherhood business fades, is almost over.
I begin to reckon its half-life.
I count its tears, its expended tissues,

And I remember everything, I remember
I swallowed the egg whole, the oval
Smooth and delicately trembling, a firm virgin

Sucked into my oral chamber
Surrendered to my mouth, my mouth to it.
I recall how the interior gold burst forth

Under pressure, secret, secret,
A pleasure softer, crazier than orgasm.
Liquid yolk spurted on my chin,

Keats's grape, and I too a trophy,
I too a being in a trance,
The possession of a goddess.

Multiply the egg by a thousand, a billion.
Make the egg a continuous egg through time,
The specific time between the wailing birth cry

And the child's hand wave
Accompanied by thrown kiss at the airport.
Outside those brackets, outside my eggshell, and running

Through the parking lot in these very balmy
October breezes—what? And who am I?
The world is flat and happy,

I am in love with asphalt
So hot you could fry an egg on it,
I am in love with acres of automobiles,

None of them having any messy feelings.
Here comes a big bird low overhead,
A tremendous steel belly hurtles over me,

Is gone, pure sex, and I love it.
I am one small woman in a great space,
Temporarily free and clear.

I am by myself, climbing into my car.

Blues for M. F. Jacobowski

You know it's time, Jacobowski, when
sneezing from chalk dust
or paper cuts are the most note-
worthy parts of your day, and

the girls in your eighth grade
class say you are just like their grandfather,
and your grandfather says its a shame
you never had a real job.

When your wife starts to call it a ten week
vacation and you thought you were laid
off for two and a half months, and

the president of the union
lectures the teachers on
schoolboard time.

It's time, when rookie teachers come to you for advice
and actually listen when you say something, and

when you start to teach the kids of the kids
you taught your first year, and
the kid you coached at third base in little league
teaches science in the room beside yours.

It's time when the Xerox machine breaks down and
the principal pages you over the squawk box
to fix it.

When the schoolboard psychologist tells you
he can't help you with your last period
class because, "You can't rehabilitate what
ain't been 'bilitated,'" and

kids won't fight in your class
because they're afraid you'll get hurt
breaking it up.

When you tell the superintendent what "M. F."
stands for and, "Five hundred black kids
can't be wrong," and

the Viet Nam vet quit
twenty years ago to reenlist
after teaching three periods in your middle school.

It's time if the junkyard dog
in the school library
doesn't even make you sign out
the swimsuit issue of *Sports Illustrated*.

And the teachers who used to play ball and drink
after school on Fridays don't
even drink when you offer to buy, now.

You know it's time, Jacobowski,
when the kids keep getting younger,
quicker, and blonder,
and you get greyer and slower and
older.

EXCERPT FROM

For a Living

What I did for a living
was type on crisp white paper with
an onionskin chemise of carbon
and send it into gray metal
mailboxes in rooms with black flint signs
hung over pastel or wooden doors.
I would duck in to leave a signal:
  "for your signature,"
  "for your information."

What I did for a living was
crank a breadbox of tan metal
with black rubber wheels and an alcohol
fluid wick to ink blue words
from John Donne, from Issac Newton,
  from Nico Tinbergen

What I did for a living was
sit very still in small, slat-windowed
rooms full of smoke and
write down all the words
I could catch slinging from
statement
  to conversation.

What I did for a living
was write rows of blue and
red numbers on pale yellow
paper through green lines
and red columns until all
the multi-carbons rested
at pink order copy and yellow check copy.
Then I tapped slowly into the humming
calculator box, the cash-
registering interests, making

a white curl of paper as
broad as my thumb arch
   over the desk file
   and float down to the floor

What I did for a living
was stare through the written blue
words until my hands at the keyboard
jerked smoothly under
the restless fling of impressions.

What I did for a living
was sit over thick catalogues
while students told me of their
lives and we adjusted their
bright prospects of choice
   to required graduations.

ALICIA PRIEST

Working while Others Sleep

I love with a secret joy to watch
over the sick as they sleep—the
halls tunnelling into darkness, the doctors
banished at last to their beds, the
night opening like a desert before me.

I enter the room, flashlight
dead in my hand, and there the moon dances
on four silent faces.
How beautiful you all are.
Even you Mr. Willoughby, face divided
in day by bitterness, a mind unforgiving
of its body, even you
can't help yourself fall
like an infant angel into the
lap of the mother.
Your face on the pillow, a
flower, can no longer hide the
tenderness you've denied ever having.

And you McPhee, your creased hand crooked
in the corner of your neck,
fingers curled like a fiddlehead around
some forest shadow. I want
to slip my hand in yours and
feel the river of dreams returning.

But Henry, you are my favourite,
in sleep you fall so far that
everytime I hear you take in the night
and then give it back
I leave the room brimming
with the mystery of sleeping life.

Job Description

care for Mr. Crystal:
salute his eye
caress him
lift his head
to take the juice
slide the soap
along his thigh
stroke his shoulder-bone

and follow down
to powder folded loins
sting his tongue
with sweetened lemon
sweep his lips
with vaseline
dress him turn him
roll him in your arms

then
with your finger-tips
draw out his teeth
press shut his eyes
wind his ring off
and send it to the safe
tie a tag
around his toe
and another round
the plastic bag
shove him on a stretcher
and wheel him to the fridge
orderly help push
it's cold down here
hurry: hurry
close the door
kill
the lights

JACK RIDL

Coach Goes down the Hall
Wondering Where All the Men Went

Where are they, for Christ's sake,
Coach wonders as he passes
what used to pass for men
slouched against the row of lockers,
gazing. What do they think about?
Suddenly, he feels as if he wants
to punch one, ram him up against a locker,
jam him inside, slam the door, spin the lock
to a code impossible to crack.
His short hair burns. His years of bending over math
and dribbling with his lame left hand
turn to stone. What do they do? They smoke,
plan ways to escape the very things
he dreamed of. What the hell
went wrong! Dribbling mattered. So did math.
So did the nights spent cramming for the credits
he would need to hold his job,
his place in class and on the bench.
But them?
He shakes his head, and
when he sucks in his gut,
he feels the awful smirk behind him,
feels the urge to throw an elbow,
trip anyone driving for the hoop.

Ref

Heading for the next game, ref
sits behind the wheel, radio
tuned to a Big Band station.
Each job takes him away
at night, sets him on the road,
staring into the high beams
glaring into another winter storm.

"I'm the ref," he tells
the parking attendant. "They
usually reserve a spot." Inside,
he avoids everyone's eyes,
finds his dressing room, runs over
a few new rules
with his partner, and smokes a cigarette,
pulls on the gray pants,
black shoes, black and white
knit shirt, drapes the whistle
around his neck.

He knows his stuff, but also
knows that everything's a call,
some so close his mind
flips a coin before he hits the whistle.

At center court, he tries
to shut out the crowd,
but still feels the whisper
rising up his back, "You blow one,
it could cost us all."
As he tosses the ball
between the centers,
he sees the roof open,
the ball floating up into
the swirl of snowflakes. . . .

Driving home, 30 bucks
in his wallet, he listens
to the news, hears the score
of the game he called, feels
a shiver of relief for the twenty
point spread, tries to shake out
the mistakes, to picture
his wife asleep in the warm bed,
his arms around her, her
taking him, making
the game easy, the outcome
one he's sure of.

Last Ditch

for Billy Mayer

Thirty-one seconds on the clock. Coach is down on one knee, screaming at Tommy to get the ball across mid-court and call time out. We're down by one. Time out. In the huddle, Coach slaps Frank behind the head, "Look at this. Look. Now, you Frank, you get the ball to Jimmy. Frank, you hear me? Ok. Now, get the ball to Jimmy. Then, Frank, you break down the lane like you're gonna get it back. Got it? Ok. Then, Jimmy, you look for Carl who'll be breaking out to the line after Frank goes by. Frank, you're gonna screen Carl's man. Ok? Now, it's just the same as in practice. No different. No different. Just the same. Just the . . . " And all I can hear is this roar, this sense that the roof is opening and a train is tumbling slowly across the sky. I look over at Jeannie. She's shoving her fist toward the scoreboard and yelling, "Come on Blue. Come on Blue." The horn sounds. We all reach in, grab Coach's hand. "OK. OK. OK. OK. OK. OK." Frank tosses it in to Jimmy. 28, 27, 26, 25. Jimmy dribbles, left, back right; his man presses close; Jimmy keeps the ball tight to his right side, keeps his left arm out. He holds his head high, at one angle. 18, 17, 16, 15. He passes to Tommy. Tommy looks inside, fakes a pass, head fakes, tosses back to Jimmy. The train is rolling, the crowd, the clock, Jeannie is shrieking "C'mon, C'mon, C'mon." 12, 10, Jimmy's still dribbling. Coach is back down on his knee, clapping, "OK. OK. OK." Frank cuts down the lane. Carl fakes left, then starts for the line; Jimmy looks to his right, catches Carl open; Carl turns, fires . . . The last dance, "Goodnight sweetheart, well, it's time to go. Goodnight sweetheart, goodnight." And Jeannie cups her hand around my neck.

The Body

When I interviewed for my first job
as an usherette at the Fabulous Forum,
the interviewer asked, referring
to the scanty toga I would wear,
"How would you handle a drunk?"
I answered confidently,
"I know what to do.
My father is an alcoholic."
I was certain experience,
the badge I sometimes wore inviting sympathy,
had taught me something—if only
how and when to push a drunk away—
though it had taught me nothing about the body
I was pushing him away from.

No one had touched me but my father
and that had been long ago.
Yet all through high school
I had dreamed,
even as I touched no one,
even as no one touched me,
of the consequence of being touched,
the pregnancy that never ended.
But now as the interviewer spoke
I didn't mind what he was telling me
as he asked his questions.
He liked my body,
and disarmed by his directness
I began to see myself as he did.
Confident in the safety of my display,
I became a Forum girl—
only slightly sorry
that my shorter, chubbier friend,
who'd also interviewed that day, did not.

I wore my toga
every night through the war years,
through basketball and hockey and roller derby,
through rock concerts,
where I wanted those kids my age to know
given a chance I'd buy fifteen dollar tickets too
joining them in what I imagined
as the happiness of their dissent.
I wanted them to know
I did not want to link arms
with security guards and college football players
to form a barrier between them and the Rolling Stones.

I wore my gold hip-length toga
and calf-high boots with their gold trim
through Johnson declaring he would not run
and through the deaths of King and Kennedy.
I stood on the court during Laker games
with Michael, who was Black,
who went to school part-time,
who had just gotten drafted and did not want to go
because he knew a guy who'd been,
who'd come back broken.
Michael, who looked skeptically at me,
a white girl,
wondering at all I did not know,
when I suggested he flee to Canada.
At school I protested, sat in,
but two years later when Michael came back,
we didn't talk.
I didn't want to know where he had been.
I was on my way out of that place.
I had friends a thousand miles away.
I was leaving, never coming back.

You say you wouldn't know that kid
leaning in her lacquered cap,
her toga and her white boots
against the blue Chevy with a cigarette in her hand.
I'm just starting to remember her.
And when the men did approach,
when they walked the cement steps
down through the loges,
the double letters of the alphabet,
to where we stood, backs to the railing,
we never knew if he needed to know
where his seat was
or if he was going to lean suddenly,
whisper lewdly—but if he did,
I took pride in knowing how to do my job.
I exhibited restraint in the public arena,
where no one had to know what he was saying
where he got to say what he wanted to say.
After all, I was a Forum girl.

HERBERT SCOTT

Boss

I am one of the old line.
No one give me nothing.
I earned what I earned
and stole what I stole.
I know this business

like a beetle knows shit.
You got to live in it.
You got to smell it
like the sweat under your arms.
I smell groceries everywhere I go.

I love groceries,
the women coming in
lonely as hell.
The rich, the ugly,
the beautiful, the sweet,

they all walk through
them doors.
You want a education
you come to the right place.
We all got to eat.

Six-Month Review

You ain't naturally gifted
in the sales and service line.
Hell, you couldn't sell
beans to a fart hound.

You got to work on your strong points.
You can spell, but too bad
you can't write worth shit,
no one can read the signs you hang.

What can you do? Work the checkstands,
stack cans, trim vegetables, sort bottles.
I suspicion you got a head
on your shoulders. Who needs it.

Don't smart ass the customers.
Sack the cans on bottom the eggs on top.
Fill the empty shelves, don't stand
around your thumbs in your belt.

Keep your apron clean and your pockets honest.
You'll make it all right, you'll live to be forty.

The Clerk's Dream

I'm going to save
my money and someday
buy a store in the neighborhood.
Me and my wife will run it,
I'll be my own boss.
And when I take money
out of the till
it will be my money.
And I'll open when
I feel like it,
and close when I feel like it.
I'll wear a flannel shirt
and no tie, and when my kids
get home from school
they'll stock the shelves,
they'll be cute as shit
in their little aprons,
and wait on customers.
I figure I'll make
maybe twenty grand a year,
and I'll join the Junior Chamber
of Commerce, and maybe
the Lions. I'll let my wife off
one afternoon a week
to play cards with the Jaycee
Janes, and on Christmas
I'll pack a apple box
with bent cans and busted cereal,
and maybe even a turkey,
and take it to the church
to give to them less
fortunate.

Boss in the Back Room

1

I love to work the checkstands Saturdays.
The carts lined up, bulging with goods.
You weigh the produce heavy, ring the prices

high. That's where you make your wages.
Keep the customers talking. They don't know
which way their money went.

2

There's too much money in groceries.
I seen it happen in my life.
The bankers in their high hats,

they own this place.
They don't care nothing about groceries.
It's paper and ink to them.

3

I know the clerks steal.
You got to keep them happy.
Jack the prices a little,

let the customers pay.
They got their own racket,
somewheres. They take you,

you take them. Live and let live,
I always say. It ain't the worst
business in the world.

4

Marriage, that's the travesty of your life.
You spend the rest of your days
picking the fleas out of your ears.

My wife got married so young
she don't remember her maiden name.
And the women you see come in,

day after day, they ain't stupid.
Their old man's sleeping on the couch
or out playing pig's knuckle

with the boys. I'm telling you,
this world is full of lonely women.
It's a great place to be.

Boss's Lament

This ain't no business for old men.
Look around. Show me the men
over fifty. You got to be young
and easy looking. You got to have
the glad hand and the sweet hello,
a smile as pretty as a mother's fart.

Someday I'll eat shit and not spit
it out. I'll want my job too much,
or end across the street washing dishes,
a bottle in my pants. The personality boys
will take my place. No more you don't
need to know nothing about groceries.

BETSY SHOLL

The Hospital State

The smell of piss guides us down the halls,
strong aromatic to keep us scowling.
The doctor doesn't care how gracefully the blind boy
moves when allowed to walk in his preferred direction,
that is, backward to us: Just don't let him.
Make him go head-on, tripping over himself
because truth's not supposed to be pretty anymore.

Nevertheless, the hands of these spastic children
keep trying to effervesce, to lift off, chair and all—
grinning, nodding, drooling children who say *daaa daaa,*
meaning yes, in whatever language they speak
in this bald hospital where the gravity's all wrong.

Sometimes lining them up, tied to their green chairs,
my hands would laugh if I let them, just flap themselves
in huge guffaws, wanting to answer a question, any question,
like what drug would you have to take, what terrible
thoughts would you have to repeat for nine months
to produce a life so completely misconnected
it keeps jerking out of itself.

The doctor congratulates me after watching
an autistic girl yank out a patch of my hair.
From his office, over closed circuit TV
he seems to think we were trading pleasantries
in some dialect of Martian, her grabbing my hair,
my hand flying into her mouth.

In the worker's lounge, two orderlies
are out of their seats, fists jabbing the air
shouting yes YES
because—just seconds left—there's a steal,
a long pass, and a three point shot wins the game.
Bunched up in the doorway behind brooms

three smiling moon faces with almond eyes
try to understand this sudden burst of clarity.

No matter how far I drive from this place
I find I have left as collateral to a strange god
my right shoulder blade where the wing snapped off
at birth, and a certain piece of scalp that crawls
whenever I watch someone who perfectly fits,
as after a slam dunk, the guy comes back down
in slow-motion replay like a great heron folding
back exactly into himself, everything we wanted
to say. Take that.

Graveyard Shift, 22d & Tucson Boulevard

Most nights, I liked the place
fine. No schedule, no calls, no
supervisor upping some unreal
quota of keystrokes.
All I had to do was scrub floors,
stock shelves, make a little
change. No sweat.

Circle K had some
arrangement—for stores
close to the railroad,
extra patrols.

It was slow. Two cops
rousted the wino with the purple
bandanna, shoved him
hurtling across the tracks.

I checked the level
on the unleaded, shivering.
Thawed my fingers around a cup
so black I saw myself, haloed
in a strange neon moon.

I thought of the girls, asleep.
Finally, we had our own place.
No matter what,
they couldn't answer the door unless
they knew the voice.
Wished I could call. I bent

for an armload of Kent and Pall Mall,
heard the front doors scrape. *Wipe your
feet* I hollered. Wasn't a regular. He
wandered over by the back. I bent
again, then straightened halfway,

299

my eye catching
movement by the register.

He was turned away. *Hey*
you can't come back here.
It was the voice
I'd use on children, firm. He turned,
hefted a smooth, face-sized
river stone and chanted

　I'll bash
　your fucking head in.

We stood like that, his face
bloated and shaking. His shirttail
out and ripped. *Take anything*
you want. Up, up, up,
bent elbows, the stone rose
two-handed over his head,
then down
　and down
　　and down

Working Late

A light is on in my father's study.
"Still up?" he says, and we are silent,
looking at the harbor lights,
listening to the surf
and the creak of coconut boughs.

He is working late on cases.
No impassioned speech! He argues from evidence,
actually pacing out and measuring,
while the fans revolving on the ceiling
winnow the true from the false.

Once he passed a brass curtain rod
through a head made out of plaster
and showed the jury the angle of fire—
where the murderer must have stood.
For years, all through my childhood,
if I opened a closet . . . bang!
There would be the dead man's head
with a black hole in the forehead.

All the arguing in the world
will not stay the moon.
She has come all the way from Russia
to gaze for a while in a mango tree
and light the wall of a veranda,
before resuming her interrupted journey
beyond the harbor and the lighthouse
at Port Royal, turning away
from land to the open sea.

Yet, nothing in nature changes, from that day to this,
she is still the mother of us all.
I can see the drifting offshore lights,
black posts where the pelicans brood.

301

And the light that used to shine
at night in my father's study
now shines as late in mine.

EXCERPTS FROM
The Associate

1

I would read until I was sure,
then type a report.
When it came back from J. J.
I'd write the letter of rejection.

"Don't go in for criticism,"
he said. "It gets you in trouble.
Use the standard form: 'We regret
that due to the limitations of our budget
et cetera et cetera.' "

One day he called me in.
From now on I wasn't just a reader
I was to be an associate,
working with authors on their books.
The rise in status, unfortunately,
didn't carry a raise in pay,
due to the limitations
of our budget et cetera.

2

J. J. on the intercom . . .
she was with him now,
would I come right away.

The eyes she turned towards me
were like ice. "I want everything
put back just the way it was,"
she wrote to J. J.
"I haven't read my Joyce for nothing."

"Here's the culprit now," he said.
Turning to me . . . "Peter,
I know that you think as highly
of *Vows* as I do. It has greatness,
wouldn't you say? Sweep and vision?"

I had a vision of my paycheck
fading. I said yes.

           Then he and she
discussed the vanishing of greatness.
This morning's *New York Times*
carried G. B. Shaw's obituary.
"There's no one left," she sighed.

He placed a hand over hers.
"I don't agree. I may be just an optimist,
but when I read the opening pages
of *Vows,* I said to myself, J. J.,
this is it . . . what I've been hoping for."

Later, when she had left,
he spoke to me . . . as a friend.
Did I realize that all the while
I was with them I never once smiled?
It isn't enough to like to read,
you have to like people. Putting a hand
on my shoulder . . . "Stay loose."
A phrase from baseball . . . He liked the Yanks
but still rooted for Cincinnati.

"Smile," he said. I said that I would try.

4

New York wasn't the main office . . .
that was in Indiana.
We went there to present our books
to the salesmen, and pay our respects
to Mr. Sidney, the Old Man.

The town is a convention center.
Shriners, Knights of Pythias,
members of the American Legion,
fill the lobby and stand around
on the sidewalk.

                    There are three now.
One of them is leaning on a stick
that is electrically wired.
A goodlooking woman comes by . . .
he touches her with it and she jumps
out of her skin. Now she is trying
to hit him with her handbag.
"Take it easy, boys," says the policeman.

Their wives come with them.
I rode down in the elevator
with three. Their hair was blue-rinsed
the color of laundry detergent.
One was carrying a roll
of toilet paper. "Here, young feller,"
she said, and held it out to me,
"have a crap game." And all three
went into a fit of laughter.

We gave our book presentations.
Then there was lunch.
After lunch, more presentations,

with the salesmen, whose party this was,
falling asleep.

We came together again
for dinner. Between the courses
one of the salesmen, named Finneran,
walked around and stood behind you
and made a remark that was supposed
to be funny. He did this with everyone,
I noticed, except the Old Man.

Then there were toasts . . . to our President,
Mr. Sidney. To the Vice-President
in Charge of Sales. To someone else
in charge of production.
Whereupon I rose to my feet.

There are things you have said and done
that haunt you for the rest of your life.
I hear myself making a speech,
saying that we should be grateful
to J. J., for being such a fine editor.

I see the eyes of the Old Man
glaring from the head of the table.
Alice, our publicity woman,
staring at me with wide eyes.
J. J. looking down at his plate . . .

I sit down again, knowing
what a fool I've made of myself.
"Who does he think he is?" says the voice
of Finneran, loud and clear.

6

There's a picture . . . like an electric chair.
You're to put your prospective mate
in the chair and pull a switch.
The pointer swings so many degrees
and you do some calculations.

You work out both your futures
from astrological signs.

Finally you ask, are the two of you
compatible?

I'm expecting an old lady
in tennis shoes. Instead
she's a rather attractive redhead,
if you like the girl next door,
with freckles, when she's thirty-five.

As I explain why "we regret,"
the elbow she has placed
on the desk starts to rap,
and I notice that she's trembling
all over, from head to toe.

"I hear," she says, "you were in San Francisco.
What did they tell you about me?"

Finally she leaves. Bernice,
the office manager's assistant,
who shares the same cubicle,
her desk facing mine, and doesn't miss a word,
puts a forefinger to her temple
and rotates it . . . the immemorial sign
that means, "This person is crazy."

7

Walter the office manager
paces the floor continually.
The cubicle I sit in is enclosed
with frosted glass. I look up
and see, gliding above the line
of frosted glass, a pair of eyes,
watery and blue . . . in lenses
that make them look like oysters . . .
fixed on me with suspicion.
That's Walter. Am I working
or dreaming the time away?

One day, in a moment of exuberance,
I got into Walter's office
with a good review of one of our books
in the *Times*.

                  "That's not good," he says.
"Now the author will expect us
to advertise."
                  I return to my cubicle
and stand at the window
looking out. It isn't just writers
who are crazy.

We are on the twenty-third floor.
Two floors beneath there's a ledge
with heads . . . of gods and goddesses,
where they can't possibly be seen.

It isn't just the world of publishing
that's crazy. It's the world.

8

Bettina

It's 900 pages long.
"Cut 300," says J. J.

Then I am to try my hand
at three chapters in the style
of the author, to bridge the gaps.

I make an astonishing discovery.
Since the characters aren't mine
all sorts of ideas occur to me.
I reel off words with the facility
of Dumas or Walter Scott.

I have Bettina's husband lose her
in a dice game. What were the games
they played in the thirteenth century?
That's the kind of thing that would take me
days.... To hell with it! I'll make one up.

Then I have her leave the gambler
for a Scotsman ... a soldier of fortune.
There'll be the siege of a castle ...
crossbows, catapults, boiling oil.

Sex no longer presents an obstacle.
Every few pages
I take the clothes off Bettina.
No sooner does she get them on
than I start taking them off.

"Well done," says J. J. "I knew you had it in you."

9

He sits holding his manuscript
on his lap like a hurt child.
I hear my own voice far away.

Once, at the start of Fall,
I was driving from New England.
The leaves were turning red and orange,
the air was fresh and cool.

I saw a sign for a barn sale.
It was dark inside. After a while
as my eyes grew accustomed
I saw tables heaped with tools . . .
another with cups and saucers.
There were toys and souvenirs . . .
the glass ball that you shake
to make snowflakes swirl and fall.

A staircase led to a second floor
with furniture and, to one side,
bookcases, shelves of books . . .
joke books by Bennett Cerf
cheek by jowl with the Civil War.
A row of bestsellers
in the *Reader's Digest* shortened versions . . .
books that had once been praised
and now were, most of them, forgotten.
Who now reads Bulwer Lytton?
Van Wyck Brooks? Josephine Herbst?

And here's another writer.
What shall I say to him?
That life is far more wonderful
than anything we can write?

That's not what he wants to hear.
"But listen to me. Let me tell you,"
he would say, "about my life."

JEFFREY SKINNER

On a Bad Painting in the Lobby
of IBM International

for Ray Mancini

The sly artist knew what he was doing—
all color and abstraction, no obsessive
rage. I sit with my red leather notebook
on my knee, waiting to enter the maze
of partitions, to sit and calmly answer
charges of substandard service leveled
by a blond manager with a gorgeous tie
and bright future. I will not defend
the sad imbecilities of my employees
but tack the blame on money, how slim
the margin of profit, how you get
what you pay for, etc., and he'll come back
with original agreements, the contract
is quite explicit on this point, etc.,
and we'll shake hands and I'll leave
carrying the implied threat of his smile
and a list of changes in personnel.
This is only the pattern of little whips
I get paid for (same as how many million
others?), and god knows I no longer blame
the pleasant receptionist who must ask
three questions one hundred times
a day, while she wants only to return
to the rating for sexual attraction
in *Redbook;* or the manager, doing his best
to rise, someday, he trembles to think,
to an enclosed office on mahogany row,
his service awards and aged brandy
hushed and elegant in the glass cabinet;
or the ones who believed TV promises
and now sit before terminals, pale green
light like a sigh on their faces;
or the guys trading numbers in the mailroom,
half joking, half praying for the combination

that might land them in the local paper,
one arm around a woman with an uncertain
smile; or even the strong-willed ones
who descend each noon from glassy clouds,
the ones who've learned to say three things
at once without anger and appear kind,
showing their even teeth—for some are
kind, and not one of them unnatural.
My client keeps me waiting. I light a third
cigarette, check my watch. The painting
on the lobby wall is right before me, calm,
easy to look at, so little movement inside
it is impossible to describe. I touch
my forehead and my fingers smear a thin
line of moisture. The receptionist is waving.

Happy Hour with Leary

In the middle of distant conversation
Leary winks and lifts his Chivas
and a tiredness settles into his voice.
For once I am fully there,
listening. He talks about the sea,
his tour with the Merchant Marines;
he remembers the money hidden
in his sock, and the late-watch—
looking at city lights
wavering on the black water.
He explains how his wife
was a good mother, attentive
to the details of comfort,
intelligent and fair, but how
whatever once held the center
dropped away the minute
their son kept silent in his room,
their daughter flew off
to school. And his wife
would not say what she wanted
and he could not guess or, later,
care. He had drifted
into his work—Facilities
Management, a section so forgotten
by the big boys that the house
in Greenwich had to go
and he moved into a decent,
bleak four-room condo in Stamford.
He was not unhappy: *What good's
ambition,* he said, *ambitious for
what?* He had his books,
real ones, and could afford
the theater once a month,
a Day Sailor harbored in the Cove,
the best scotch. Then he paused,
wiped his mouth with his hand,

leaned back in his chair. He ordered
another drink and toasted
my new family, my new book,
continued success! . . . *Ireland,*
he leaned in and whispered,
that's where I breathed
easy. . . . His grandfather lifting a colt
at eighty, sneaking shots in the
shadows of the feed room. . . . He went on
from there in a small voice,
and good, I thought, it's
good to hear, to see a man *speak*
in the lean heart of the business
day. The waitress brought our check
on a black tray with two foil-
wrapped mints. Leary opened one
with small pale hands and chewed
as he continued—
he was back at the sea, trying
to explain precisely how it felt
to approach the port of Oslo in May,
seventeen years old, not even the need
to shave yet every morning. . . .

The Moment when the Workers of the Night
Pass By the Workers of the Day

Down at the salt marsh there is no pleading.
The sun itself begins as a seed in the cordgrass
nest, until its sudden birth spreads light
across the sea with the speed of burning cellophane,

walks inland, stepping window to window,
birdbath to gutter run-off (light has a weightless
step), until even the dark soul of the first shift
turns in its sour sleep and wakens, the panic-

bars creak and a sluggish rope of men shakes
eight hours from their clothes, trading cracks
with the day-shift coming on with the smell of fresh
shirts and Aqua Velva, measuring their thirst and desire.

But it's across town the real money's made
these days, in buildings poured level by level,
thin slabs of Italian marble facing the treated
concrete, fifteen levels of spiral linked parking

below, as if the whole were screwed into the earth.
And the sudden hush of mahogony row, puce carpet
of deepest pile, the carved wooden doors
that once opened a sacred Hindu temple, each

as large as four large men, now block the CEO from non-
essential eyes. His windows are tinted gold, and when
the sun rises to his level it looks itself goldly
in the face, clouds drifting in the mirrored plaque

like fish. It may be I am reading this all wrong.
It may be the hard moment, moment when the workers
of the night pass by the workers of the day that renders
both illegible, and the pleading I see written there

is written in me. Perhaps, like stars and reasons
for murder, such faces are not friendly to explication,
are only what they appear—subterranean,
drained white and bitter as wild onions growing

under a flat stone, sockets for the male prongs
of television, dead-tired caves so full of one thing
after another there is no room for the slightest mystery.
Down at the salt marsh there is no pleading—

on foot through black rush and salt meadow hay
to the near water zone and the lip of the estuary,
looking down—a blue crab, motionless. He has lost
one claw. But human pity is less to him than the sun

now beginning to lean hard on his fierce back
and he sidles purposefully away, hand-like, across
the shallow, as angled light throws shadows of small
rocks in his path, and he knows all the work ahead

but nothing of the hours hurtling from his body
which meet and join the hours hurtling from my body
toward the open sea. Dawn . . . Who are we always waving to?
Who flicks the light, strokes our faces, hurries on?

ELLEN McGRATH SMITH

Thinking about Moses in the Receptionist's L

My boss likes the Christian station.
All day I hear fire and brimstone, and now
the raucous radio preacher
who's always on at ten
is rending the office air with the hate-
filled way he keeps saying "Jew."
If only I were Jewish
I'd go to Human Relations, but I'm
Catholic, and supposed to like this.

I have always been strongest
when there is no need to be.
But don't leave me at this job;
put me near the ear of some great god
not the one belonging to that born-again
guy who solicits big money to run
his inner-city mission for kids
and gets awfully close when he comes
to the office, stands right between
my typewriter and me—an
impossible space.
This L I sit in
is an unfinished rectangle,
far from protective. The other day,
a supervisor from another department
came by, a concerned look on his face.
"Are you wearing a bra today?"
he asked me in his snug little
grandfather sweater.

Five days a week, in the mornings,
I say this is a temporary job,
and that gets me going, brushing
my teeth, taking the incline,
crossing the bridge. I perch
at this desk, a bird whose claws

are on the spacebar. I need to find
an Aaron who will speak for me,
who will say enough is enough,
clearly and with certainty,
because I'm losing my voice, if
in fact I ever had one.

Getaway Cars

1

Who is more hated than a meter maid?
Out there, in their raincoats,
they're just one
in a chain of command, and there I was,
downtown, a clerk in the radio room,
dry, in hose and heels,
picking up the mic
when the Boot Crew
had been called by a meter maid who thought
she had a scofflaw on her hands.

"Boot him, Dan-o," I'd say
when they had more than three
unpaids on the computer.

Sal headed the Boot Crew.
Once he brought a six-foot fully dressed
hoagie into the office, "for the girls"
he called us. Sal spoke his six-digit
sentences tough, his eyes skimmed
the license plates as if they bore names.
The Boot Crew are bona fide cops;
they carry guns.

My dad was a cop.
He said, hold onto that job, girl; you're lucky
I knew somebody.
Dental,
eye care,
pension, Major
Medical, etc.

2

I was arrested for drunk driving.
The turnkey was nice enough; *yeah-yeah*
I know your father,
the sergeant,
let me call him.
We'll get you outta here alright.

I screamed, turned over the box-spring
in the cell, multiplying
my bruises.
I got in a fight with a prostitute
who wanted, in her tiger-print halter,
to sleep.

I insulted the matron,
who also knew my father, called her fat
I believe. And I convinced them
with my hundred-proof raving
that I did not,
under any circumstances, want them
to call my father.

They took me up to I.D.

In the morning, I had to call in sick.
The matron handed me the phone.
I told my boss I was downstairs
in jail.

3

Then she started to act like I owed her,
like A.R.D. isn't really for

first-time offenders. Like I hadn't
paid my fines, joined AA,
started therapy.

She made me write her letters
though I wasn't paid
to be a steno,
then she'd berate me—"These
big words, come on, now
this don't sound like me."
One day she called me a jagoff
cause I asked her to repeat
what she wanted on her pizza.

My desk was in the middle
of the pool. My pension
was sizable. My father
was pleased I was paying
my bills. And on my feet
I was feeling the clamp
and the pull. All day long,
whether Xeroxing
or smoking in the snack bar,
it was there:
the thought of those stuck cars
out in Schenley Quadrangle,
left overnight
after everyone was gone,
the bright orange chomp,
the Denver Boot across one tire,
those cars so seemingly
like all other cars,
immobile now,
their windshields X'd.

I'd see cartoon bubbles
coming out of their grilles,
and everything became
a joke I could live with.
The cars would mutter,
"Who's my driver?";
They would grumble,
"Who owns me?"

City

I was called a spy last week by
a fifty-year-old co-worker
who has raised three whole children.

It doesn't surprise me.
The mayor didn't hire me, the controller
didn't hire me; I hired myself to spy
on the stale paranoia that comes
with twenty years of doing exactly
the same job, administration after
administration.

I spy
on Evelyn vomiting booze
in the ladies' room
at nine A.M., on homeless people
pressing all seven stops
on the elevator just to stay
warm longer; spy
on the looks that say
"you got a job" with accusation,
on my fingers moving faster
on the keys when my mind
moves slower, on women
stealing Xerox
for their churches.

Through espionage,
I learn of the proprietary way
people who get paid more call themselves
"professionals." I learn to plan my sick days
strategically. I try to accrue my one-half
personal day every month.

Every time I get my paycheck,
I hope I don't get caught.

But if I hadn't spied
on the woman who called me a spy,
enough to understand
how she can be so bored and petty,
I might be taking swipes at her
in the coffee room,
which has happened before
and which would put me on probation.

302 Arrest Warrant

The first thing she does is pour cereal for
the three children Youth Services took away
from her. A cigarette, a cigarette, a
cigarette. She neglects to wipe the sleep
from the inlets of her eyes. A smoke at the table.
One near the window. A cigarette, and what time
is television? The floorboards' gaps . . . and she
is so mad at her mother. The dead, funky Frig-
idaire, the leaking pipes still shuddering all over
one flush last night, and her eyelids scorch for
how mad her children's defenders are at her.
The sky is flat drywall, no sun for her to curse
today. She starts her day in a house that is
condemned, and she is no more disoriented than
a spider that's built its web outside a dim
apartment window. Her skin crawls. She'd like
some lotion. Yesterday, police sirens outside
made her hot for a man, or the impact of one.
She'd have only had to whiz, and it would have stopped.
But she got herself some, rubbing up against a chorus
of six people on the bus who were saying she was
trifling, against the blue pole of the mailman rushing off
before she got to the door, against the low rim of
the kitchen sink she ground up hard against the facts,
news traveling fast like grass pollen—she can only
hear the bad reactions—these things and more drove up
hard in her, and she could hear them coming, then
her children, like elves, came in to wipe her thighs,
or so she got herself to dreaming.

Sanity is a drumskin pulled out tight over a life.
Some don't be a drum, and that is how they stay
all right. But the ones that be drums: well, they have
to be drums or else how you gonna have a band at all?
She was the rhythm for a jazz tune one summer
at fifteen. Walking down the street, it seemed like

she was opening up a number, setting the tempo
with her hips, and it wouldn'ta been at all if she'd stayed in
back then. When her people started backing up
was when she was the ritual downbeat, rage stripping
her naked. Maybe the babies throwing off all her
chemicals, maybe just plain a blown fuse, but all of East
Pittsburgh smoked in ruins 'round her savage red heart,
and she tore up . . .

This morning, a form has been signed by a judge.
Mental Health has been notified, the police. There's a
petition for her 302 arrest. The house is unfit.
She refuses to leave. She is a squatter in her mother's
house. Her mother is afraid of her. Her children grow
up through someone else's roof. They tear up. They
tear up, and she has no idea that paperwork
is rustling, that anyone is coming, or she'd be behind
the window's heavy curtain, her eyes and ears listening.
Her scalp is itchy, the humidity. The magistrate's
signature blouses out like a lasso. Get ready for a heavy
jam. She'll be arrested, but she will not know why but
that voices, hands will bash her like bongos again.
She gets mad and she gets happy too fast, knows the set
lasts for seventy-two hours. I am a clerk and I am her
agent, for I typed out the memo that booked her.
The keys did a scat across her straight brow, straight
because they look her in the eye and look for her to go
off, but she is going to try not to. The skin on her face
reverberates in bass. You can really hear it.

Check-up

Grey sheets where are you? Sure this door is unlocked before paralyzed. Once I have it, like it. Where is Dr. Lipman I'm looking for Dr. Lipman? I'm Dr. Lipman, what are you waiting for? My wife's here. If we're disconnected, get undressed and put on a gown. Anita speaking. What's wrong with her? All the records be right back. What's not wrong with her? Savoring it, that's why you don't want to read. Short. Not on you, all of them. If my Mother my older sister would be alive I will tell both of them go to hell. What is your social security number? Thieves and all that. Ask her for an idea. You know I was going sickness, doctor medication and with all that acupuncture they would still be here if all these people are waiting for him. Mr. and Mrs. Growl come back in please. Didn't know looks nice Mommy's car you wouldn't fit in mine. I was home with my Mother, doctor away, small town before Yom Kippur. O.K.? Alright. O.K.? Bye-bye. Used to write letters then when they would come—don't lose my place, did I leave a woman's place over there? answer them a big beautiful light so they made a soup in room 3 starved because they didn't feed them. What'd they say, not ready for her? So they got indigestion. Thank you, you won't be called for a while. My daughter still talking to Dr. Lipman? I'd like to see him don't think I'm her Father. A long time twice a week haven't made them the whole family used to a lot of my friends. Should be out in a minute. Take two but break them in half. Breakfast? No such a thing! Put you on some medication once a day with arthritis and with dinner. Anita pick up the phone. Tell him there's a uh really? That, I thought that? Tell me when you do what you do what are you wait wait wait doing? 96 I have to sit here till he's finished with the old people? The other one was in the back also. Breathe—the answer is no. Don't forget the chart, God and Revelation on the 18th. Make sure how often she takes the most 22 a day. Naomi come sit on the table so I can take your blood. Slowly spring is coming it'll last ten years. O.K. is he finished with you now? I'll give you a 101 shot. Get up, talk about it, take your pant-ies off, yes, all the same thing. Back problems. Well I hope so! You know in the beginning get yourself a book with some steamed vegetables a pinch of curry. Anita, where is that left lumbar—hold and breathe x-ray naturally it's healthier. Excuse one one minute. Hi! Dr. Lipman? Be with you soon. Stuff to return, so can I go? Maybe put somebody in there. Both too tight. What-ever I say tell him somebody you know, an x-ray, isn't it a sin waiting? Dr. Lipman pick up on 2. A good thing you didn't. Be home, call me. Go ahead.

Switched her from penecillin to diarrhea not more than twice a day careful she's going to get constipated with a really take it for just but this alright I do I'd like to see you right there O.K. so I'll see where'd she go? Missing my lunch, Doc. Don't worry, your left reflex is gone. Thanks, but you're depressing my What I'm going to have you do is stop breathing But Let's practice You have Open every back problem known But not ethically right to be come on operated by a 2nd opinion Sesame stick out your tongue say ah!

Today

Today I slept until the sun eased
under my eyelashes. The office phone
rang and rang. No one answered.
Today I wrote songs for dead poets,
danced to Schubert's 5th Symphony,
(which he never had time to finish),
right leg turning andante con moto,
arms sweeping the ceiling as leaves fell,
green and golden, autumn in Paris.
I sat in a bistro and sipped absinthe
while Cesar Vallejo strolled past,
his dignity betrayed by the hole
in his pants, and I waved, today

and the dictaphone did not dictate
and the files remained empty
and the boss's coffee cup remained empty
while the ghosts of my ancestors
occupied my chair and threatened all
who disturbed their slumber

today, when I sat in bed, nibbling
croissants and reading the New Yorker
in San Francisco, and I did not make
my daughter's lunch, I did not pay
the PG&E bill, I did not empty the garbage
on my way out the door to catch the bus to
ride the elevator to sit at my desk on time
because today I took the day off.

And rain drenched the skins of lepers
and they were healed.
Red flags decorated the doorways
of senior centers, and everyone
received their social
security checks on time.

And I walked the streets at 10
in the morning, praised the sun
in its holiness, led a revolution,
painted my toenails purple,
meditated in solitude,
today, on this day, when I took,
with pay,
the day off.

DAVID E. THOMSON

Deadline

No time to think, to revise
when the presses roll. Not in the press
room when the foreman screams
for the final proof

of a story that needs another
edition. Not on the city desk,
when twenty inches have to hold
three stories and only two can be

jumped. Not in the front
office, where the publisher damns his
sales staff to fill sixty percent
with ads and circulation to deliver

delinquent payment notes. Not at home
where the office lingers over dinner
like cigarette smoke in wools.
Not in bed, when the phone still rings

you to sell or cut or add, to connect
with your sources or check out
when the governor will dissolve
the legislative session. No, you may pour

a cup of coffee as you're carried
to the last moment you can file
a report. But to taste the dark or light
roast, to smell the steam, to lean

back and watch the wisp of it
as someone passes by, to be
out of the time machine for you don't
know how long? That's another story.

An Alternate Ending to a Temp Job

Her Co-worker Talks

I'm still trying to put it all together.
From what I hear she was just down on her luck.
She was trying to get an advanced degree
but didn't have
a lot of money or confidence in herself.
She'd been too nervous and too broke to do her work,
so she left school to get a full-time job and finish
at night. After looking for work for a few
weeks and finding nothing, she was getting scared.
I guess a friend told her about this place,
a temp job collating papers at this warehouse
on the west side of Manhattan. It was one of those
old buildings with windows that always shook
when you stepped down too hard, windows so caked
with grime and soot it always seemed dark outside.
Her friend told her sure, it was a shit job,
but if she just took it for a few weeks she'd
get Unemployment and be o.k. . . .
Yeah, I needed money too, needed money bad.
Why else would anyone work there?

Right after we got there we heard about a lot
of crimes in the neighborhood. A lot of drugs,
a lot of pimping on the street. But like I said
we all needed money, and you always tell yourself
you'll be all right.

I didn't know what to think about her.
She was what, 24? Well, she looked a lot younger.
With that hair she cut herself, that baby face,
and God she was tiny! Every day she wore
overalls and carried a knapsack with a thermos
of coffee, lunch and *The Complete Milton* in it.
Can you beat that! . . . She seemed depressed.

Everybody in a place like that's depressed,
but she seemed like she really had something
on her mind. . . . Lunchtime she'd go back
to the loading dock where it was really quiet
and read that Milton. Said she was working
on a paper or something. Was trying
to get some money together (on that salary!)
and go back to school. I'd invite her
to eat lunch with me, or go out for a walk,
get away from the dust. It was early September,
still sunny and warm. You could feel
like a human being just walking down 14th Street,
maybe buying some cheap blouse
you'd probably never wear. But no, she'd
just sit on that unused loading dock,
drinking that dank instant coffee and eating
American Cheese, and doing whatever
she was doing with that book and a lot of notes.

That's where it happened.
Two guys shot her, execution style.
They took her just inside the loading area,
told her to lie down and fired three bullets
into her head. Police say the motive's
robbery, but I don't know about that.
She was so little, and it doesn't look
like she struggled. She probably would've
given them everything she had.
Why'd they have to kill her?

An Academic Fantasy

I still have hope
that one day after,
please, not too many more
years of teaching all day
writing all night
I'll get that job.

And after
seven more years
multiplied by how many
aspirin, how many valium,
how many exhausted arguments,
wavering between crying and
screaming, hugging and
hating my husband—
or how many years alone
my drooping head propped
in my own iced hands—

After all these years
I'll get tenure,
I'll never drink another
cup of coffee. Never eat
dried cheese while running
down the street.
My body will sway
in the freedom of daily
jazz classes. I'll lie
in a chair, feel the sun's
rays warm my eyelids to resting.

I'll have my own money,
my own health insured,
my own title will inscribe
my own office door.

I'll fill my shelves
with dusted books.

That childhood crying unheated
under an old winter coat of
a blanket,
closing my eyes to the muffled
sounds of my mother's cries,
that childhood, those years
expiated.
They'll see it, point to me
dream of me, the American Dream.

And I will tell them no, no.
I will tell them dreams
require sleep.

Working into Night

Reading my writing after writing all day,
my neck, shoulders slacken;
I push my fingers into my temples,
feel the pulse of my blood
while chiseling a paper
for MLA, for San Francisco,
for the state with the fault line
jagging into its earth.

Sometimes as I sit quietly my heart
doubles its pace, the result
I've been told of a defective valve
prolapsing, refusing to seal
as it pumps blood.

I might sit here as blood cakes
around my heart; a displaced, renegade
platelet lodges itself in a vessel.
I might lose control of one arm,
peripheral vision in one eye,
or have a major stroke and lose
everything I know as me.

I've seen pictures of the fault line;
the two plates shifting, trembling,
setting off periodic shocks measured
by seismographic waves, by changes
in the behavior of cats, by the
fluctuations of the moon.

There are labs of people studying
the earthquake; they know its patterns,
its fault line veins, approximate
its force on a scale; they know
everything but when it will strike.

In San Francisco there's a woman
going to the MLA; she'll get on BART,
jot down busy notes as the train
rushes through the tunnel under the bay,
and she jots down busy notes till the shaking
begins below the earth, till water rushes in.

My heart beats to the speed of the words
I read aloud from the paper I present
at San Francisco
while leaning forward in a folding chair
tapping my foot on the solid floor.

A Woman Writing in America

People tell me I'm lucky
my husband makes real money.
I know I am.

How many days
I went out
looking for work.
The summer sun,
an unrelenting spectator,
glared above me
as each block resounded
in those heeled pumps
or the winter froze
blood in my lips.
I could not wrap
a scarf tight enough
against a throat
swallowing hard.

How many days
I hoped to exhaust
the streets for
a little more money.
Most of the time
the streets won.
How many days
I went home
to blank walls,
blank splintered floors,
blank sheets pulled over
the cot, blank paper
at the typewriter.
My eyes closed, my mind
burrowed under my pillow.

There may have been
rich material,
powerful images here.
But they soaked away
in sweaty nightmares.

In my own office
filled with heat or
cooled air, where
I can press my toes
into the carpeting,
writing's easier.
I can pick for words
like pens. Can face
a blank with images
I'm not terrified
to conjure.

But when
we applied to buy
this home, I knew
I'd applied to buy
what my salary, my
history could
never buy.

At the interview
I sat till
the building sponsor
turned to me: "And do
you intend to work? . . .
O, you do work . . .
You write . . .
You teach English . . .
I barely speak that."

JOHN UPDIKE

Back from Vacation

"Back from vacation," the barber announces,
or the postman, or the girl at the drugstore, now tan.
They are amazed to find the workaday world
still in place, their absence having slipped no cogs,
their customers having hardly missed them, and
there being so sparse an audience to tell of the wonders,
the pyramids they have seen, the silken warm seas,
the nighttimes of marimbas, the purchases achieved
in foreign languages, the beggars, the flies,
the hotel luxury, the grandeur of marble cities.
But at Customs the humdrum pressed its claims.
Gray days clicked shut around them; the yoke still fit,
warm as if never shucked. The world is so small,
the evidence says, though their hearts cry, "Not so!"

JUDITH VOLLMER

The Gesture

The first time I dreamed about the Oak Ridge donkeys
making their circle, brains damaged,
making their circle watched by scientists & tourists
down the road from the plant, I tried to count
them away like sheep. But they couldn't jump
or disappear and I was forced to watch the circle
like a lesson, like my father's gesture

when he was flat on his back sleeping after work.
You wouldn't know he was alive unless you watched
the stretch of his fingers twitching
the air above his chest.
"This is the cleanest work I've ever done,"
he'd say, home from the plant
tight as a vault.

A man he knew
tried filtering contaminated water,
burnt the flesh off the bones
of his fingers. "This is absolutely new,"
my dad would say, designing
controls & loops at the kitchen table.

My father had a strong body when he was young.
A mind like a vault.
He was graceful holding the pencil.
He was happy rising up from sleep.

The Nuclear Accident
at SL 1, Idaho Falls, 1961

My father remembers a nurse
talking from her hospital bed,
off-limits in her dome, like a ghost
or captured angel, still full of what
she'd managed to do: climb the ladder,
free the man so hot they had to wait
before burying him, till they scraped
his skin and cleaned his bones.
After three weeks she was still alive
and slowly dying, telling the
ridiculous bad luck of it:

A guy's standing, settling the fuel bundle
into the reactor
and his buddy comes up and gooses him.
The bundle jerks, the lid of the great
vessel slides open and off. The guy
is blasted up
impaled to the ceiling
by a shaft of steam & a metal rod
his white-suited body
stuck up there
and no one,
all of them evacuated,
can get him down till
days later the medical team
enters the containment
in jumpsuits & booties.
My father remembers the nurse
entering the dome, pretty & bright.
It takes brilliance to be a heroine
& something secret & stupid.
She walks across the shining floor.
She places her foot on the first rung
then the next, climbs up.

She must know how stupid this is.
It's only a body up there
and the air is invisible
with what will kill her.
Has anyone given her anything to take along
on this trip? Rabbit foot? Heart on a chain?
Can she see anything in the face looking
down at her? She holds herself
up. She pulls him down.
She walks to the ambulance & lead coffin.
She knows what she is doing.
She knows what she has to do.

It Was My First Nursing Job

ar.d I was stupid in it. I thought a doctor would not be unkind. One wouldn't wait for a laboring woman to dilate to ten cm. He'd brace one hand up his patient's vagina, clamp the other on her pregnant belly, and force the fetus through an eight-centimeter cervix. She tore, of course. Bled. Stellate lacerations extend from the cervix like an asterisk. The staff nurses stormed and hissed, but the head nurse shrugged *He doesn't like to wait around.* No other doctor witnessed what he did. The man was an elder in his church. He chattered and smiled broadly as he worked. He wore the biggest gloves we could stock.

It was my first real job, and I was scared in it. One night a patient of his was admitted bleeding. The charge nurse said *He won't rip her—you take this one.* So I took her. She quickly delivered a dead baby boy. Not long dead—you could tell by the skin, intact—but long enough. When I wrapped him in a blanket, the doctor flipped open the cover, to let the mother view the body, according to custom. The baby lay beside her. He lay stretched out and still. *What a pity* the doctor said. He seized the baby's penis between his own forefinger and thumb. It was the first time I had ever seen a male not circumcised, and I was taken aback by the beauty of it. *Look* said the doctor *a little boy. Just what we wanted.* His hand—huge on the child—held the penis as if he'd just discovered a lovecharm hidden in his grandmother's linen. And then he dropped it.

The mother didn't make a sound. When the doctor left, she said to me in a far flat voice, *I called and told him I was bleeding bad. He told me not to worry.* I don't remember what I said. Just that when I escorted her husband from the lobby, the doctor had already gone home. The new father followed me with a joyful strut. I thought Sweet Jesus Christ. *Did the doctor speak to you? No ma'am* the father said. I said quick-as-I-could-so-I-wouldn't-have-to-think: *The baby didn't make it.* The man doubled over. I told him all wrong. I would do it   all   over again   say   *Please sir. Sit down. I'm so very sorry to tell you—* No. It's been sixteen years. I would say *I am your witness.* No. I have never told the whole truth. Forgive me. It was my first job, and I was lost in it.

Baby Random

tries a nosedive, kamikaze,
when the intern flings open the isolette.

The kid almost hits the floor. I can see the headline:
DOC DUMPS AIDS TOT. Nice save, nurse.

Why thanks. Young physician: "We have to change
his tube." His voice trembles, six weeks

out of school. I tell him: "Keep it to a hand
you'll be OK." Our team resuscitated

this Baby Random, birth weight
one pound, eyelids still fused. Mother's

a junkie with HIV. Never named him.
Where I work we bring back terminal preemies.

No Fetus Can Beat Us. That's our motto. I have
a friend who was thrown into prison. Where do birds

go when they die? Neruda wanted to know. Crows
eat them. Bird heaven? Imagine the racket.

When Random cries, petite fish on shore, nothing
squeaks past the tube down his pipe. His ventilator's

a high-tech bellows that kicks in & out. Not
up to the nurses. Quiet: a pigeon's outside,

color of graham crackers, throat oil on a wet street,
wings spattered white, perched out of the rain.

I have friends who were thrown in prison, Latin
American. Tortured. Exiled. Some people have

courage. Some people have heart. *Corazon.*
After a shift like tonight, I have the usual

bad dreams. Some days I avoid my reflection in store
windows. I just don't want anyone to look at me.

A Twenty-Four-Week Preemie, Change of Shift

We're running out of O$_2$
screaming down the southwest freeway in the rain
the nurse-practitioner and me
rocking around in the back of an ambulance
trying to ventilate a preemie with junk for lungs
when we hit
rush hour

      Get us the hell out of here

You bet the driver said and pulled right onto the median strip
with that maniacal glee they get

I was too scared for the kid and drunk with the speed
the danger—that didn't feel like danger at all
it felt like love—to worry about *my* life
Fuck that

      Get us back to Children's so we can put a chest tube in this kid

And when we got to the unit
the attending physician—Loretta—was there
and the nurses
and the residents
they save us
Loretta plants her stethoscope on the kid's chest
and here comes the tech driving the portable X-ray
like it's a Porsche—*Ah Jesus* he says
the baby's so puny he could fit on your dinner plate

X-ray says the tech
and everybody backs up, way back
except for Loretta
so the tech drapes a lead shield over her chest

X-ray says the tech

348

There's a moment after he cones down the lens
just before he shoots

you hold your breath, you forget
what's waiting
back at your house

Nobody blinks
poised for that sound that radiological
meep

and Loretta with her scrub top on backwards
so you can't peep down to her peanutty boobs
Loretta with her half-Chinese, half-Trinidadian
half-smile
Loretta, all right, ambu-bagging the kid
never misses a beat
calm and sharp as a mama-cat who's kicked the dog's butt
now softjaws her kitten out of the ditch

There's a moment
you can't even hear the bag
puffing
quick quick quick
before the tech shoots
for just that second
I quit being scared
I forget to be scared

God

How can people abandon each other?

Before Penicillin

to the memory of E. S. Waring

The doctor steps into the room.
Light is December dusk. Sleet clouds
bunched up. All the beds are here
in this one-room shack, pushed

up against the wall, and even in this shambling
light, he reads the diagnosis
in her face. Gray-green.
Bone-stiff.

The parents
pull up a straight-back chair for him.
Her brachial pulse runs in a thread
so thin it would fray if you blew on it.

He takes the hand of a child he delivered
thirteen, fourteen years ago.
It's all right, Evie.
Then he folds the army blanket down.

The girl's entire abdomen is abscessed.
Burst appendix, rotting for days and now
spread. She opens her mouth and the
smell—

He listens to her chest, tucks the blanket
back under her chin.
Let me get her to the hospital.
In 1932, there is no such thing as

penicillin.
No Sir, Doctor, the father says. *You take her
over there, she'll die.* They quarrel
and the mother says *Please,* once, then is still.

When the doctor finally steps outside,
he can hear the younger children begin to keen.
He tugs the brim of his hat down low. His wife
will be angry again, at him and the house

and the bank in town which has filed
to foreclose and their four small girls
whiny with colds and the sleet which will needle him
wicked *thwik* on the road and in the ditch

the nine miles home. He can hear
the younger children begin to scream. He washes
his hands on the bristling grass, runs them
under his mare's black mane, and leans on her neck,

on her fragrant, inculpable neck.

TOM WAYMAN

Marketing

for Jacqui and Mike

A book isn't a TV dinner.
Unlike food, nobody has found a way
to preserve books:
you can't freeze them, or dry them,
or add chemicals. So if I keep a title in stock
more than two or three months
they mostly go bad. Look at this one:
Arlene found it this morning
in the fiction section.
It seems fine on the outside,
but open it—see how soft these pages are?
And back here—*ugh*—
rotten, brown, gooey.
What customer is going to want this?

I understand that under the best possible conditions
in a publisher's warehouse
books now have a maximum storage time
of two years. But if I was going to carry
part of a publisher's backlist
how would I know how long
a book had been sitting before I got it?
On our shelves, it could go bad in a day.
Publishers will take returns,
but not if the books are what we call 3-D:
diseased, damaged, or decayed.
Look at the spine of this:
mold. Already.
Excuse me. *Arlene! More here to clear out.*

We have some titles around longer:
anything that steadily sells.
But that's turnover: new copies have to be printed,
shipped, stocked, and then sold by us
at a rate that assures no individual copy will deteriorate.

A single volume of a best-seller
has the same shelf-life
of any slower moving title. If sales slack off,
I've got to get rid of them, too.

The mass market people
are the most considerate: all they ask
is a chance to display their wares.
If a title doesn't sell in twenty days,
they tell us to just tear the covers off,
return the covers for full credit
and pulp or otherwise destroy the rest of the book.
These people are good for the consumer, too.
I hear that without being requested to by the government
they're going to start putting on each book
one of those labels to tell how fresh it is:
Best before such-and-such a date.
And there's talk in the industry
they plan next to list the ingredients of each book
on the cover: *girl meets two men, marries one,*
some explicit language, that sort of thing.
But I don't think they'll ever do that:
people seem to like to be surprised by what's in a book
when they read it. After all,
a book is not a TV dinner.

Students

The freshman class-list printouts
showed birthdates so recent
Wayman was sure the computer was in error.
One young man, however, was curious
about Wayman's mention near the start of term
of his old college newspaper:
"You were an editor *when?* Wow,
that's the year I was born."

The wisdom of the students
hadn't altered, though.
Wayman observed many clung to
The Vaccination Theory of Education
he remembered: once you have had a subject
you are immune
and never have to consider it again.
Other students continued to endorse
The Dipstick Theory of Education:
as with a car engine, where as long as the oil level
is above the add line
there is no need to put in more oil,
so if you receive a pass or higher
why put any more into learning?

At the front of the room, Wayman sweated
to reveal his alternative.
"Adopt The Kung Fu Theory of Education,"
he begged.
"Learning as self-defence. The more you understand
about what's occurring around you
the better prepared you are to deal with difficulties."

The students remained skeptical.
A young woman was a pioneer
of The Easy Listening Theory of Learning:
spending her hours in class

with her tape recorder earphones on,
silently enjoying a pleasanter world.
"Don't worry, I can hear you,"
she reassured Wayman
when after some days he was moved to inquire.

Finally, at term's end
Wayman inscribed after each now-familiar name on the list
the traditional single letter.
And whatever pedagogical approach
he or the students espoused,
Wayman knew this notation would be pored over
with more intensity
than anything else Wayman taught.

Surplus Value: Chalk White

The students wander into class
I wait by the door
and think of the fees they paid in September:
admission charges
to my act today,
to a whole term of performances.
Yet this show is also subsidized
by taxes: deducted from shifts the students worked
last summer, or the past few years,
plus everybody else's time
including the hours I am employed.
All this money
—suitably apportioned of course—
might be my salary.

Except
there's the building to pay for
and heat and light
and keep clean, and someone
to admit, counsel, record,
write letters, purchase supplies,
plan residences, hire and fire,
argue with the Ministry, invite the Mayor
to tour the premises . . .

So,
like the expensive office tower
of steel and glass
filled with men in suits
that rises from the work
of a young man on a sidehill
in the mud, kneeling to pull a choker cable
under a fallen spruce,
these people stand
on the back of my voice
in the seminar room now, on my papers

356

scrawled with my notes for today.
Among these men and women
is one who decided
he should receive twice my wages
for his work
and his secretary should get half
and the person who waxes the floor, half.
This man takes
from their work and mine
to fatten himself,
he seizes from the labour all of us do
—all equally necessary—
more cash for himself.
At the end of each month he hands me
an envelope
and announces: "This is what you're worth."
He says it at the end of each week
to the others employed here.

But this is not what we're worth.
This is not
what we earned.

Wayman among the Administrators

After some years of teaching
Wayman discovered that the gentle moss of administration
formerly coating the tree of knowledge
had transformed itself into a virulent fungus.
Memos from financial vice-presidents and
deputy service managers
began to cover Wayman's desk
like spores. These contained phrases such as
"educational delivery systems"
as if the college was a cartage and storage enterprise
or perhaps a railroad. Also present were terms like
"cost-effectiveness per student-hour"—
a figure apparently obtainable by reading the dials
implanted into the skull of each enrollee during registration.

Meanwhile, a froth of busyness
emanated from the front office
as carpenters and electricians rebuilt adjoining classrooms
into more cubicles for freshly hired personnel
deemed necessary to oversee the dwindling number of courses offered
due to the lack of funds available for public education.

And the newcomers established themselves
by memo. "We're having trouble identifying people
by the two initials they've been using on internal communications,"
one circular read. "Henceforth all memos
must be signed by *three* initials.
Please memo me back indicating
the three initials you will use."

The campus director, a man from the old days,
attempted feverishly to match his superiors' and inferiors' memos
with messages of his own. One Monday Wayman arrived at work
to receive a note from the director duly routed
to all administrative, teaching, and support staff
which read in its entirety: "Good morning."

When managerial functions were reorganized yet again
and the ratio climbed dangerously closer to
an administrator for each faculty member
Wayman concluded maybe these men and women were right.
Perhaps the job here really did depend on
them holding meetings with each other
and writing up the results of such gatherings for circulation.
Never one to stand in the way of progress
Wayman sat down at his typewriter on a spring afternoon
and produced a memo he hoped was equal
to any issued that day.
"I," Wayman wrote,
"quit."

Holding the Line

Eleven days that September
under umbrellas and vinyl raingear
the faculty are out to support
the custodians, library clerks,
secretaries on strike
for a new contract.
We clump together now and then
to exchange rumours about
how the talks are progressing, morale,
and who crossed. The slow four hour shifts
pass in the damp cold.
Occasionally a student

hurries through our line to seek the services
he or she wants to purchase.
On their return, some take the soggy leaflets
which detail our reasons
for being here,
others ignore us,
a few want to argue:
you'll never make back
the money you lose by striking.
"Figure it out," says Barb,
a steward.
"If I work another few years,
the increase we'll get more than pays
for these weeks. And if we don't ask
for more, they sure won't ever
raise our wages."

But these students intend
anger, not debate
and they head off along the street.

Then a Monday after supper
I get a phone call: "It's settled.

Classes as scheduled tomorrow.
Show up at eight ready to teach."
When I drive onto campus next morning
the rain has stopped.
I leave my car and walk back
to stand at the edge of the road
where we lived for days.
No one is here.
The picket signs have vanished; traffic
rushes by.
Nothing remains of our actions
except where, inside,
some people
go on
holding the line.

Paper, Scissors, Stone

An executive's salary for working with paper
beats the wage in a metal shop operating shears
which beats what a gardener earns arranging stone.

But the pay for a surgeon's use of scissors
is larger than that of a heavy equipment driver removing stone
which in turn beats a secretary's cheque for handling paper.

And, a geologist's hours with stone
nets more than a teacher's with paper
and definitely beats someone's time in a garment factory with scissors.

In addition: to manufacture paper,
you need stone to extract metal to fabricate scissors
to cut the product to size.
To make scissors you must have paper to write out the specs
and a whetstone to sharpen the new edges.
Creating gravel, you require the scissor-blades of the crusher
and lots of order forms and invoices at the office.

Thus I believe there is a connection
between things
and not at all like the hierarchy of winners
of a child's game.
When a man starts insisting
he should be paid more than me
because he's more important to the task at hand,
I keep seeing how the whole process collapses
if almost any one of us is missing.
When a woman claims she deserves more money
because she went to school longer,
I remember the taxes I paid to support her education.
Should she benefit twice?
Then there's the guy who demands extra
because he has so much seniority
and understands his work so well

362

he has ceased to care, does as little as possible,
or refuses to master the latest techniques
the new-hires are required to know.
Even if he's helpful and somehow still curious
after his many years—

Without a machine to precisely measure
how much sweat we each provide
or a contraption hooked up to electrodes in the brain
to record the amount we think,
my getting less than him
and more than her
makes no sense to me.
Surely whatever we do at the job
for our eight hours—as long as it contributes—
has to be worth the same.

And if anyone mentions
this is a nice idea but isn't possible,
consider what we have now:
everybody dissatisfied, continually grumbling and disputing.
No, I'm afraid it's the wage system that doesn't function
except it goes on
and will
until we set to work to stop it

with paper, with scissors, and with stone.

CHARLES WEBB

Mr. Kyle the Banker

takes the jack out of his new Mercedes
Benz and starts lugging it with him
everywhere. "I think he's just fond

of his car," says Tess the Teller.
"It's like carrying a picture of your kids."
"Or sleeping with one arm across

your lover's thigh," adds Carol, Tess's
best friend. "Naw—he used it, and forgot
to put it back," Fred, the Loan Officer, says.

"Sometimes my wife'll scream at me
'Where are my glasses?' and they're
sitting on her nose the whole time."

"It's self-defense," Hannah, the Office
Manager, believes. "That thing'd put
some bad hurt on some mugger's head."

"The poor man's lonely," says Maxine
in Customer Service. "He wants
to meet a lady in distress."

"It's sexual," says Ann, who's working
on a Masters in Clinical Psych.
"You know what 'jack' means."

Business gets worse and worse.
One by one, pink slips go out;
employees go home. Federal agents

move in to find Mr. Kyle alone
in his office, jack in hand,
cranking as his ship sinks under him.

C. K. WILLIAMS

Chapter Eleven

As in a thousand novels but I'll never as long as I live get used to this kind of thing,
the guy who works as director of something or other in the business my friend owns and who,
I'm not sure why, we're out, my friend and I, for an after-work drink with, keeps kidding around,
making nice, stroking us, both of us, but of course mostly my friend, saying "Yes, boss, yes, boss,"
which is supposed to be funny but isn't because joke or no joke he's really all over my friend,
nodding, fawning, harking hard, and so intense it all is, with such edges of rage or despair—
is my friend letting him go? is his job as they put it in that world, that hard world, on the line?—
that finally even my friend who must have suspected something like this was going to happen
(why bring me then?), gets edgy, there are lapses, we all shift, then my friend says something,
"I don't feel great," something, "I have a headache," and, without thinking, I'm sure without thinking,
it happens so quickly, the guy reaches, and, with the back of his hand, like a nurse or a mother,
feels my friend's forehead, as though to see if he has a fever, and my friend—what else?—
jerks back, leaving the hand hung in mid-air for a moment, almost saluting, almost farewelling,
until finally the poor man hauls the hand in, reels it back in, and does what with it?
Puts it for a moment lightly on the back of his head, lightly on his collar, the table, his drink?
All right, yes, the back of his head, lightly; lightly, his collar, the table, his drink.
But what does it matter anyway what the poor man does with his poor marooned hand?
Besides, he's fine now, we're all fine, it was all just a blink, the man's folded his hands,
you'd think he was just saying grace or something, and probably nothing happened at all,
you probably just blinked and drifted and imagined it all; if you asked the man how he was,
what would he say, except "What do you mean?" and what would you do but shut up and smile,
this isn't The Death of a Salesman after all, nobody's going to turn into a Gregor Samsa;
if you were him wouldn't the last thing you'd want be for someone like me to me-too you?
My friend signals, the check arrives on its salver and my friend stares down at it hard.
"I'm dead," he says finally: "I'm on such a short leash with the bank, I can't make a dime."

IRENE WILLIS

Easy Hours

From my mother's womb I fell into the State.
—Randall Jarrell

I didn't fall into this job
the way some did.
Actually, I just walked in
off the street, I guess you could say—
up some granite steps and through
a glass door taped against the wind.
The first thing I noticed was the way
that door was taped, some of the windows too.
And a guy walking up on the flat roof
in the rain, fooling around with some wire.
Later I'd watch him from the twelfth floor
window while I waited for somebody to come up
and crack it open, give me a little air.
I've got allergies. Doctor says to watch it
or it might turn into asthma.
But those fumes from the copying machine
and the cigarette smoke from the hall
near the elevator bother me something awful.
I get all congested.
Still, it's better than what my parents had.
Great benefits.
My dad worked an assembly line.
My mom too—a defense plant during the war.
Later she became a union organizer—my little mom.
Hard to believe, you know what I mean?
When the war was over she went to selling clothes
in a big department store. That's why her feet
are so bad today, they wouldn't let her sit down.
No chairs on the sales floor.
Lila in that corner office over there, her mom
cleaned houses, she never got over it.
I don't know who took it worse, Lila or her mom,
because Lila never stops talking about it.
I mean, it's like a punctuation mark: cleaning

Miss Anna's kitchen. "It's better than cleaning
Miss Anna's kitchen," is what she always says.
I clean my own kitchen after work.
Don't get me wrong. This job with the State is
good. Easy hours. You get to sit down all day,
take a vacation once in a while. Hey, look,
in three years I'll be vested.

Wall Street

Getting money, not poems
from these spit-thin streets

Searching out the grains for bread
among these cornices
these pigeon roosts
this stone of money dark Manhattan

The poem never leaves me out of itself

The poem recites me from sidewalks and windows
from cracks of sunlight over a city
foreign to me as Asia

Its voice calls down to me from glazed hand-lettered doors
the half-truths of my ambitions . . .
the years go forward on my hungers
like a narration.

Getting my bread
just that
eating it, fleshing out, decaying

Bread must be the poem that always exists
my body's meaning
moving me through hallways
past marble where spring hides
past rivers locked in wood

The secretive insistent meaning
of the elevators the clocks
the faces of clerks
the cop retired to his bank job
the desk the telephone
the white shirt
the window's question

"Why not get out of here?"
the numbers crawling across the walls
the poem

Getting my bread, the poem
can never deny me
its voice.

Winter Loafing

I leave work early, out of step
with the rhythm of these office buildings
gathering steam until they could burst,
their glass hands clapping against the sky.

I drift downstairs with the snow.
Outside, the trees uphold the rhythm
of space and seasons—
black indications of long rests
in a movement of silence. The lights go on
as secretively as the tuning of a harp.

I guess I'm afraid of my death,
of missing out,
of never being able to taste the fruit of idleness,
and so I stand on corners, stand and look
that the day may not die,
and see the people pour from the office buildings
in a dark bright stream,
and the sun
like an old man's pink face, like a rose among graves.

The Fee

Dear Author:
We are preparing
the definitive, illus-
trated catalogue
of our international
exhibition, "Urns
Around the World"
for publication.
May we, The State
Education Department
of New York, The Uni-
versity of the State
of New York at Albany,
Time/Life Books and their
subsidiaries, the
Smithsonian Institution,
and the licensees
of the foregoing
have permission to use
your poem, "Ode on
a Grecian Urn,"
throughout the world
in all editions of our
catalogue and in any
material based on it
for all printings
of all editions?
The press run of our
catalogue is 150,000 copies
in cloth and 300,000 copies
in paperback. The volume
features 200 full-color plates
and will be printed
on 90 lb. glossy stock.
These editions
will sell for $98.00

and $45.00 respectively.
Due to the fact that
so many authors
will be represented
in the catalogue,
we cannot offer
remuneration. However,
upon publication we will make
copies available to authors
at a ten percent discount
(postage and handling
not included).
Of course we will
make certain that you
receive credit in these
publications for the use
of your material.
If you agree to
the terms of our contract,
please sign below
and return this form
at your earliest convenience.

Work

To have done it thirty years
Without question! Yet I tell myself
I am grateful for all work;
At noon in my air-conditioned office
With a sandwich and a poem,
I try to recollect nature;
But a clerk comes in with papers
To be signed. I tell myself
The disruption does not matter;
It is all work: computer runs,
Contracts, invoices, poems; the same
As breaking shells, hunting woods,
Making pots, or gathering grain.
Jazzmen even refer to sex as work.
Some primitive people believe
That death is work. When my wife asks
What I am doing, I always answer,
I am working, working, working.

Now I know I will spend the rest
Of my life trying for perfect work,
A work as rare as aurora borealis,
So fine it will make all other work
Seem true, that will last as long
As words will last. At home
In my room, I mumble to myself
Over my poems; over supper I talk
To myself; as I carpenter or paint
Or carry the groceries up the steps,
I am speaking words to myself.
"What are you doing?" my children ask.
I am working, working, working.

CONTRIBUTORS

Aɪ (b. 1947) writes, "I worked my way through college doing office work. My mother and grandmother were a maid and a cook respectively. This poem is only loosely based on the Tawana Brawley incident. It was really inspired by a film called *The Big Carnival* by Billy Wilder about a reporter whose career is in decline and who has been exiled to New Mexico from New York. One day he's on the scene when there's a cave-in at a mine where a guy's been digging for artifacts. The reporter decides this is his big chance and decides to take the story as far as he can. After a while it all spirals out of control and ends on a profoundly dark note. I thought it would be interesting to write a poem about a TV reporter who in essence does the same thing. She rides her horse, her story, until it stumbles under her, then she shoots it and moves on without remorse. Very cynical, huh? But real." Ai, who lives in Tempe, Arizona, has published four books: *Cruelty, Killing Floor, Sin,* and *Fate.*

MAGGIE ANDERSON (b. 1948) writes, "My parents were both teachers who left West Virginia as soon as they had education and opportunity. I was born in New York City, but after my mother died, my father moved our family back when I was thirteen to be near to his three sisters. The men in my father's family worked on the Baltimore & Ohio railroad. 'Sonnet for Her Labor' was written for my aunt Nita Anderson Craig, who kept house for her husband and brother and who herself worked intermittently as a dispatcher for the B&O. She was the person in my family most interested in my writing. The poem is a sonnet because she liked best 'poems that look like poems, poems that rhyme.' In this way I have tried to honor her, to thank her." Author of *Years That Answer, Cold Comfort,* and *A Space Filled with Moving,* Anderson teaches at Kent State University.

RANE ARROYO (b. 1954) writes, "I'm a Puerto Rican poet and playwright who has had over thirty-five addresses and as many jobs in my life, currently a teacher in Pittsburgh. As a Gay man and a Hispanic, I'm committed to writing and reading the world with my own strategies. 'Juan Angel' is dedicated to my Uncle Rachel, yet another casualty during the AIDS war; to misquote the Bible: 'The dead you will always have with you.' My Uncle and other Latin men gave me models of strength and dignity." Arroyo's most recent book is *Columbus' Orphan.*

JOHN ASHBERY (b. 1927) has worked as a reference librarian for the Brooklyn Public Library, a copywriter for Oxford University Press and McGraw Hill Book Company, an art critic, and a professor of English. He is the author of several books on art and many poetry collections, including *Self-Portrait in a Convex Mirror,* which won the 1976 Pulitzer Prize, National Book Award, and National Book Critics Circle Award.

JAMES A. AUTRY (b. 1933) has worked as copy chief and as editor of *Better Homes and Gardens,* as editor of the magazine *New Orleans,* and as editorial director of Meredith Special Interest Publications. He is the author of *Nights under a Tin Roof, Life after Mississippi,* and the business book bestseller *For Love & Profit: The Art of Caring Leadership.*

JIMMY SANTIAGO BACA (b. 1952) is a Chicano poet and writer from New Mexico. Born to an impoverished family, he grew up in an orphanage and as a runaway in the barrio, eventually landing in prison, where he first taught himself to read and write. His haunting verse autobiography, *Martin & Meditations on the South Valley,* won the 1988 American Book Award of the Before Columbus Foundation. Baca's most recent project is a feature film from Disney's Hollywood Pictures called *Bound by Honor,* which he co-wrote and produced.

LENORE BALLIRO (b. 1954) has worked as a stitcher, assembler, shipper/receiver, waitress, clerk, and display designer. Currently she is a teacher-trainer and English as a Second Language instructor in adult literacy programs throughout Boston.

WALTER BARGEN (b. 1948) lives and works in Missouri. He notes, "These poems were written in response to my first desk job, which I have never gotten over." His most recent books are *Yet Other Waters* and *Mysteries in the Public Domain.*

JANE BARNES (b. 1943) says a partial list of her jobs includes baby-sitter, shrimp sheller, file clerk, store clerk, credit investigator, slide film processor, krumhorn assembler, technical writer, tour guide, and secretary to symphony orchestras, a German painter, lawyers, architects, and professors. "I've put a lot of work into disassembling the tableau presented in this poem. The speaker is now happily married to an artist with whom she plots out how to do as little as possible in order to do the REAL WORK—writing/making. On our last 'business trip' we had a picnic in the tower of a cemetery overlooking a thousand dead New England artists and made many contacts."

DOROTHY BARRESI (b. 1957) grew up in Akron, Ohio, where she began her work life at age twelve with baby-sitting jobs, moved on to waitressing jobs and a variety of others, including work in the decontamination and sterilization department of a hospital. "Not until I was a teacher," she writes, "did I feel that I had stepped out of the shadows of demeaning work. My poem is based upon a friend of a friend, whose sometimes glamorous, sometimes awful experiences as a back-up singer led me to write about what it is like to inhabit the second position, always, in one's work. I also mean the poem to be a metaphor for all women who have had to 'take one step backwards' in the service of someone else's dream." Barresi, who teaches at California State University, Northridge, won the 1990 Barnard New Women Poets Prize for her book *All of the Above*.

JACKIE BARTLEY (b. 1951) worked for sixteen years in hospital laboratories around the country where, she claims, "this poem happened to me everyday, but I didn't write it down until I left laboratory work. I don't know why." Currently she teaches writing and literature at Hope College in Holland, Michigan.

JAN BEATTY (b. 1952) has waitressed "fast food places, franchises, pizza joints, dive bars, fine restaurants, and jazz clubs in Pittsburgh for the past ten years. My true heroes are 'lifers' and diner waitresses." She teaches poetry at Carnegie Mellon University.

JUDITH BERKE (b. "won't tell") worked as a secretary for many years before becoming a poet. Her books are *White Morning* and *Acting Problems*. She lives in Miami Beach, Florida.

KAREN BRODINE (1947–87) majored in dance at the University of California, Berkeley. She then worked as a dancer, and after a congenital knee problem ended her career, as a dance instructor and a part-time writing instructor at San Francisco State University. However, her main livelihood came from the typesetting trade, in which she worked from 1975 to 1986, and this background inspired "Woman Sitting at the Machine, Thinking." An activist, she was involved with Radical Women, the Freedom Socialist party, and she cofounded the Women Writers Union in San Francisco. Her book *Woman Sitting at the Machine, Thinking* was published posthumously in 1990.

DAVID BUDBILL (b. 1940) grew up in a working-class neighborhood in Cleveland and was the first in his family to complete high school. He has worked as a short-order cook, gardener, carpenter, day laborer on a Christmas tree farm, and a freelance writer. Of his poem "Jeanie" he writes, "It began one morning in November 1986 in a greasy spoon in Jamestown, New York, when I heard a waitress say, 'Holy Kripes! I'm twenty-seven years old and I'm still livin' at home.' The rest is not history, but I hope it is poetry." Budbill's most recent collection is *Judevine: The Complete Poems.*

MICHAEL J. BUGEJA (b. 1952) writes, "I was reared in the arts and media capital of the world—the New York metropolitan area—two miles from physician-poet William Carlos Williams in Lyndhurst, New Jersey (bordering Rutherford). I became state editor for United Press International in 1976, a professor of journalism in 1979, and a serious poet a few years later." His most recent book is *Flight from Valhalla.*

DEB CASEY (b. 1950), in her own words, is a "marker/maker/mother/teacher/worker who lives up a bumpy road in Eugene, Oregon, with my family." She is completing a poetry manuscript called "Dream of a Working Mother and Her Daughters."

DAVID CHIN (b. 1953) was born in Jersey City, attended Jersey City State, Antioch (B.A., Biology), SUNY College of Optometry, Columbia University (M.F.A., Writing), and SUNY Binghamton. Between Columbia and Binghamton he spent a decade working as a lab tech, research assistant, research associate, and staff scientist performing basic research at Sloan-Kettering, Cetus, Bristol-Meyers, and Proctor and Gamble.

MICHAEL CHITWOOD (b. 1958) was born and raised in Redwood, Virginia. He writes, " 'Talking to Patsy Cline' is about the intersection where Technology Avenue crosses Honeysuckle Lane."

DAVID CITINO (b. 1947), a native of Cleveland, is director of the Creative Writing Program at Ohio State University. His poem "Basic Writing, Marion Correctional," he says, "comes from a year-long writing course sequence which it was my privilege to teach at the state penitentiary in Marion, Ohio. I grew close to my students, and in so doing I learned that I had a great deal in common with them, and that for all its frustrations, teaching is a noble profession."

JAN CLAUSEN (b. 1950) writes, "The Beats inspired me with a vision of the nobility of simple labor, which for them meant cruising timber—surveying stands of trees, usually for a lumber company—but for me turned out to mean frying donuts and emptying bedpans. I worked at the Winchell's Donut House at 12th and Hawthorne in Portland, Oregon, first as a counter girl, then night baker. It was a family-run franchise characterized by feudal relations of production; at the end of my stint, a self-styled Wobbly came in and tried to organize the place." Author of *Books & Life* and *The Proserpine Papers,* she now lives in Brooklyn.

RICHARD COLE (b. 1949) writes, "I have worked at the usual variety of blue-collar and white-collar jobs, enjoyed a brief and exceptionally unsuccessful career as a screenplay writer, and now work as a technical copywriter at a large advertising agency in New York City." His first collection of poems is *The Glass Children.*

WANDA COLEMAN of South Central Los Angeles writes that she is "under fifty and for most of my adult life I have been the working mother of three children, having had a wide-ranging number of jobs: medical billing clerk/ transcriber, typist, waitress, scriptwriter, magazine editor, and dancer with Anna Halprin's Dancers' Workshop in San Francisco." She is cohost of "The Poetry Connexion," an interview program for Southern California's Pacifica radio station. She is also a recording artist with three CDs on New Alliance Records: *High Priestess of Word, Black & Blue News,* and *Berserk on Hollywood Blvd.* ("released just before L.A. burned," she says). Her sixth and most recent book of poems is *Hand Dance.*

STEPHEN COREY (b. 1948) hails from the "white-collar, middle class—always enough, never any extravagance. Summer work in electroplating, die-casting, and furniture factories reinforced for me the life I didn't want; subsequently, I've earned a living in journalism, teaching, and literary editing." Of his poem "Domestic Life: Nurse and Poet," he writes, "I often find myself wondering how different I would have been if my daily shoptalk at home had not been focused, for twenty-plus years and counting, on sickness, injury, aging, pain, dying, and death." Corey is the author of *All These Lands You Call One Country.*

BARBARA CROOKER (b. 1945) says her first job was as a carhop at Patty's Charcoal Drive-in for $.85 an hour plus tips. She also worked her way through college as a waitress. Her newest books are *The Lost Children* and *Obbligato.* She lives in an old apple orchard in eastern Pennsylvania.

JIM DANIELS (b. 1956), a Detroit native, writes, "Most of these poems come out of various minimum-wage jobs that I have worked: soda jerk, liquor store clerk, stock boy in a department store, janitor, bank bookkeeper, short-order cook, and assembly-line worker in an auto plant. I enjoy writing in persona. When I wrote about factory work, I developed a character, 'Digger,' to explore in depth the effects of that work on an individual. Now that I have taught for many years in a university, I've created a new character who's lost perspective on his job, 'The Tenured Guy.'" Daniels is the author of *Places/ Everyone, Punching Out,* and *M-80.*

MARK DEFOE (b. 1942), who now teaches in West Virginia, has also worked as a farmhand, a bellman, a waiter, a circulation manager for a large newspaper, an advertising copywriter, and a free-lance writer. His two books of poetry are *Bringing Home the Breakfast* and *Palmate.*

TOI DERRICOTTE (b. 1941) for several years taught mentally retarded and disturbed children in the Detroit public schools and for twenty years worked as a master teacher in the New Jersey Poets-in-the-Schools Program. The work of giving birth is reenacted in this excerpt from *Natural Birth,* a book-length poem sequence exploring her own experience as a middle-class, African-American, unwed, young mother. Derricotte's most recent book is *Captivity.*

CORNELIUS EADY (b. 1954) is the author of *Kartunes, Victims of the Latest Dance Craze, Boom Boom Boom,* and *The Gathering of My Name.* Born and raised in Rochester, New York, Eady currently teaches writing and is director of the Poetry Center at the State University of New York, Stony Brook.

KIRSTEN EMMOTT (b. 1947) lives in Vancouver and works as a mother and a family doctor. She is the author of *Are We There Yet?*

GALE RUDD ENTREKIN (b. 1948) teaches English at Diablo Valley College in California, where she lives with her husband, poet/computer analyst Charles Entrekin, and some of their five children. She is the author of *John Danced.*

MARTÍN ESPADA (b. 1957) was born and raised in Brooklyn. He has worked as a night desk clerk in a transient hotel, a groundskeeper in a minor league ballpark, a bindery worker in a printing plant, a bouncer in a bar, a welfare rights paralegal, and until recently as a tenant lawyer. He now teaches at the University of Massachusetts, Amherst. His most recent book is *City of Coughing and Dead Radiators.*

LYN FERLO "(b. apparently) is an artist who has also become proficient as a plasterer, wallpaper remover, wallboard hanger, carpenter, floor sander, painter, paperhanger, floor tile layer, etc. ad nauseam who intends, when it is All Over, to do very little more than lie on the couch and eat chocolates! In the meantime she works as a secretary at a major university, the latest in a lifelong string of 'because I need to eat' jobs."

ALICE FULTON (b. 1952) writes, "My poem is not autobiographical. It is a 'fiction of the feminine,' suggesting 'woman' as cultural construct rather than a 'natural' or archetypal being. It is also a fiction in that I researched and then reimagined the scene and the people described, hoping to explore the dynamics of power between them. In researching the poem, I was struck by the anger and contempt both patrons and workers expressed toward one another. I was also interested in the way humor can be used both as a strategy of self-preservation and as a means of degrading or oppressing the other." Fulton's collections of poetry include *Dance Script with Electric Ballerina, Powers of Congress,* and *Palladium.*

TESS GALLAGHER (b. "impending") writes, "My parents were loggers in the Pacific Northwest. I was the oldest of five children and I shared the housework with my mother from an early age. It was the time of wringer washers and clothesline drying of clothes in the yard, of work shirts in faded blue. 'I Stop Writing the Poem' relates most directly to the tenderness of women in the household work they do. In this case the shirt being folded is that of my dead mate, but it echoes back to my childhood where I remember learning at my mother's elbow how to fold clothes. There is the sense that doing this work is as holy as the writing of the poem, and that a woman's creative life is more intermittent, full of pauses and duties, interrupted yet sustained by certain not to be disparaged useful gifts to order the household." *Moon Crossing Bridge* and *Portable Kisses: Love Poems* are two of Gallagher's most recent books.

GARY GILDNER (b. 1938) writes, "The three Polish poems resulted from the fourteen months I lived in Poland (1987–88) teaching at the University of Warsaw and coaching the city's baseball team. My background is northern Michigan, Polish and German, farmers and lumbermen. After World War II we moved down to Flint where my dad worked as a carpenter and I grew up wanting to play pro baseball. At age sixteen I threw a no-hitter in American Legion ball and was scouted, but two years later my arm died, as they say." Many of his poems are collected in *Blue like the Heavens.*

DANA GIOIA (b. 1950) writes, "I was born in a working-class section of Los Angeles. My father is Sicilian; my mother is Mexican and Native American. I grew up in a little pocket of Sicilian-speaking relatives and was the first in my family to attend college. 'In Cheever Country' is a view of the New York suburbs as seen by someone who doesn't take the comforts of the suburbs for granted. Borrowing certain images from the work of John Cheever, the poem celebrates this central American landscape that most poetry ignores or despises. 'The Man in the Open Doorway' is a glimpse into the mentality of a corporate executive—written, I should add, with my insights from fifteen years of working in large corporations." Formerly a vice-president for marketing in the Desserts Division of General Foods, Gioia in 1992 left business to be a full-time writer. He is the author of *Daily Horoscope, Gods of Winter,* and *Can Poetry Matter?: Essays on Poetry & Culture.*

ALBERT GOLDBARTH (b. 1948) writes, "My upbringing took place in the lower middle-class, demi-Jewish neighborhoods of Chicago, where my father was a penny-ante shlepper of life insurance for Metropolitan Life and my mother a housewife and secretary. Like many childhood friends, I was the first generation to go to college; like many poet friends today, I earn my living in academia. 'Elbee Novelty Company Inc.' isn't journalism, nonetheless Louie Berkie and his warehouse kingdom are real, though it's been years since I've ventured down its aisles of oddments." His most recent book is *Heaven & Earth, a Cosmology.*

LEONA GOM (b. 1946) has been a secretary, waitress, tombstone cutter, and teacher, "the latter at levels from grade one to university." She is the author of books of poetry and three novels.

JUDY GRAHN (b. 1940) is the daughter of a cook and a photographer's assistant. She has worked as a waitress, short-order cook, clerk, bar maid, artist's model, nurse's aide, typesetter, editor, publisher, and teacher. Her books include *Another Mother Tongue: Gay Words, Gay Worlds, Mundane's World: A Novel, The Work of a Common Woman: Collected Poetry,* and *The Queen of Wands,* which won the American Book Award of the Before Columbus Foundation.

SHARON HASHIMOTO (b. 1953) writes, "I am a third-generation Japanese-American. My grandparents worked in hotels and as farmers, whereas my parents worked for the V.A. Hospital and for Boeing. I have worked at several unusual jobs, taking obituary notices being the most delicate. Failing the Seattle Water Department's lift and carry exam taught me a lot about what I can and can't physically accomplish. For the past several years I've made my 'official' living as a literature and writing instructor for Highline Community College in Seattle."

LAURIE HENRY (b. 1958) has worked as a court stenographer, a bilingual secretary, a book editor, and an English teacher. "I wrote this poem," she writes, "after learning that a high school classmate lost his police-dispatcher job. I feel as sympathetic to the sheriff in the poem as I do to the speaker; neither person was in an easy situation. As far as I know, the poem's speaker has not worked since 1985."

EDWARD HIRSCH (b. 1950), a Chicago native, writes, "No one grows up wanting to be a 'commuter.' It's a role one puts on and takes off. In this one-sentence poem the speaker is overcome by slight waves of panic and nausea—of dissociation—as he watches himself fulfilling a role that is becoming his life." Hirsch teaches at the University of Houston and has published three books of poems: *For the Sleepwalkers, Wild Gratitude,* which won the National Book Critics Circle Award, and *The Night Parade.*

JONATHAN HOLDEN (b. 1941) writes, "I was raised in suburban New Jersey, around these kinds of people in 'The Crash.' The poem arose from my reading William Greider's 'Annals of the Federal Reserve' in the *New Yorker* and my realizing that money does not exist."

LYNDA HULL (b. 1954) teaches in the M.F.A. program at Vermont College. Her books of poetry are *Ghost Money* and *Star Ledger.*

DAVID IGNATOW (b. 1914) grew up in Brooklyn, the son of a Ukrainian Jewish immigrant skilled in the art of bookbinding. He worked in his father's bindery and as a shipyard handyman, public relations writer, salesman, and eventually as treasurer and president of a bindery firm. He is the author of fourteen books of poetry, most recently *Despite the Plainness of the Day: Love Poems.*

DENIS JOHNSON (b. 1949) is a poet and fiction writer whose books include *Angels, Fiskadoro, Jesus' Son: Stories,* and *The Incognito Lounge.*

LAWRENCE JOSEPH (b. 1948) is professor of law at St. John's University School of Law and the author of three books of poetry: *Shouting at No One, Curriculum Vitae,* and *Before Our Eyes.* "My objective in 'Any and All,'" he writes, "was to reinvent, in a poem, the equivalent moral and social impact of Herman Melville's 'Bartleby the Scrivener.' (A legal scrivener in Melville's time served the same function as an associate in a law firm today.) The poem, like 'Bartleby the Scrivener,' is ultimately concerned with language, identity, and power."

MAXINE HONG KINGSTON (b. 1940) who lives in Oakland, California, writes, "I have worked laundry, bookkeeping, sewing and mending, baby-sitting, tutoring, tax preparation, insurance adjusting, typing and filing, housewifery, restaurant, substitute teaching, crafts fairs, high schools and colleges, TV and radio, lecturing, and writing. My poem 'Restaurant' is entirely and exactly autobiographical." She is the author of *The Woman Warrior—Memoirs of a Girlhood among Ghosts,* winner of the National Book Critics Circle Award for nonfiction, and *China Men,* winner of the National Book Award for nonfiction.

SUSAN KINSOLVING (b. 1946) was born in Illinois and now lives in Connecticut. She has taught poetry at California Institute of the Arts and currently administrates some poetry programs for the New York Public Library. Her first book is *Among Flowers.*

EDWARD KLEINSCHMIDT (b. 1951) lives in San Francisco and has worked as an orderly in a cancer ward, an apple picker, a miller in a paint factory, and a construction worker. His book *First Language* won the 1989 Juniper Prize of the University of Massachusetts Press. He teaches at Santa Clara University.

TED KOOSER (b. 1939) is an executive for a life insurance company in Nebraska. He writes, "Seeing these poems gathered together, I am reminded that it is often impossible to separate people from their work, for so often people are their work and can't be extricated from it." His most recent book is *Weather Central.*

MARILYN KRYSL (b. 1942) writes, "I served as artist in residence at the Center for Human Caring at the Nursing School in Denver in 1987, during which time I researched and wrote about the work of nurses. I am a professional writer and a professor of English at the University of Colorado, Boulder, where I've worked for twenty years."

BRAD LEITHAUSER (b. 1953), who holds a law degree from Harvard University, is a poet and fiction writer whose books include *Cats of the Temple, Hence, Equal Distance, Hundreds of Fireflies,* and *Mail from Anywhere.*

PHILIP LEVINE (b. 1928) writes, "As a young man I was an industrial worker, a member of the United Auto Workers, the American Federation of Labor, the Teamsters, and even the Brotherhood of Railway Workers. From age thirty to sixty-five I taught English and creative writing. My poem reprinted here, 'Buying and Selling,' is based on work I did in the Bay Area in 1957 and 1958 when I first came West." Levine's *What Work Is* won the 1992 National Book Award for Poetry.

JULIA LISELLA (b. 1961) has worked delivering newspapers as well as writing and editing them; currently she teaches writing and is completing a Ph.D. at Tufts University. Of her poem she writes, "Jean and Jules, now in their midseventies, still work at the Queen of Peace Nursing Home and their work values continue to be my model and constant source of inspiration."

THOMAS LYNCH (b. 1948) writes, "For the past twenty years I have been the funeral director in Milford, Michigan, as was my father. My father's work gave him a certain anxiety about the tragic and untimely deaths of children. Whenever my brothers or I would want to do something—anything—he'd say, 'You can't do that. I've just buried a kid who did that. . . . ' We lived uneventful and protected lives. Now, as a parent, I find my children leading likewise protected lives." Lynch is the author of *Skating with Heather Grace*.

FRANCES MCCUE (b. 1962) writes, "In 'The Stenographer's Breakfast' a court reporter transcribes a deposition into her steno machine. A group of male lawyers is interrogating a widow about her husband's death. The stenographer, the only other woman in the room, has an ethical dilemma: to follow the rules of a dutiful reporter and take 'dictation' from the men, or to help save the widow from the attorneys' cruelty and to interfere with the proceedings. I myself was a paralegal for five years, and I wrote poems during lunch hours and at night. What I wrote had nothing to do with my working life, until finally, I realized that the office was a rich arena of social contrasts. Once I embraced my work during the day *as part of* my work as a writer, the poems grew." McCue's book *The Stenographer's Breakfast* won the 1991 Barnard New Women Poets Prize.

ROBERT MCDOWELL (b. 1953) is editor and publisher of *The Reaper* magazine as well as Story Line Press, both devoted to poetry. He is the author of *Quiet Money*.

MICHAEL MCFEE (b. 1954) has worked as an editor, librarian, free-lance writer, and book reviewer, but mostly as a teacher of poetry at colleges, including Cornell, Lawrence, and now the University of North Carolina, Chapel Hill. His most recent books are *Sad Girl Sitting on a Running Board* and *To See*.

CAMPBELL MCGRATH (b. 1962) has worked as a dishwasher and a dockhand. He currently teaches creative writing in Chicago, where he lives with his wife and child. His books are *Capitalism* and *American Noise*.

DAVID MCKAIN (b. 1937) writes, "I helped to start an organizing collective, served as chair of a HUD Citizen's Advisory Committee, was president of an environmental education committee, and conducted public workshops on housing—all in New London, Connecticut. A friend and I translated the New London housing code into Spanish, distributed the translations, and tried to start a tenant's union. My poem came out of that experience." McKain is the author of several collections of poetry and a memoir, *Spellbound: Growing Up in God's Country*.

MIKE MAGGIO (b. 1952) currently works in Saudi Arabia where he administers an overseas scholarship program. He has also worked in Jordan and the United States teaching English and counseling foreign students. " 'Found Poem #40,' " he writes, "was 'found' while I was registering students at the University of Southern California using the software program dBASE."

STANLEY MARCUS (b. 1954) lives in New York City where he works as the managing editor of *American Artist,* a large-circulation art magazine. He writes, "In the evening, I write poetry, often about how ill-suited I am for the corporate world."

PAUL MARION (b. 1954) works as a writer and cultural affairs consultant in Lowell, Massachusetts, where from 1984 to 1989 he was cultural affairs director of the Lowell Historic Preservation Commission, U.S. Department of the Interior. His poem grew out of a documentary survey project conducted by the American Folklife Center of the Library of Congress in the late 1980s. For the record Marion notes, "I played right field for the 1988 championship Burgess Construction team."

SUZANNE MATSON (b. 1959) grew up in Portland, Oregon, and now teaches at Boston College. Her books are *Sea Level* and *Durable Goods.*

SUZAN MILBURN (b. 1954) has worked as a swimming instructor, baker, deli person, and teacher at a French preschool in Vernon, British Columbia. She now "works as a student at Okanagen University College."

JOYCE CAROL OATES (b. 1938) writes, "My father worked for General Motors for forty years, in Lockport, New York, and was a member of the United Auto Workers. The poem is not drawn from life in any specific way but is an imaginative reconstruction of a world I've known intimately." Oates is the author of many books of fiction and poetry and is the winner of the 1970 National Book Award for fiction.

ED OCHESTER (b. 1939) writes, "My family worked as cops, firemen, insurance salesmen, typists, truck drivers, and clerks; I was the first one to complete college. For most of my work life I've taught at the college level (and am currently director of the Writing Program at the University of Pittsburgh), but I've also done time as a teamster, warehouse clerk, waiter, advertising copywriter, and receptionist. This poem is about the receptionist job; it happened 'just as it says,' except that the names are changed." His most recent books are *Changing the Name to Ochester* and *The Pittsburgh Book of Contemporary American Poetry*.

SHARON OLDS (b. 1942) is the author of *Satan Says, The Dead and the Living* (winner of both the 1983 Lamont Poetry Award and the National Book Critics Circle Award), *The Gold Cell*, and *The Father*. She teaches poetry workshops at New York University and Goldwater Hospital on Roosevelt Island in New York. Olds writes, "I am happy to see these poems of parenting included in an anthology about *work*."

ALICIA SUSKIN OSTRIKER (b. 1937) writes, "My background is Jewish Socialist. My parents both got degrees in English, but never made it out of the working class, and in fact never really wanted to. 'Mother in Airport Parking Lot' is a (premature) farewell to the labors of motherhood. 'Taking the Shuttle with Franz' is an intellectual (or do I mean ineffectual?) worm's-eye view of the type of men who run American business." Ostriker's most recent books of poetry are *The Imaginary Lover* and *Green Age*.

WALT PETERSON (b. 1943) grew up on Pittsburgh's South Side and worked construction jobs before attending college. Of his poem he writes, "M. F. Jacobowski's insights have come from my own twenty-two years as a classroom teacher in the Pittsburgh Public Schools."

FRANCES PHILLIPS (b. 1951) has worked as a secretary, administrative assistant, and fundraiser for an aerospace company, a drug and alcoholism treatment center, a state university, and a public relations firm. She writes, "This excerpt is part of my long poem 'For a Living,' which is about quitting my first full-time office job after graduate school. At the time I also was active in the Women Writers' Union, and along with Karen Brodine, Nellie Wong, and others, I was working to bring into poetry the textures, distractions, and power relationships that shape secretarial work." Currently she is executive director of Intersection for the Arts, San Francisco's oldest alternative arts center.

ALICIA PRIEST (b. 1953) worked as a registered nurse in hospitals throughout British Columbia. Currently she is a features writer for the *Vancouver Sun*.

JACK RIDL (b. 1944) has poems here from a collection that follows life in a small town as the high school basketball team goes through a winter full of losses. His father was the head basketball coach at the University of Pittsburgh and at Westminster College. Ridl himself is a retired point guard and shortstop who currently teaches at Hope College in Holland, Michigan.

MAXINE SCATES (b. 1949) grew up in a working-class neighborhood near Los Angeles International Airport. While in college she worked as an usherette at the Forum and the Long Beach Arena and also as a cashier and ticket taker at the Queen Mary. Her first book of poems, *Toluca Street,* won the 1988 Agnes Lynch Starrett Poetry Prize and also the 1990 Oregon Book Award for Poetry. Currently she lives and works in Eugene, Oregon.

HERBERT SCOTT (b. 1931) writes, "My first job, seventh grade, was grinding sausage, slicing lunch meat, and sweeping up in a small store in Norman, Oklahoma, for fourteen cents per hour. I worked for A&P in Chicago at ages nineteen–twenty. Then I worked eleven years with Safeway in Oklahoma and California. I worked all jobs but meat market. Liked best: produce; least: working empty bottles. The clerk's dream was my dream at one time, what Robert Bly would call a 'daydream,' until my grandmother reminded me that I wanted to write and teach. 'Boss' is based on Acie Leon Bryant, a renegade manager who loved the business, whom the clerks loved, who ended up across the street washing dishes because he wouldn't eat shit, who was replaced—as he predicts—by someone who doesn't know 'nothing about groceries.' "

BETSY SHOLL (b. 1945) writes, "When I was a student I volunteered at a state hospital that looked like a prison outside and a warehouse, a dungeon inside. There was a day room with thirty Down's syndrome kids, no window, no toys. All day I'd 'work' with kids who were autistic or had cerebral palsy, kids who didn't talk; some were totally unresponsive, some sweet and smiling. Then I'd drive back to my school and walk into the cafeteria, which was full of conversations, the first words I'd heard all day. The shift of worlds often made me weep, suddenly unfit for either one. For years I tried unsuccessfully to write about that place, then finally this poem came together. I didn't make up those children." Sholl's *The Red Line* won the 1991 Associated Writing Programs' Award Series in Poetry.

PEGGY SHUMAKER (b. 1952) writes, "I grew up in a working-class family, daughter of a salesman/truck driver/musician and an office worker/waitress. I have worked in banks, a halfway house for girls labeled incorrigible by juvenile court, in publishing, prisons, and universities. The event depicted in my poem happened to my sister, then a clerk in a convenience store. As his weapon the thief hefted a big rock. Incidentally, he robbed seven stores in this way, and using a rock constitutes armed robbery." Shumaker's most recent book is *Wings Moist from the Other World*.

Louis Simpson (b. 1923) writes, " 'Working Late' is about Jamaica where I grew up and my father Aston Simpson, a lawyer. He worked hard . . . too hard. He had a reputation for preparing a case thoroughly and for his skill at cross-examination. I came to the States when I was seventeen, studied at Columbia, and served in the U.S. Army, in the infantry. That was work. After the war I worked on the night shift of the *New York Herald Tribune* as a copyboy, while taking courses at Columbia, then as a packer for an import-export firm. The first really serious, full-time job I held was as a reader, then 'associate editor' at the Bobbs-Merrill Publishing Company in New York (the poem 'The Associate' is about this). In the mid-1950s I got out of publishing, obtained a Ph.D., and went into teaching, from which I retired recently." Simpson won the 1964 Pulitzer Prize for poetry. His most recent book is *In the Room We Share*.

Jeffrey Skinner (b. 1949) has worked as a private detective, as a security guard on the night shift, and as vice-president and general manager of a security guard company. "These poems come from my experience," Skinner writes, "and they reflect the blur of time and ambition, the day-to-day routine that becomes central to so many lives." His most recent book is *The Company of Heaven*.

Ellen McGrath Smith (b. 1962) grew up in Pittsburgh the daughter of a policeman, and she has worked in public relations and a variety of clerical jobs. She notes, "Though the poems here look at civil service jobs in a somewhat negative light, these jobs and my co-workers sustained me in many ways."

Miriam Solan (b. "won't tell") has performed in the theater, worked on the editorial board of a poetry magazine, and taught children's writing workshops. Her poem "Check-up," she hopes, depicts modern medicine in the pre-Clinton era only. Author of the poetry collection *Seductions,* she lives in Scarsdale, New York.

Carol Tarlen (b. 1943) writes, "My father is a retired truck driver and Teamster Union member; my mother was a Rosie the Riveter and member of the Machinists Union. I am a clerical worker and member of AFSCME, Local 3218. I wrote this poem on a paid vacation day that I took to celebrate the completion of a Master's Degree earned while I worked full time as a secretary. I wrote it in pseudo-biblical language because paid days off are rare and miraculous and holy!" Tarlen lives in Sausilito, California.

DAVID E. THOMSON (b. 1964) grew up in Oklahoma and worked for the *Enid Morning News*. Of "Deadline" he writes, "The poem addresses the conflict I've encountered since I declared a double major in English literature and journalism at Oklahoma State University—that ever-present tension between the documentary and interpretive." Currently he teaches at Francis Marion University in Florence, South Carolina.

MICHELLE M. TOKARCZYK (b. 1953) writes, "Before beginning my work for the Ph.D. in English, I held jobs as an office temp, bookkeeper, library assistant, receptionist, and copywriter. 'An Academic Fantasy' and 'Working into Night' come out of my continuing reflections on the precariousness of being untenured. 'A Woman Writing in America' grapples with both the discrepancy between my own status/income and my husband's and the actuality of being an artist and intellectual in a capitalist country. 'An Alternate Ending to a Temp Job' expresses the nightmare fantasy I had when I worked in a dangerous neighborhood." Tokarczyk's book of poems is *The House I'm Running From*.

JOHN UPDIKE (b. 1932) writes, "My father was a public-school teacher. As a boy I worked briefly in a factory and for several summers as a copyboy for the local newspaper. In the mid-1950s I wrote for the *New Yorker*'s Talk of the Town Department, and that was my last formal employment. Which doesn't mean I've been loafing all this time. 'Back from Vacation' is based on the tan the local druggist sported one winter." Updike, a prolific writer of fiction, poetry, and criticism, is two-time winner of the Pulitzer Prize for fiction. His *Collected Poems* appeared in 1993.

JUDITH VOLLMER (b. 1951) worked for several years as a newspaper reporter and editor and now teaches writing at the University of Pittsburgh, Greensburg. "The nuclear industry in the 1950s," she writes, "pioneered the non-blue-collar dreams of my Eastern European, lower middle-class family. The voice in these poems tries to articulate the dreams, the excitement, and the complete terror of that time." Her book *Level Green* won the 1990 Brittingham Prize in Poetry.

BRONWEN WALLACE (b. 1945), a Canadian, has worked as a teacher and writer. Her books include *Marrying into the Family* and *Signs of the Former Tenant*.

BELLE WARING (b. 1951) worked for fifteen years as a registered nurse in Washington, D.C., hospitals. "These poems," she writes, "are an attempt to show how it really is in there—the good, the bad, and the ambivalent. 'Before Penicillin' honors my grandfather and points out that part of being a doctor is to help people to die as well as to live." Her collection *Refuge* won the 1990 Associated Writing Programs' Award Series in Poetry.

TOM WAYMAN (b. 1945) has worked various jobs including college teaching, construction, and assemblyman in a truck factory. He is the author of several collections of poetry and editor of three anthologies of mostly Canadian work poems: *Paperwork, Going for Coffee,* and *A Government Job at Last.*

CHARLES WEBB (b. 1952) worked for ten years as a rock musician, but is now professor of English at California State University, Long Beach, and a licensed psychotherapist. Of "Mr. Kyle the Banker" he writes, "Columbia Savings, where I banked, was taken over by federal regulators as part of the savings and loan bailout. Watching that process, coupled with job instability due to budgetary problems in the CSU system where I work, inspired the poem."

C. K. WILLIAMS (b. 1936) is the author of several books of poetry, including *Tar and Other Poems, Lies, Flesh & Blood,* and *A Dream of Mind.*

IRENE WILLIS (b. 1929) writes, " 'Easy Hours' began when I looked out of my twelfth-floor window in a state office building and saw two workmen on the roof across the way. It merged with a scrap of conversation about hours and benefits." She has taught English and was director of an alternative high school in New York State. Now an educational planner and policy analyst for the state of New Jersey, she lives in Princeton.

ROBERT WINNER (1930–86) worked for many years in the financial industry on Wall Street. Two of his published volumes are *Green in the Body* and *Flogging the Czar.* An edition of his complete works is now in preparation.

BILL ZAVATSKY (b. 1943) writes, "I have worked as a factotum in a factory, pianist in bands playing everything from weddings to jazz clubs, but for the past twenty years I have taught all but the unborn and the dead how to write, for the last six years at the Trinity School in New York City. 'The Fee' was written in fits of hilarious despair when editors of two anthologies couldn't understand why I had objections to letting them print my work for free and in perpetuity." Zavatsky's books include *For Steve Royal and Other Poems* and *Theories of Rain and Other Poems.*

PAUL ZIMMER (b. 1934) writes, "I have been working full time for forty years. Before I became a book publisher I worked as a warehouseman, shoe salesman, technical writer, stockbroker clerk, steel-mill electrician, college teacher, news reporter, and bookstore manager. I grew up in a mill town and my folks both worked six days a week as retail clerks. Sometimes I am pretty tired when I finally find time to work on poems, so I don't feel 'inspired.' Occasionally when this happens, I write poems about 'work,' because it is very much on my mind." His most recent book is *Big Blue Train*.

NICHOLAS COLES was born in 1947 in Leeds, England. He holds B.A. and M.A. degrees from Oxford University and a Ph.D. from the State University of New York, Buffalo. His summer jobs in school and college included work as a farmhand, a dishwasher, and an office boy in a law firm, as well as stints in construction, a wall-board factory, and an engineering plant. For the past twenty years he has worked primarily as a teacher, first in preschool and since 1980 as an English professor at the University of Pittsburgh, where he directs the Western Pennsylvania Writing Project. He teaches and writes about composition, working-class literature, contemporary poetry, and teacher-research. His articles have appeared in *College English* and other journals and collections. He is co-editor with Peter Oresick of *Working Classics: Poems on Industrial Life* (1990), also published by the University of Illinois Press. He lives in Pittsburgh with his wife, Jennifer Matesa, and son Jonah.

PETER ORESICK was born in 1955 in Ford City, Pennsylvania. He earned a B.A. in education and an M.F.A. in writing from the University of Pittsburgh. His summer jobs in college included working on the line in a glass factory and as a trash collector for the city of Pittsburgh. He later worked as a high school teacher in the Pittsburgh Public Schools, a writer-in-residence for the Pennsylvania Council on the Arts, and for five years as a full-time househusband caring for his then-preschooler sons. In 1985 he joined the staff of the University of Pittsburgh Press, where he is assistant director and promotion and marketing manager. His books of poetry are *Definitions, An American Peace, Other Lives,* and *The Story of Glass.* He is co-editor with Ed Ochester of *The Pittsburgh Book of Contemporary American Poetry,* an anthology featuring poets in the Pitt Poetry Series. He lives in Pittsburgh with his wife, Stephanie Flom, and sons Bill, Jacob, and David.

ACKNOWLEDGMENTS

The impetus for this anthology was the enthusiastic response to our first, *Working Classics: Poems on Industrial Life* (1990, University of Illinois Press). We owe thanks to those many readers who encouraged us, especially Fred Pfeil. In his April 1991 *Voice Literary Supplement* review of *Working Classics* he first suggested an updated anthology to reflect "the rise of service industries, with all of their minimum-wage slots for gas jockeys and mouseburger franchise workers." Richard L. Wentworth, director and editor-in-chief of the University of Illinois Press, was quick to believe in the new project and to offer us a contract. Two student interns, Alice Chiao and John Leitera, helped us sort and organize the voluminous submissions we received from poets and with typing, filing, indexing, and library research. Stephanie Flom and Jennifer Matesa closely read drafts of the Introduction and notes, offering many valuable suggestions, and Stephanie Flom also assisted with the tedious proofreading.

We especially thank the hundreds of poets who sent us poems for consideration and who were patient with us while we made our selections. The poets included in *For a Living* were most helpful in securing permission to reprint their poems and in providing biographical notes. Special thanks to Frances Phillips. After months of agonizing deliberation, we appropriated our main title, *For a Living,* from her wonderful poem and 1981 poetry collection of the same name, which we recommend to all.

There is much good work that we did not have room to include in *For a Living.* We hope that readers will seek out individual collections of poetry by the poets at bookstores and libraries.

AI. Excerpts from "Evidence: From a Reporter's Notebook" from *Fate* by Ai. © 1991 by Ai. Reprinted by permission of Houghton Mifflin Company. All rights reserved.

MAGGIE ANDERSON. "Sonnet for Her Labor," reprinted from *A Space Filled with Moving* by Maggie Anderson, is used by permission of the University of Pittsburgh Press. © 1992 by Maggie Anderson.

RANE ARROYO. "Juan Angel," first published in *Kenyon Review* (Winter 1992), is reprinted by permission of the author.

JOHN ASHBERY. "The Instruction Manual" from *Some Trees Poems* (New York: The Erro Press, 1956), reprinted by permission of Georges Borchardt, Inc. for the author. © 1956 by John Ashbery.

JAMES A. AUTRY. All poems are reprinted from *Love and Profit: The Art of Caring Leadership* by James A. Autry. © 1991 by James A. Autry. Used by permission of William Morrow & Co., Inc.

JIMMY SANTIAGO BACA. Excerpt from "A Song of Survival" is reprinted from *Immigrants in Our Own Land and Selected Early Poems* (1990, New Directions Books) © 1982 by Jimmy Santiago Baca. Reprinted by permission of New Directions Pub. Corp. "There's Me" is from the book of poems *What's Happening* by Jimmy Santiago Baca. Published by Curbstone Press, 1982. © 1982 by Jimmy Santiago Baca. Reprinted by permission of Curbstone Press.

LENORE BALLIRO. "French Restaurant, 1982" is published here for the first time by permission of the author.

WALTER BARGEN. "Heavenly Host" first appeared in *Farmer's Market* and "Another Hour" first appeared in *Ascent*. They are reprinted by permission of the author. "Thomas Hill Power Plant Car Pool" is reprinted by permission of the author from *Mysteries in the Public Domain* (1990, BkMk Press). © 1990 by Walter Bargen. "What We Want to Hear" is published here for the first time by permission of the author.

JANE BARNES. "Right Now" is reprinted by permission of the author from *Extremes* (1981, Blue Giant Press).

DOROTHY BARRESI. "The Back-up Singer" is reprinted from *All of the Above*. © 1991 by Dorothy Barresi. Reprinted by permission of Beacon Press.

JACKIE BARTLEY. "The Midnight Tech's Meditation" is published here for the first time by permission of the author.

JAN BEATTY. "A Waitress's Instructions on Tipping or Get the Cash Up and Don't Waste My Time" is used by permission of the author.

JUDITH BERKE. "Ms" is reprinted from *White Morning*. © 1989 by Judith Berke, Wesleyan University Press. Reprinted by permission of University Press of New England.

KAREN BRODINE. All excerpts are reprinted by permission of the publisher from *Woman Sitting at the Machine, Thinking: Poems 1978–1987* by Karen Brodine (1990, Red Letter Press). © 1990 by Red Letter Press.

DAVID BUDBILL. "Jeanie" is published here for the first time by permission of the author.

MICHAEL J. BUGEJA. "Hove" first appeared in *Nimrod* and is used by permission of the author. © 1987 by Michael J. Bugeja.

DEB CASEY. "ZOOOOOOOM: A Familiar Story: Drop-off/Pick-up Panic" first appeared as "Justification" in *Calyx: A Journal of Art and Literature by Women* (vol. 12, no. 3, Summer 1990). The other poems are published here for the first time by permission of the author.

DAVID CHIN. "A Seven Day Diary" first appeared in *Mississippi Review* (vol. 19, nos. 1–2, 1990). Used by permission of the author.

MICHAEL CHITWOOD. "Talking to Patsy Cline" is reprinted from *Salt Works* by permission of the author and Ohio Review Books.

DAVID CITINO. "Basic Writing, Marion Correctional" is reprinted from *The Discipline: New and Selected Poems, 1980–1992* by permission of the Ohio State University Press and the author. © 1992 by the Ohio State University Press.

JAN CLAUSEN. "Sestina, Winchell's Donut House" first appeared in *Waking at the Bottom of Dark* (1979, Long Haul Press). © 1979 by Jan Clausen. Used by permission of the author.

RICHARD COLE. "Business Class," "Dignity," and "Success Stories" first appeared in *The Literature of Work: Short Stories, Essays, and Poems by Men and Women of Business* (1991, University of Phoenix Press). "Waiting for Money" first appeared in *Denver Quarterly* (Fall 1988). "Working Late," "The Business Life," and "Recession, 1992" are published here for the first time. All poems used by permission of the author.

WANDA COLEMAN. All poems are reprinted by permission of the author from *African*

SUBJECT INDEX